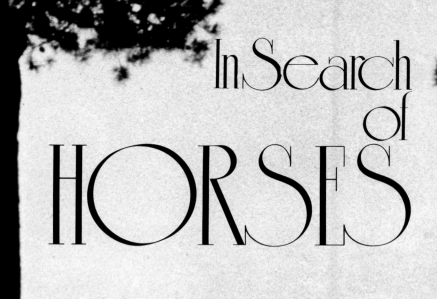

In Search
of
HORSES

For Paul White
a friend in need
(and fond of horses too)

In Search of
HORSES
Caroline Silver

EXCALIBUR ✚ BOOKS · NEW YORK

Contents

Introduction	5
To Topaz, a Filly	7
Horse Sense	15
Small, Vigorous and Lively	19
A Matter of Forgery	26
Natural to Man	29
Galloping Mania	32
They're off	36
Wild Horses	47
Drinkers of the Wind	56
The Competitors	62
Drums and Trumpets	75
The Hireling	82
Horses at Work	84
End of the Day	94
Acknowledgements	96

Series edited by HOWARD LOXTON
Picture research by ANN DAVIES
Produced by Elsevier Publishing Projects S.A., Lausanne
Published by Excalibur Books

Introduction

Lord Poseidon, from you this pride is ours:
The strong horses, the young horses; and also the rule of the deep.
According to Greek mythology, the first horse came from the sea. His name was
Arion and he was the son of Poseidon, the god of the sea and brother of Zeus.
In the Old Testament it says: "Hast Thou given the horse strength? Hast Thou
clothed his neck with thunder? He paweth in the valley and rejoiceth in his strength."
Such tributes have been paid to horses throughout the ages of man. But why
should man care so much about an animal that James Thurber humorously
described as having "one leg at each corner"? Why should babies, in some cases,
say "horse" before they say "Mama"? Why do equestrians sacrifice many
so-called essentials such as automobiles before they give up their horses?
The answer, if there is an answer, has to do with the reverence that thousands
of years ago showed itself in the myth of the centaur, the manhorse as one being.
It is the deep delight that rejoices the mind of anyone who has ridden a good horse
on testing country, watched a thoroughbred move freely over open pasture,
or touched the neck of a milk float horse and been rewarded with the richness
of its texture and its scent, the horse's patience, trust, and strength.
This book is meant as a communication between those of us who feel that way.

To Topaz, a Filly

To the human observer, the pattern of the horse's life begins at birth more than for any other domestic animal. There is no building of a nest, no anxiety, no altered behavior pattern to inform us of what is up with a pregnant mare. Some mares get fat, some don't; and many an informed horseman has gone hunting on his mare, not knowing what she was up to 11 months before—when she met a stallion on the quiet—only to find her in the box next morning with a foal at foot. The guilt he feels at having ridden her hard in that condition is unneeded: she does as many generations of her forebears have done in the wild—moves on from day to day, foals, gets up and moves again.

The process of birth is the same from breed to breed, affected only by the degree of human anxiety, emotional or financial, which fractionally alters the circumstances in which the foal is born. The following true story of a birth to Topaz, though involving the close attendance merited by a racehorse foal worth many thousands of pounds, applies fundamentally just as well to a carthorse or to a Shetland pony.

In thoroughbred racing circles the ruling is that the mare (described as "visiting") goes to the stallion (described as "resident"). The famous stud where Topaz was to foal had known many great stallions, the residents at the time of her arrival, for example, both being winners of the English Derby. Visiting mares usually foal at the stud and are then served at their first heat after foaling, this is the case on most thoroughbred stud farms. Thus Topaz, a 19-year-old chestnut mare, in foal to yet another Derby winner, arrived a few weeks before foaling so that her body could acquire immunity against local infections which might be dangerous to her foal.

Topaz belonged to a famous American owner-breeder. She was a big old mare with only one eye—the right eye had been lost through an infection—and a stomach distended by ten foalings. She was once (hard to imagine in her big-bellied old age) a winner on the racecourse.

Northern hemisphere racehorses are begotten unusually early so that they can benefit as youngsters from the artificial birthdate set for all at January 1. During the second week of March Topaz's udder "bagged up" full of milk. On March 21 she "waxed"—

a thickish secretion oozed from each milk canal and hardened into wax-like blobs on her teats. Drops of milk fell from her udder. On the morning of March 24 the muscles around her tail looked hollow and slack. Slackening, caused by the hormone *relaxin* which softens the ligaments to ease the passage of the foetus, occurs 12 to 18 hours before the foal is born and is so slight that it is easily overlooked. Topaz's excellent stud groom noticed it, however, and moved her into a foaling box.

With so much money at stake dependent on a successful birth the comfortable foaling boxes were fitted with television cameras, monitored by a control set in the sitting-up room where someone was always on watch during the foaling season. On March 24 a Dutch girl sat with the mares. At 7.45 p.m. she noticed that Topaz had broken out in a light sweat on the neck, soon spreading to a heavy sweat on the neck and girth which steamed in the cool air of the box. She called in the stud groom.

Topaz seemed calm and easy in herself. "These old mares don't upset themselves much," the stud groom explained. "Topaz knows a lot about it." At 8 o'clock she got down in her straw and rolled, breathing in short snorts of discomfort because her stomach was so large. Then she got up quickly. Colostrum, the important first milk containing antibodies to immunise the foal against disease, spurted from both teats. The groom milked a little of it into his hand, found that it was mainly milk and that Topaz had already lost most of her colostrum. He wasn't worried: he had spare colostrum in the deep freeze, milked from mares who had had plenty, and Topaz's foal could have a bottle of that.

8.10: The mare went down again, rolling. The groom reckoned that she knew the foal was not quite in the correct position and she was rolling to get it right. He washed his arms up over the elbow in warm, disinfected water and reached into her vagina to check. Topaz knuckered to him softly. Her birth canal was blocked by the partly-ejected water bag, which he burst with his hand so that he could reach through and feel that the foal was in the proper position (if not, this would be the moment to straighten it). Water poured out of Topaz, and one of the foal's forelegs stuck out from under her tail, encased in thick white membrane. The groom felt the other foreleg, lying a little behind the first and touched the head, lying neatly along both legs like a diver's. Satisfied

The birth of a thoroughbred. The mare's tail is bandaged to keep loose hairs from getting in the way.
Right: The foal's forelegs are emerging in the correct position.
Far right: A moment of rest at the end of labor. The foal's hind legs are still in the birth canal but the amniotic sac is partly off and the foal has begun to breathe.

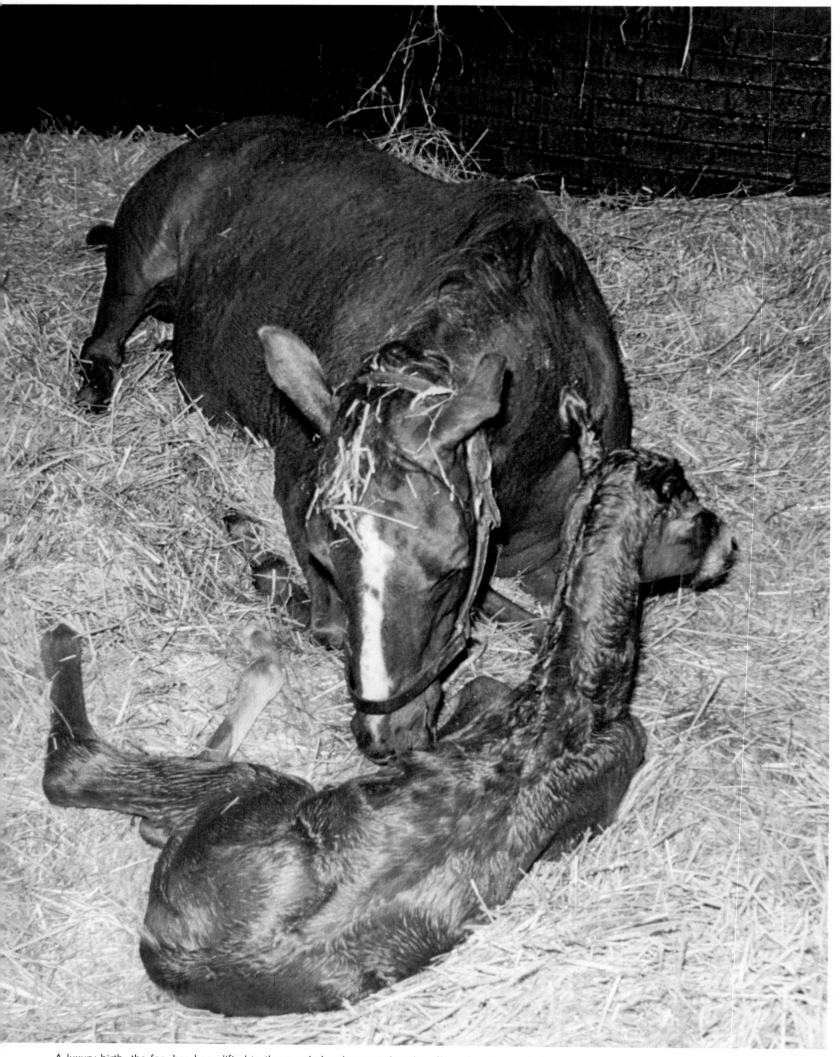

A luxury birth: the foal has been lifted to the mare's head to save her the effort of getting up to inspect it.

that the foal's shoulders would pass on a slant through the narrow pelvic area and that its nose would not get stuck against the roof of the vagina, he withdrew his arm and left the mare to get on with it by herself.

At 8.15 the other foreleg showed, just behind the first. Topaz began to work, a contraction every few seconds drawing her stomach up from underneath. She stopped and panted, blowing with pain, then stretched out on her side again. Discomfort made her twist her head so that her nose pointed towards the ceiling, and her upper lip curled back to show her teeth. One of the foal's hooves burst through the amniotic sac. The end of its foot was white and soft, and looked like flabby gristle at the tip.

8.24: The foal's head appeared, covered in membrane. When the contraction passed and Topaz had relaxed the groom pulled gently on the second foreleg, which was dragging back into the mare. The foal's nose stuck out clear of the amniotic sac, nostrils closed and tongue hanging out; it wasn't breathing yet. Lying in the straw, Topaz turned her head and hummered (her attending groom's word for the intimate voice a mare uses to her foal). "Not there yet, old girl," he told her.

Topaz bore down hard. She stuck her legs out stiff, and curled her lips back over her gums in effort. At 8.29 the foal slipped easily out, and as its ribcage slid clear of the constricting vagina it gave a little gasp and started to breathe. The groom cleared the water from its nostrils with his finger, which he said wasn't really

A strong cart mare with her newborn foal. She has given birth in the field without the watchful attention given to valuable thoroughbreds.

Horse and pony foals are always hungry.

necessary. As the foal's hind legs slipped away from the mare she got up fast and turned, eager to see her foal, snapping the umbilical cord which bled in spurts. The groom held the end of it tight between finger and thumb until the bleeding stopped.

Topaz bent over the foal, hummering to it and licking it dry.

It was a bay filly, daughter of a Derby winner, a sticky little effort with a wisp of beard hanging from its lower lip and a hide soaked wet with fluid. It lay in the straw limply, buffeted from side to side by Topaz's tongue.

The mare's huge empty belly looked no smaller, but her sides were hollow below the hip. The empty placenta draggled down behind her, and the groom tied it up with binder twine to keep her from kicking at it or stepping on it.

Eight minutes from birth the foal tried to get up, rocking backwards in the straw with its forelegs splayed out in front while Topaz, hummering, licked its face. A spurt of pain got her down in her bed, rolling as the tired muscles of her stomach contracted. The stud groom and his Dutch assistant hurried to pull the foal out of the way, afraid she might roll on it accidentally.

Most foals take an hour to stand, but Topaz's strong filly was up on its feet, wobbling, in only 17 minutes. Three times it crabbed over backwards on to its bottom, but it would not give in. Topaz continued to dry it, talking to it all the time. "Funny old girl," the groom said. "You'd think an old mare like that would be used to it, but she's like a kid with a Christmas present." Topaz began to frisk a little, raising her elderly body in tiny rears of delight.

At 8.58 the afterbirth came away and the groom removed it, checking that it was complete as a partly-retained placenta can cause infection in a mare. The foal, walking now, stuck its nose out questingly towards him. "I'm not your mother," he said to it. It lurched away to Topaz, feeling along her side for the teat. It had no notion where to look. It poked its mother in the armpit, hard; she swung her head around and pushed it away, kicking out fussily. Saliva ran down the foal's lips in a fine white hungry foam; it licked its mother's udder, but didn't drink. Topaz blew air down her nose impatiently.

At 9.44 it found the teat and began to suck.

What happened thereafter is very much the same for any young foal. It is put out to pasture with its dam and with other mares and foals,

coming in at night if the weather is inclement and it is high born and roughing it outside without much harm if it isn't. It learns fast, vitally, to manage its long legs at a trot and canter, swings away up the pasture to rear and box with the other young foals; picks curiously at the grass, forelegs straddled so that it can get its short neck close enough to the turf, not really eating, more in imitation of its dam. Horses learn by imitation—so much so that a riding horse should never be fostered on a carthorse because it will pick up a clumsy galloping action.

As the summer days lengthen and the sun gets on its back it grows big and fit and starts to graze properly. In the natural way of life, today left open to very few animals, it will continue to drink from its mother either until she gets fed up with it and drives it off or until the stallion of the herd chases it away. It behaves very much as a human would under similar circumstances—hanging around miserably on the fringes of its own society, getting bitten and kicked by the bigger fellow, until eventually it joins up with a group of contemporaries or with another herd that will let it tag along. Most foals are more kindly weaned by human agency at about six months old, forcibly separated in a traumatic few hours of squeaking and screaming which is most humanely done by keeping the mare and foal out of earshot of each other; then, if lucky, turned out the next day with other foals of about the same age. The mother–child bond breaks decisively, and within only a very few weeks the mare and foal will appear not to recognize each other if they meet.

The lapse of time between weaning and breaking in a young horse varies with the purpose for which it has been bred. Horses come to full physical maturity at about four years old, and a heavy weight put upon their backs before that age can cause permanent damage to the spinal column. Under the silken skin of many flat racehorses who are broken in and ridden and, in North America, even raced as yearlings, fused vertebrae are often found, though luckily this seldom seems to cause pain to the horse or affect its racing or stud career. Most horses are left to mature slowly, never feeling the weight of a human or the constriction of a saddle until they are three or four years old. During this gentle seasonal rotation of growth —through the shedding of the foal coat as the first winter approaches, the loss of the remnants of the curly foal tail which still linger in the yearling, the awkward, gangling stages in which the body grows unevenly, sometimes shooting up behind then growing up in front and looking sway-backed until the middle grows up to the same height, the growing in of a full set of temporary teeth and their slow replacements by the permanent teeth of a mature animal—the inquisitive young horse learns from experience and by examples from its associates. Wise handling, if the owner has the time to do it, means that the horse is constantly associated with man, learning elementary lessons such as to wear a halter and be led or to pick up its feet when asked and hold them steady for the hoofpick during the first few months of life, coming to the paddock gate when called and getting accustomed to the sudden buzz of traffic. (It is of immense value if a young horse can be pastured in a busy area with a wise old horse who shows no fear when a heavy truck grinds past or a train hisses and rattles at shattering speed on a nearby railway track.)

Fear of the unfamiliar is natural to a horse, whose whole survival instinct is bound up with the ability to flee from anything potentially dangerous, not pausing to make the inquiring inspection that may prove fatal, and to buck a predator off its back. Sudden movements and sharply raised voices will startle a young horse, and the good horseman is gentle and quiet in all his movements. Carrying a rider is a grotesque outrage of all a horses instincts

Mares usually bear a single foal. Twins are exceptional in horses. The young stay with their mothers until they are about six months old.

for self-preservation. A wild range horse, saddled and ridden for
the first time with little if any preparation for the nervous shock
of the terrifying weight which in the natural state would likely
be that of a mountain lion or other big cat, puts up a frenzied display
of desperate bucking and jumping that movie audiences throughout
the world associate with bucking broncos.

The more usual method of training, which wise old horsemen
often like to refer to as "gentling" rather than "breaking" the animal,
involves a slow process which begins with lightly girthing a strap
round the horse's middle, tightening the girth gradually as the horse
becomes accustomed to moving with the unfamiliar restriction
and comes to know that it will not harm him. Later a saddle
is substituted, again girthed only to the point where it will
hold in place; then the horseman slowly lies across the horse's back
in a gradual easing of weight from leaning *against* to leaning *upon*
and taking the feet off the ground so that the whole weight
of the man is taken by the horse, easing a leg over to sit upright,
always talking soothingly and always with another person at the
horse's head. Next the horse can be lead away slowly, so that it adapts
to the shifting weigh at different gaits. After schooling on gradually
over one year or many the horse acquires the degree of sophistication
needed of it—which will obviously be much more elementary
in a pony for a young child, which needs only to be kind and quiet
and sensible in traffic, than in a dressage horse or show jumper
whose advanced training program takes several years to carry out.
One might marvel at the superficial precocity of the racehorse,
who appears on a public track a year or two before most horses
are even ridden, were it not that the flat racehorse is required
to do only one thing: to carry a lightweight man at a gallop, without
much regard to brakes or steering. Many of these horses are not
taught properly to walk or trot, are not "mouthed" in the way
that makes a pleasing riding horse accept the bit, never learn
to stand up on ploughed land, negotiate a fence, or stand at ease
on tarmac in a busy city. Racehorses, crammed full of high protein
food from weaning, so that their physical development accelerates
more rapidly than that of their less valuable relations, and handled
with intense attention from the moment of birth, are bred in
most cases to prove their ability on the racetrack at the earliest
possible moment. Having done so they spend the 16-20 years of their
mature life at stud, where the value of an outstanding winner and
proven sire amounts to millions of dollars.

It is for this reason that the likes of Topaz, for example, visit a
stallion rather than risk taking him to the mare when she might
be out of heat while other mares come ready for his services.

It is because of the value of the stallion that the normal courtship
display in which a wild horse singles out a mare and pays attention
to her for the brief few hours that would put her in the mood
to want him is omitted—hours in which she might kick or bite him
until he wins her over to his need. Because the stallion is so
valuable that no damage can be risked to him, mares have their
hind shoes removed and are fitted with felt boots that take the zest out
of a kick, and every possible care is taken to avoid harm to either
horse. The racehorse mare is first tested by a "teaser"—a stallion
of no value who will win her through the early, grumpy, proud displays
of pseud disinterestedness and then she is presented to the
stallion who is expected to cover her across a padded board.
When the brief how-do-you-do is over and the stallion shows signs
of arousal she is held by two men with a foreleg lifted off the ground
so that she cannot kick out when he mounts her. After she
has been covered, stallion and mare are led quickly away from
each other so that no opportunity for harm occurs. Then she waits
again, 11 months, fat-fed on good pasture and dried food, until
once again the moment arrives for the foal of a Derby winner to take
its first breath and for life to begin all over again in a horse.

Horse Sense

I am that merry wanderer of the night,
I jest to Oberon, and make him smile
When I a fat and bean-fed horse beguile,
Neighing in likeness of a filly foal.
       William Shakespeare:
        A Midsummer-Night's Dream

Horses communicate with each other and with man by a variety
of different signals which can be interpreted by such elementary
phrases as "Who are you?" "Welcome," "Is anyone around?" "I am
afraid," "I absolutely will not," "Don't go away," "I need you,"
"I am king," "Let's play." The messages are passed not just by the
sound the horse makes but by his physical stance, his air and manner,
at the moment of delivery. Many messages are purely visual:
ears cocked forwards can be taken as "I am interested," "I am happy,"
"Welcome," "What on earth is that?" depending on the circumstances
at the time. Ears laid back flat mean "I hate you," "Go away,
or I will do you harm," "I won't," or laid half back may signal
simply "I am bored," "I am thinking about something else,"
"I am dozing off."

A horse whose attention is caught by a sudden interest pricks up not just his ears but his head, focussing his whole attention on the object that attracts him. If nervous or unsure, his body tenses into a quivering alertness to run away if need be, and if very worried indeed he sweats in light patches on the neck, behind the ears and between the hind legs. His nostrils flare to their fullest extent to pick up any scents that may help him analyze what worries him, and his breath comes in short, audible snorts that communicate his fear to any horse within earshot.

Comfort from horse to horse is expressed in the mutual scratching of each other's backs and necks with a gentle rhythm of the teeth; reassurance by a head laid across the other horse's neck or by a comforting whickering of the breath. Horses are herd animals, dependent on the company of their own kind to an extent where they become uncertain, lonely and unhappy when pastured by themselves. The main line of communication, the voice, ranges from the carrying whinny of loneliness, through the short, sharp squeal of anger that usually precedes a kick, to the contented, hummering whicker of a mare encouraging her foal.

No matter what action a horse is about to take, he can be absolutely relied upon to signal his intention in advance in a recognizable, time-honored horse form. Other horses depend upon these signals for their information, and so does the observant horseman who wants to stay on board.

Talking to horses, beyond the constant soothing mutter of the horseman, begins with the horse "How do you do?" of blowing into each other's nostrils. How far the horseman wants to take it on from there is between him and his horse.

Breathing into each other's nostrils is the horse way of greeting and mutual scratching a common gesture of comfort. An arm across its neck will reassure a horse or it will feel like another horse's gesture.

Small, Vigorous and Lively

Ponies range from the maximum permitted height of 14.2 hands (58 inches) high—beyond which magic size, their build and disposition notwithstanding, they are for some reason unknown to me automatically called horses—down to the tiny Falabella breed of Argentina, which stands less than 7 hands (28 inches) at the withers. Their brains seem often in inverse ratio to their size, and the strength of their comparatively tiny bodies as well as the wide range of their intelligence has caused many generations of humans to marvel that so much complex ability should dwell in so small a compass of a horse.

A traveler to the far north of the British Isles, the Reverend John Brand, was certainly not the first to be struck by the aptitude of the Shetland pony which is indigenous to the Islands of Shetland and the Outer Hebrides; but this account of the breed, taken from his *Brief Description of Orkney, Zetland, Pightland-Firth and Caithness* and written in 1701, sums up some of the surprise that many of us have felt when first coming to know a pony: "They have a sort of little Horses called Shelties, than which

no other are to be had, if not brought thither, from other places, they are of less size than the Orkney Horses, for some will be but 9 or 10 Nevis or Handbreaths high, and they will be thought big horses there if eleven, and although so small yet are they full of vigour and life, and some not so high as others often prove to be the strongest, yea there are some, whom an able man can lift up in his arms, yet will they carry him and a woman behind him 8 miles forward and as many back; Summer or Winter they never come into an House but run upon the Mountains in some places as flocks, and if any time in Winter the storm be so great, that they are straightened for food, they will come down from the Hills when the Ebb is in the sea, and eat the Sea-Ware (as likewise do the sheep). They will live till a considerable age as 26, 28 or 30 years, and they will be good riding Horses in 24 especially they'll be more vigorous and live the longer if they be 4 years old before they are put to work . . .

"The Coldness of the Air, the Barrenness of the Mountains on which they feed and their hard usage may occasion to keep them so little,

The pupil tries to lead the teacher: at this stage the pony is usually wiser than the child.

for if bigger Horses be brought into the Country, their kind within a little time wil degenerate; and indeed in the present case we may see the Wisdcme of Providence, for their way being deep and Mossie in many places, these lighter Horses come through when the greater and heavier would sink down; and they leap over ditches very nimbly, yea up and down Mossy braes and Hillocks with heavy riders upon them, which I could not look upon but with Admiration, yea I have seen them climb up braes upon their knees, when otherwise they could not get the height overcome. so that our Horses would be but little if at all serviceable there."

Being by and large less valuable than horses, ponies have had a far greater chance to develop in the wild by natural selection, and consequently the native breeds of pony which inhabit practically every country are hardy in the extreme. The huge, shaggy winter coats that turn cold climate ponies into animals that would make a sheep feel under-dressed protect them against all weathers. They are far healthier living out, given a windbreak of some kind, than sweating it out in a stuffy stable. They are also instinctively greedy. Generations of plucking a living off the poor land to which so many in the past were banished when man chose the richer soils to farm has caused them automatically to put their heads down when there is anything edible at foot. For this reason a pony pastured on rich grass needs constant watching because it will stuff itself to the point where its body weight becomes more than its feet will bear and serious lamenesses, such as laminitis, will occur. A common and poignant roadside sight is that of a pony, hopelessly outclassing its child passenger, with its head stuck greedily down into a hedgerow and its rider tugging futilely at the reins.

In the past, before the industrial revolution changed the order of agriculture and the motor engine replaced the horse as common transport, ponies were used for a variety of different purposes throughout Europe and Asia. The hardy Fjord pony of Norway, one of the few breeds to have kept its identity recognizably throughout the centuries, has changed little from the horse the Vikings bred and used for horse-fights. Today it endures as a work horse in areas that are too steep or too cold for a tractor or a lorry, though its attractions as a weight-carrying riding pony have caused large numbers to be exported. The Danes, especially, are fond of it and breed it widely.

The Austrian Haflinger, a long-lived, tireless and surefooted breed, has for centuries made its living doing pack work in the high mountain passes of the Tirol. Being of a docile disposition, it has also worked

A variety of European ponies.
Top: New Forest ponies at a sale.
Above: Dales ponies at a stud in northern England.
Right: Hafflinger in Switzerland.
Top right: Welsh Mountain ponies in their natural habitat.
Far right: New Forest ponies.

Iceland ponies.

well between the shafts; and it is still occasionally so used today, though it is more common as a riding animal.

The immensely frugal Mongolian pony survives on next to nothing in the way of food. It is one of the most antique of pony types and also one of the few breeds of pony still used mainly as a working animal. It is bred in large numbers by the nomadic tribes of Mongolia, Tibet and China, and is used for herding, riding, carting, in agriculture, and for pack work. It further provides meat and milk for its masters: for the first three months after foaling the mares are regularly milked and the milk is made into cheese or fermented into *kumiss,* an alcoholic drink, on equine dairy farms. It is thought that yogurt was a Mongol invention made originally from mares' milk.

The British Isles has developed a surprisingly large number of pony breeds for its small area. The Dales pony is a strongly-built riding or cart pony which for many years carried the local doctor on his rounds. Like its slightly smaller close-relation, the Fell, its survival in quantity in modern times is largely due to its suitability as a trekking pony in the high moorlands of northern Yorkshire. The tiny Welsh Mountain pony is strong and spirited enough, although only about 12 hands high, to carry a farmer hunting all day; while the even smaller Shetland, which so surprised the Reverend Brand, was widely used down the coalmines of northern England and, when well-matched, was sometimes seen between the shafts of ladies' phaetons.

But the working uses of the past are largely disappearing. Today, the pony has become the doormat of the future equestrian, its first function being that of teaching young humans how to ride. For this it is ideally suited once the first few years of its own perilous surprise at the world has been overcome. A pony of three years old is far superior in brain power and experience to a child of the same age, and it is not until both have reached the age of nine or ten that the mental levels equal out and the child begins to have control of who goes where, and why.

Ponies are first class teachers for a young rider. For the very young and squeaky, the older the pony is the better it will put up with the frightening, frightened demands of the pupil on its back, though very old ponies are not all that keen on carrying out the wishes of the more advanced who want to hunt all day. They are quite capable of turning round and going home before the rider has had half the fun he wants. Ponies' homing instincts are extraordinary, exemplified as much in the hunting pony who, when tired, will take you home by the shortest route from any point of the compass if you loose the reins on its neck as in the renowned

Iceland pony who will carry a visitor to any destination and, turned free, will come home of its own accord within a very short period of time.

Apart from the simple ability to ride a horse—an enthusiasm that may not necessarily continue into adulthood—ponies teach children a host of things that are useful to them in later life. More than any other animal or any other form of sport, owning a pony can teach a child patience, discipline, responsibility, courage, tact, and respect for another species. A pony needs two or three hours a day of attention, at regular times of the day and in all weathers (in cases where this responsibility was not made clear before the pony was bought, many a parent has had cause to regret ever having made the purchase).

Maintenance such as daily exercise and foot care, brushing over to keep the coat attractive (deep grooming in the grass-kept pony is unadvisable, as it removes essential oils and dust which protect the animal against rough weather), regular feeding when snow covers the ground, when the pasture is too sparse to support the animal, or when hard work such as hunting is being asked of it is all fairly obvious to the casual eye. Other things that are often not taken account of when a person first thinks of purchasing a pony include the cleaning and repair of harness, routine searching of the pasture and surrounding hedges to remove poisonous plants, repairing broken fencing, providing windbreaks where necessary and maybe building a shelter of some kind so that hay can be economically fed (if simply scattered on the ground the pony will trample it, and in wet weather much of it will become soggy and unpalatable).

If all this sounds like a lot of work—well, so it is; but almost all of it is enormous fun. The miserable hours spent trailing round a field trying to catch a pony who isn't in the mood for it are made up for when the pony comes to meet you at the gate. Incidentally, it is more likely to do this if it is caught up at the same time every day, since ponies, like horses, are creatures of routine.

Right: Ponies in the Mongolian winter.
Below: Fell pony stallion.
Below right: Norwegian Fjord foal.

The thrill of padding along behind a pack of hounds, feeling a bit proud to be there and a bit apprehensive in case you commit some awful social bunder such as getting in front of the Master; the soft summer evening rides after school is finished; the triumph of your first rosette in a local gymkhana; the warm comfort of curling into a pony's neck when everything in life seems to have gone rotten; the friendly welcoming whicker and sweet, steaming breath of a hungry pony on a frosty night—these things, and many like them, are what make owning a pony special.

Ponies have a look in their eyes that is both kind and wise, fur that turns the favourite teddy bear back into the stuffed toy it really is, a friendly solidarity of body that strengthens and reassures, and an ability to move with speed and grace across country that gives you a feel of the freedom of clouds chasing each other across the moon. They are the first true friends of many children, a permanent anchor in a changing, growing world.

Pony events at shows. Gymkhanas provide excellent training for young riders, offering a variety of events calling for dexterity in horsemanship.
Left: The sack race calls for mounting and dismounting at speed.
Below left: Musical poles requires a controlled canter round the outside of the ring with, when the music stops, a quick turn and dash for the pole, ending with an abrupt halt from full gallop.
Below: The magnificent four-in-hand of Shetlands, a more sedentary use of the pony than gymkhana games, requires an adult skill in driving.

A Matter of Forgery

Farriery is one of the oldest trades in the world still to be practised today in a form that is not so very far from the original. The abundance of blacksmiths who must have worked in villages throughout Europe during the Middle Ages can be guessed at from the enormous quantity of people surnamed Smith or Schmidt, so great that trying to pin one down in a telephone directory in any European or North American city if you have only a vague idea of his street address is a waste of time.

Not so long ago, not so far back in recent history that most adults cannot remember having seen them, nearly every village had its resident blacksmith. The forge building with its permanent coke fire always kept red-hot just under the surface, the bellows waiting to blow it into life, the familiar heavy anvil and often a line of horses quietly waiting to be shod was part of country life. After the Second World War the increasing disappearance of the farm horse in favor of the tractor led to the increasing disappearance of the smith. Many sustained themselves for a time by sideline jobs such as the working of wrought iron, but gradually smithy after smithy closed down and the farrier seemed to have departed, an important part of a vanishing past.

The smith, in fact, did not so much vanish as metamorphose. With the growing interest in riding and the boom in horse breeding that occurred in the affluent sixties, the farrier reappeared in a traveling van, driving from stable to stable upon request— all modernized, with horseshoe sizes graded in numbers just like

human shoes. Shoeing a horse cold became the done thing; though hot shoeing, which ensures a better fit, is still practised whenever possible.

A horse needs shoes to protect the working surfaces of his feet against excessive wear, the more especially so if he is used on metaled roads. The horseshoes, usually made of iron, last from four to eight weeks depending upon the amount of roadwork the horse does. During that time—generally after four weeks, but it varies with the horse—they will need removing and replacing so that the constantly-growing wall of the hoof can be pared down. If the wall of the hoof was allowed to grow out over the shoe, the tendency would be for it to split up the sides, cracking too near to the sensitive interior of the foot.

Racing shoes, called racing plates, are a different matter altogether. Aimed at giving the horse the least amount of weight to carry during a race, they are made of aluminum. Racehorses are usually "plated" the night before or upon the morning of a race, and have their work shoes replaced within a day or two because aluminum has very little durability on tarmac.

As well as making and fitting horseshoes, the skilled farrier will perform tasks requiring judgement and intelligence, such as shoeing a young horse with a shoe built up to one side to correct a bend in the leg or a faulty action.

What the old truism "a horse is only as good as its feet" really means is that a horse is only as good as the man that shoes it.

Left: Turning a hot shoe on the anvil.
Center: Trying a shoe for fit before the final alterations are made.
Above: Trimming excess nail ends from the wall of the hoof.
Right: Cold shoeing on a farm.

Natural to Man

On a clear day, when you can see forever, there usually isn't much scent about. The smell of a fox lies best on wet earth; holding earth which doesn't dry out in the sun or the wind; damp earth under a lowering sky, on a day when the pungent smells of moss and bracken steam fragrant from the hedgerows and a fine mist hangs over ponds and puddles. On such a day in any country in the temperate zone, when you hear the huntsman calling up his hounds, the occasional short, sweet blast of the horn, the deep, incessant dog-talk of his voice and the throaty answer of the excited pack; on days like this, clattering along a country road with your horse sweating up ever so slightly with anticipation, his ears pricked, his heart as high as yours, on such a day you know you're on a winner. Riding to hounds, as the expression goes (rather than riding "at" hounds, or "through" them; the last of which will probably get you sent home for bad behavior, satisfies a variety of different instincts in many men. There is the pleasure of watching a pack of hounds working a line; the thrill of a challenging fence on a good galloping horse; the independence of going off alone, judging the course the fox will take from the direction of the wind, the lie of the land, and your own intimate knowledge of the countryside (this is called "taking your own line," and your knowledge of the country had indeed better be intimate or the hunt will perform that well-known queer manoeuvre by which a half-hundred dogs, horses and people are swallowed into a landscape without trace or sound). After, there is the peace of the hot bath, the pleasure of the well-exercised body that has been tested and come through the sharpened appetite for supper and the deep release of sleep. For one reason or another most people prefer foxhunting or

staghunting. For myself, the choice falls with draghunting, a relatively
minor sport in which hounds pursue a strong man-laid scent over
a predetermined line with artificially-built fences. The attraction
of draghunting, with its obvious limitations, is a horseman's joy
in getting around the course, finishing over a 10-12 mile point
with as many fences as are in the Grand National. A good drag line,
being fast and guaranteed, usually requires the sort of hunter
used in the "best" hunting country—the well-drained, well-fenced
open grass that dominates the landscape hunted by such famous packs
as Ireland's Galway Blazers, England's Quorn, or the great,
timber-fenced, bold country of Maryland and West Virginia.
For this, a near-bred blood horse is the sort of animal best suited;
but a "hunter" may be any sort of animal, a good one being a horse
that can act on the available going, whether it is the deep alluvial
plough of East Anglia or the trappy, hilly country hunted by the
sporting Welsh farmer packs.
After draghunting, I am inclined to rate cubhunting next for pleasure,
though of an entirely different sort. Cubhunting, in which
young hounds are taught their job on young foxes, precedes the season
proper by some two or three months. It begins in late August or
early September, starting early in the morning before the sun
has burned the dew off the grass and the scent has vanished in a
steam of early autumn mist, and involves those few riders who
turn up to stand around a covert and turn the cub back rather
than let him loose to run a line.
Cubhunting could be rather boring were it not for the quality of early
morning light, the long shadows cast by a rising sun in a new day,
the curious, mellow scent of autumn in the air. Getting up before
the first light marks a horizon in the sky, going out in the dark
to rouse a hunter blinking sleepy in a stable under the sharp,
electric light; saddling up and clopping off into a gradually increasing
lightness, the cobwebs on the hedgerows etched in dew: these things
are part of hunting, and hunting, as Surtees' famous Mr. Jorrocks said,
is natural to man.

Galloping Mania

Most European countries go in for amateur racing of one sort or another. Germany and France are notable for it, rivaling each other in the number of flat races, hurdle races and steeplechases open to the non-professional rider. Great Britain and Ireland go one step further (or may be it is one step back) by staging point-to-points, which are fund-raising hunt steeplechases limited to hunt subscribers and to horses which have been "regularly and fairly hunted". This last requirement is often a bit of polite baloney, because good hunters mostly wouldn't succeed on a steeplechase course and good chasers would be useless in the hunting field. The thrill of riding in a race for the first time, no matter whether as amateur or professional, must be much the same for all, and I suspect that the following personal account of a first ride in a race is fairly universal.

Competition for a ride in a point-to-point is very keen, and for the non-horse-owner with no previous experience of racing the chances of being offered a mount are about as thin as a cockerel's eyelash. Thus it was not until I was 30 that, by means of unscrupulous pulling of strings, I managed at last to get it set up. The horse, which was called Poorernie, belonged to a Mr. Bert Doggrell and was entered to run in a three-mile race with 18 fences at the back end of the season. I was told that Poorernie was a safe ride and experienced, which was just as well since either horse or jockey should have some knowledge of the job, and I refused Mr. Doggrel's kind offer to let me school it over fences in cold blood in case I fell off it.

In February and March I went to all the local point-to-points, where I saw several nasty accidents and two horses so badly injured that they had to be shot. I learned that in these races riders sometimes fall off from exhaustion; that horses often fall through tiredness; that experienced point-to-point riders expect one accident in every 10 rides.

I knew that I had to spend the next two months in training. Getting fit took two hours a day on a racehorse (for the development of general riding muscles); 25 minutes daily with a skipping rope (lungs); 25 minutes of push-ups and lifting weights (for arm and back muscles needed on a strong horse); and two miles a day

Summer racing at
Bad Harzburg, West Germany.

of running, or alternatively sprinting and jogging (lungs again).
May came around at last, blossoming with a flippant insouciance
that I was much too terrified to share. I gathered up my hired
racing clothes and jangling nerves and drove to Larkhill, where the
meeting was, to stay the night before the race. It was a wet evening
when I arrived; on the top of Salisbury Plain the fences stood out
big and black against a grey, wind-tossed sky. Away in the distance
where the course went out of sight were clumps of newly-leafed trees
and a group of pines. In a flurry of May rain I began to walk
the course, inspecting each fence as I went.

The Larkhill course, unlike many point-to-point courses which
run over open farming land, was fenced on both sides and was used
only for racing. It was beautifully kept, with 13 neat birch stick
fences banked with gorse on the take-off side, and the course
secretary told me that £400 a year was spent on maintaining
these fences alone.

Competitors had to race round the course one and a third times
to cover the full distance of 3 miles 228 yards. The finishing post
was at the south-east end of the course, with the start a mile away
to the north-west so that the runners passed the crowd at the finish
on their first circuit, went away to the right into the country,
and came back past the start to jump the first five fences over again.
Fences 3 and 11 were open ditches—a dry ditch in front of the usual
fence—and since fence 3 was also fence 16 one had to jump
three open ditches in a race. At the far end of the course, between
the twelfth and thirteenth fences, the ground sloped sharply downhill
on a right-angled bend where I thought a horse going too fast
might easily slip, and then there was a long, slow uphill pull over
the thirteenth fence back past the start. Any horse left behind
on the hill might be too tired after the uphill pull to make up
the ground again back on the flat.

The following day I met the owner at the declaration tent. He was
calm and cheerful and had the tact not to ask if I had ridden in
a race before. This was a question I had been avoiding. He filled out
the declaration form, which is a formal announcement that a horse
will run, and handed me over to his son, Michael, for instructions
about how to ride the race. Michael told me Poorernie would judge
the jumps himself but that I must push him to keep up with the
leaders throughout. He said that at the top of the hill, passing
the start for the second time, I must move up and take the lead and
kick Poorernie on.

We went to look at Poorernie waiting in his horsebox. I had not seen
the horse before and could not see much now as most of him
was hidden under blankets, but there was an amiable chestnut face
and longish teeth, a shiny firm neck. I found out that Poorernie
had belonged to the Doggrells since he was a yearling 12 years before,
and that he was rather a family pet.

I had to change and weigh out. I was to wear Mr. Doggrell's
gold cap and black jersey, with gold hoops and blue sleeves, and
a hunting stock tight round my neck for support if I fell. In the ladies'
changing room I met the four other riders, including young
Mrs. Alderton who was down to ride a horse called Gay Quadrille,
a combination that had won me money many times before at
point-to-points.

Dressed, we went separately to weigh out, stepping on the scales
with our saddles and weightcloths. Michael handed me his
14 lb-saddle, then 7 lbs in weights (ladies must all ride at 154 lbs)
and the Clerk of the Scales nodded "OK." Then there was nothing
to do but hang around discreetly—I was told it was bad form to go
and look at the betting once you were dressed in colors—until
it was time to go into the paddock.

When Michael called me I followed numbly into the paddock.
The other owners and riders were already there, with the horses
circling round in front of a tight-packed crowd. The bell to mount

After the race is over there is the weary journey home in the horsebox,
usually unloading in the dark. Tired muscles relax with a warm
bran mash in the loosebox overnight, and by the following morning
the horse has often stiffened up. If the weather is good the horse
may be loosed for a short period in a paddock to ease his body.
Given this opportunity, almost all horses will opt for a roll, grinding
the tight, itchy bits of skin on back and sides into the rough winter grass.

sounded, and I had just a glance at my horse before I got on him.
Poorernie looked splendid, a gleaming chestnut with the muscles
standing out tight under his silken coat. He seemed at the peak
of condition for a race. Michael gave me a leg up and I was led off
round the paddock and out on to the course. As we left someone
called out to me, "Has anyone told you Gay Quadrille jumps
across to the left?"

I had the reins short and crossed on Poorernie's neck in case
the horse wanted to gallop off too fast, but as we broke into a canter
I was glad to find that, while nicely on the bit, he didn't take much
hold at all. He had a lovely stride, a very comfortable horse
going well up into his bridle, and the manners of a perfect gentleman.
A few drops of rain had fallen on us in the paddock but now
the sun was shining on the lush May grass. I cantered down to the
start feeling fine and clear-headed, Poorernie's ears pricking with
pleasure and his muscles moving rhythmically beneath his golden coat.
We walked to the first fence and looked at it together; I patted
his firm neck and spoke to him. Then we trotted back to the start,
joining the other riders who were walking in a circle behind
the Starter.

The Starter called us into line—I was second from the inside,
with Gay Quadrille on the extreme left because Mrs. Alderton
sportingly didn't want him in a position to jump across another horse
—and we all broke into a trot as we came up level with the
white flag. It fell and we were off at a gallop, Lady Allison, a gray,
leading from Gay Quadrille, Red Trawler, then me.

we went past Red Trawler and pushed on after Lady Allison and Gay Quadrille, who seemed to be going impossibly fast.

We came round the bend to the fifth fence on the inside, me kicking Poorernie to keep up with the leaders, flew over the straight in front of the crowd, over the sixth, and swung away into the country right-handed to meet the seventh. At our 30 m.p.h. speed the wind felt strong in our faces and our lungs were working overtime to meet a fence every 18 seconds. Gay Quadrille and Lady Allison were still in front of me, Gay Quadrille jumping well clear to the left and me on the inside following Poorernie's inclination to keep tight on the bends.

Poorernie was the perfect horse, sensible, talented and enjoying himself, and he seemed also to know the Larkhill course very well. We swallowed up the seventh fence, and at the eighth the leaders were only two lengths clear of us and I had a searing pain in my lungs. Round the S-bend between the eighth and ninth we flashed through bright gorse, the gray Lady Allison three lengths in the lead and Gay Quadrille's muscular bay quarters about a length ahead of us. Poorernie was going superbly, jumping straight with never a mistake and still cutting all the corners.

Over the twelfth Lady Allison still had a three-length lead over Gay Quadrille, who was a little ahead of me but now in touch. Then downhill to the slippery right-angled bend, and Lady Allison nose-dived on the wet grass and almost sat down: I shouted out something fatuous like, "Well sat," to her rider, who was magnificently still in the saddle, and she called back with something equally neurotic which sounded like, "Don't let that old b . . . . jump across me," and we shot past on the inside.

At the long climb up there was only Gay Quadrille in front of us, and for the first time it occurred to me that we might win.

It happened very fast—one moment we were trotting into the start and the next we were racing at the first fence (my first dilemma: the horse needed a clear view to judge the fence correctly, whereas I needed not to see the huge thing looming up). I let Poorernie alone to see how he would take it. We were on the fence in a flash and he left the ground so early that I, accustomed to indifferent jumpers, wasn't really ready and was lucky to stay on. He flew over the fence in a huge, smooth leap, making up ground in the air. It watched the second fence and the first open ditch come up and disappear beneath us, and between the third and fourth fences

Ladies suffer from racing nerves just as badly as the men. In many countries, because of the severely limited opportunities for women to race, the tension of the inexperienced jockey is visible at the start of the race, as can be seen in the picture above. It's allright once you get settled down (*right*), but the first few seconds of a race can be horrific. Connoisseurs of the art of swearing are advised to stand by the first fence in any ladies' point-to-point and listen: it is one of the surest venues in the world for a guaranteed demonstration of rough language.

I gave Poorernie an extra shove with the legs. He moved straight up level with Gay Quadrille at the thirteenth fence; we came over the top of the hill together back in sight of the crowd and raced neck-and-neck for the next four fences. There was a great sense of aloneness and exhilaration—the horses behind us were lost in the rushing wind and I was aware of a peculiar mixture of sensations. The thudding of our flight. Sun. A lark's song borne back towards us. Poorernie's straining muscles. The fences rising up at us and flashing by underneath like breaking waves. Exhaustion. At the sixteenth fence, the open ditch again, Mrs. Alderton and I were six lengths clear, and, I believe, having some sort of silly chat about how to get fit. At the seventeenth, with only the right-hand bend and one fence left before the winning post, Gay Quadrille jumped left as usual and this time simply disappeared out of my field of vision. Turning to the right with Poorernie hugging the rails I had the extraordinary sight of no one in front. Just one jump to go and a noise coming up from the crowd; I felt very much alone. Now there was only me and Poorernie with his game pricked ears and his clever feet.

I pushed him a bit with what strength remained and we were over the last. Still 200 yards from the finish, Poorernie slowed down, seemed to lose momentum. I hit him lightly down the shoulder and called out to him, and he leaped forward with a fine burst of speed to the post.

At first I thought only: we've got where we had to go. Poorernie knew it too and pulled himself up without help from me. Other members of the field, still galloping, went past us; and in my stupor I envied them because they had been riding in a point-to-point. Finally it hit me that we had won. Gay Quadrille was second, Lady Allison third.

Then Poorernie turned himself around and headed for the winners' enclosure, and Michael Doggrell came up and said I must take the saddle off myself so that no one could be thought to have tampered with the weights, and must take the saddle and the weight cloth and weigh in—which I did, at 5 lbs lighter than before the race. I told Bert Doggrell that I hadn't ridden in a point-to-point before, and he said that was all right because he hadn't told me that the horse had never been raced by a woman before and that the last time Poorernie had run at Larkhill he had fallen at the second open ditch. So we laughed, and had champagne.

Above: Racing at Frankfurt. *Left:* Hurdle racing. A fall over a small fence can be just as nasty as a fall over a big one. But one man's disaster can clear a nice gap for the horses following behind—always provided that the faller does not trip them up.

They're off

In winter, the first lot goes out with the first light, stirred out of sleep by the bustle of the stable lads and the strong, authoritative voices of the trainer and head lad. Usually it's all a bit of a rush, a sharp change from dozing in a warm straw bed to the cold bit in the mouth as the bridle is lifted up over the ears. The overnight rugs come off and are piled into a corner, the saddle is girthed in place and a work blanket is fastened neatly over the top to keep the frost from getting at the thin, silk hide. Mane and tail are brushed in place, the hooves picked out, and the racehorse is led out into the sharp, exhilarating blast of morning, bucking and kicking with excitement under his featherweight exercise boy.

When they are all assembled in the stable yard they go out on to the racetrack, the exercise grounds, the downs, or indoor school, depending on the country and the weather. The colts go first and then the geldings the fillies trailing off behind to keep their scent from getting to the young stallions up in front. Youth, high protein, and the morning wind stir up their blood so that even

a rustle in the dead, dry grass will take them wheel away, whip round, rear up, kick out; and if they drop their riders, off they go, floating with easy grace along the track or turning in towards the string to make the other horses jump and kick and play. Mostly at this time of year they only walk and trot, because (except in sub-tropical regions such as Florida and southern California) there isn't any flat racing until the spring comes in and so there is no call to be hard fit. Steeplechasers, though, being in the middle of their racing season, come up the gallops one by one, moving at a steady half-speed gallop with perhaps ten lengths between each horse.

When the hour-long exercise is done the lads dismount and lead

Morning exercise on Newmarket Heath, greatest of the British training grounds. In the first light, at a walk, all horses are potential winners and all stable boys potential jockeys. But, though they serve the full five years of their apprenticeship, very few of these lads will ever see a racecourse except on foot.

Ploughed gallops (*below* and *far right*) are strips of gravel deeply turned and raked. Steady work on the plough, with each foot sinking in to fetlock-deep, builds muscle on the horse more quickly than the easier travel over grassland (*center*).

the last mile home to ease their horses' backs. Shut up in their looseboxes again the horses get the sweat and mud cleaned off them, their hooves picked free of stones and dirt, their coats brushed over and, if wet, dried off. Then the indoor rugs are buckled into place, the hayrack filled, fresh water brought, and finally a rich, sweet breakfast feed is poured into the mangers and the horses are left in peace to eat and sleep until the time arrives for evening stables.

After the lads themselves have breakfasted the second lot goes out. In most flat stables this will be the yearlings, accompanied by a wise old horse or two to lead them and to teach them manners. Wandering a little from side to side as they fail to get their balance quite correct, they learn to walk and trot and canter in single file,

and after that to work upsides in threes and fours. They are the unknown quantity in racing; the young, unproven, who have never seen a racetrack. On average only one out of four will ever win a race of any kind, but at this stage there is always an owner or a stable lad who thinks each horse a budding superstar. A few of them will never see a racetrack, breaking down in wind or limb in training and may be going straight to stud. Others may become "morning glories"—horses who work well enough at home, but at the racetrack in the afternoon have lost their early morning zest. Some will prove too slow, or will be entered in the wrong races (one of the most important skills of a great trainer is to enter a horse against others that it is likely to beat, and this requires, apart from talent, an intimate knowledge of all racetracks and all other horses likely to compete). Many more are simply not competitive. Any fool can get a horse to gallop, but if the urge to win is not instinctive to it he'll never make a racehorse.

There are horses who do best at certain seasons of the year. Early runners, tearing up the racetrack in the spring, grow lazy and lose their form when the summer sun gets on their backs. Others take weeks or months to come to their peak, only really running on when the season is more than halfway over.

Within the general type called "racehorse" there are many different kinds of animal. There are sprinters, on the small side and compactly built, who can jump out of the starting stalls at a tearaway pace and maintain their speed for short distances not exceeding a mile. There are stayers who, though they cannot live with a sprinter over five or six furlongs, yet have a steady,

remorseless stride which brings them home in front over two miles or more. The most desired among the flat-race horses are those who, at three and four years old, beat the best of their age group at a mile and a half, thus showing a mixture of the sprinter's turn of foot and the stayer's strength of heart and limbs. The most valuable prizes —the American Triple Crown, the French Arc de Triomphe, and the English Derby—are designed for horses of this sort, and it is the winners of these races who later command the greatest price at stud.

Steeplechase horses, who are expected to cover long distances and jump big fences, come into their prime at about eight years old and are a somewhat different sort of thoroughbred. Although they may be bred along very similar lines to the flat horse they are slower to develop, and when they reach maturity often show greater depth and more bone. These horses must have stamina, sense and courage. At their best they compete for England's Cheltenham Gold Cup, the greatest honor in chasing; and stiffer and more widely-known trials exist for them, so dangerous that the owners of some top chasers will not permit their horses to be entered. These are the Aintree Grand National, held in northern England, and Czechoslovakia's dramatic Grand Pardubice. Both are held annually, the National in the spring and the Pardubice in the autumn, and both are run over roughly 4½ miles with 30 or so fences; though the Pardubice, which is run on both plough and grass, has, unlike the National, a variety of different sorts of fences to be jumped and is therefore more suited to the kind of horse with a leaning towards cross-country work and less to the big, bold sort of chaser

that might win the National. The world's most horrifying fence, the Taxis, occurs in the Pardubice. A natural hedge 5 feet (1.5 metres) high and 5 feet wide conceals from the approaching horse a ditch 16 foot 5 inches (5 metres) wide and 6 foot 6 inches (2 metres) deep on the landing side. Many, taken unprepared, fall into this ditch, and many more fall over the fallers.

The most popular of all types of racing, trotting, does not involve the true thoroughbred horse, although the Standardbreds of America, the Orlov and Métis Trotters of Russia, and the French and German Trotters mostly carry more thoroughbred blood in their veins then they do of any other breed. Trotting racing seems to have evolved separately in several different countries as a natural part of such activities as taking the gig to market and seeing if you could out-trot the other fellow. The craze in Germany, where trotting is twice as popular as thoroughbred racing, began in the second half of the 19th century. The first trotting club, the Altona, was formed in Hamburg in 1874, and the basis of the modern German Trotter was the Russian Orlov, 18th-century brainchild of Count Alexius Grigorievich Orlov (who may also have been the murderer of Czar Peter III). Massive doses of American Standardbred blood, so-called because each performer must achieve a minimum standard of speed over one mile before it is allowed on the racetrack, and more recently of that of the French Trotter has built the German horse into a high-calibre competitor. The German record over 1,000 metres of 1 minute 17.3 seconds is held by Permit, who is by Epilog, one of the most famous of the German Trotter sires.

Starting stalls, a modern development that is now in almost universal use (*top:* Newmarket, England; *center:* Arizona, USA; *bottom:* Germany), ensure an even break for all. From there on in factors of speed and skill soon sort them out.

Right: Passing the finishing post, Marseilles, France.

Thoroughbred racing varies from country to country, and about the only generalisation universally true of a trainer's working day is that it is never done. In the smaller European countries, horses are trained at the trainer's own establishment and are shipped out to race as they come ready, sometimes staying overnight but never away from home for more than a day or two. During the racing season, normal work for the trainer will entail getting up in time to see the first lot work, and soon after that usually having to leave for a far-away racetrack to see one of his horses run or to learn the form of other runners. It is for this reason that the horses who are most imminently ready to race go out with the first lot, and for this reason that the first lot has to be over and done with and back in the stables by about 9 o'clock in the morning. After the first lot, if the trainer is having a rare easy day, he goes out to watch the second lot. More often he drives or takes a light aircraft to the racetrack, arriving in time to saddle his runner and to give instructions to the jockey. In the Paddock he may meet the owner of the horse, with whom he goes over the animal's probable performance, and, later, its actual performance. After racing he rushes home in time for evening stables, when his lads are cleaning and mucking out the horses, and inspects every horse in his charge. If this were not enough, there is a lot of paperwork to be done. Corn, hay and straw must be chosen and paid for; veterinary and farriers' bills debited to the right horse so that owners' accounts can be made up fairly; entries made long in advance and the forfeit stages noted; horseboxes organized and accommodation reserved for horses and lads who will stay overnight at the races. There are also written reports on the progress of horses to be made up and sent out, telephone calls to owners and time spent socially with them.

Yet, if the European trainers seem to have a hard life of it, American and Russian trainers can make them look almost indolent. Because of the vast tracts of territory involved, horses are trained on the racetracks; and trainers, having horses working at three or more tracks simultaneously, fly from place to place, living like jet-set gipsies in motels and airplanes. In America the racing season goes on relentlessly all the year round. A trainer is likely to live in Florida from January until the end of March, then move up to New York for racing at Belmont and Aqueduct in the spring. In August there is the Saratoga meeting in upper New York State. Meanwhile the trainer may be running horses in Chicago, or flying one across for a big race on the West Coast, or living temporarily at Hollywood Park. In the fall it is back to New York, and at the end of November racing begins again in Florida. All this, plus the paperwork and so on. Training racehorses is not a job but a dedicated way of life, an avocation that consumes at the expense of all other interests.

The only reason for it has to be the peculiar fascination of the racehorse. Man has been drawn to racing horses since time out of mind. The first recorded instance of a race appears on Hittite cuneiform tablets dated 4,000 years BC, and before the days when man could write it seems likely that he raced his horses against his neighbor's. Though it has since become a multi-million dollar industry, the hard core of racing remains the same: a delight beyond price in the speed and courage of a horse.

Above left: Accidents are more likely when the horse is tired. This faller is coming over the last jump on a course with a slight uphill gradient.
Top right: Very few even get to the last in the gruelling British Grand National. In this picture, taken during the 1975 race, L'Escargot (blinkered), the eventuel winner, fights it out with Red Rum, winner in '73 and '74.
But even where no fences are involved, nothing is certain to stay on its feet. A slip on the snow at St. Moritz (*left*) or a tangle of Canadian wheels in the trotting race (*center right*) or chuck wagon race (*right*) could cause a nasty pile up.

Wild Horses

This is the age when the old saw about "wild horses couldn't drag you away" has finally come true. It isn't that the wild horse has developed a bad case of cold feet; it's simply that there aren't enough wild horses around to do a proper job. The truly wild horse is near extinction, and with its passing a vanishing dream becomes a legend.

Millions of years before man began, great herds of horses roamed freely over the face of the earth. They had the wind to tell them where the water was; the knowledge, passed from horse to horse by demonstration, of the summer pastures high up in the hills. Distances meant little to them, and the migration down the mountainside when winter stung them round the ears, the haul across the plains to shelter where the snow was thin enough to scrape a living, was just a part of normal life. They ran instinctively from natural enemies, shying at logs and ditches which could conceal all manner of invader and approaching water holes with caution. Some, adapted to the scrub forests of northern Europe, were elk-like in the head and browsed off trees. Others, more like the modern horse to look at, grazed on the steppes and plains of central Asia.

Hungary: A free-range herd is brought in. The tamer headcollared pair in the center have been loosed to guide the others and to help them settle down.

Each herd was governed by a king, a stallion, proud of his mares and foals, diligent in driving off the intruder, forever on the watch against attack or danger. Often he was challenged by a rival horse, a colt or loner paying court to some of his mares, and only by strength and brainpower could a stallion maintain his herd. Gradually, and largely through the agency of man, the horse grew taller and its territory increased. Only in the last few centuries have there been horses in Australia or America, and it is largely there, to the small extent that they exist, that the truly wild horse remains. The Australian Brumby—whose name is probably derived either from a pioneer horsebreeder called James Brumby, from "baroomby," the Queensland aboriginal word for wild, or from Baramba, the name of a station and creek in Queensland— still carries on in microscopic numbers because it is almost impossible to train, and so, once caught, is scarcely worth the effort. The curious thing about the Brumby, which is now a genuine wild horse of considerable intelligence, is that it originated only just over a century ago from feral horses when the great Australian gold rush

Left: The two oldest breeds of horse still known to man—the Tarpan (*above*) and the Asiatic Wild Horse (also called Przewalskii's Horse). Few now remain, and their survival is due largely to their interest for zoos and wildlife parks.
Below: A Brazilian remuda, semi-wild, is brought in from the ranges.

of the mid-nineteenth century caused many domestic horses to be turned loose on the ranges to breed as they chose. They proliferated rapidly, accelerated by the redundancy of twentieth-century horses which were sent to join them when mechanisation became the thing, and since World War II have been heavily culled because of the damage they did to agricultural land, so that now very few are left. Something of the same story happened to the North American Mustang. Horses were introduced to the Americas by the Conquistadores of the fourteenth to fifteenth centuries. Those that escaped, or were let loose, quickly deteriorated on the ranges from high-quality Spanish stock into plain scrub horses which, from natural selection, became very tough and brainy. These were the ponies the Indians used, conforming to no special color, size or shape, and they were also the original cow ponies. They have been culled for agricultural reasons, shot for dog meat and for glue; and today there would be no Mustangs left were it not for government laws ensuring their protection.

Two of the original types of wild horse still exist, or just about. Both, in height, are only ponies, and both exude a ferocity unknown in the tractable domestic horse that has been a friend of man for centuries. One type, kept alive by zoos and wildlife parks and living semi-wild in a Polish herd at Popielno, is the Tarpan, an Ice Age horse which was once widespread in Europe and Asia. It formed part of the make-up of many primitive horses, and so

is a basic part of the ancestry of the more sophisticated modern breeds. It is a curious horse, having sometimes the striped coat that would make it invisible in the forest and occasionally turning white in winter, as Arctic animals do.

The Tarpan appears to have divided into two groups, one wandering in eastern Europe and the other grazing on the steppes of the Ukraine. It has been hunted for food for millennia; much as deer were hunted, but more ruthlessly because the Tarpan stallion would attack his domestic rival ferociously. Tarpan meat was regarded as such a great delicacy that by the end of the eighteenth century it had been hunted almost to extinction.

Left: The famous white horses of the Camargue, which run loose in the marshes of the Rhône delta and are the mounts of the local gauchos. The Camarguais, technically a pony because of its short stature, owes its fame more to its highly-photogenic surroundings than to its ability.

Above: A frightened Dülmen weanling is separated from the herd.

There is a Mongolian legend of Tarpan which concerns the Torguls, a human tribe descended from a Tarpan stallion. On the day of the birth of Torgut, son of lovely Irgit and magnificent Tarpan, stallions, mares and foals came from all points of the compass to witness the event. After a fierce fight with wolves, in which the stallions routed 20,000 of them, Tarpan, immortalized, trotted proudly away with the young prince on his back.

The other still-extant primitive wild horse, the Asiatic Wild Horse (also known as *Equus Przewalskii Przewalskii Poliakov,* or Przewalskii's Horse), still just about survives in the Tachin Schara Nuru Mountains, the Mountains of the Yellow Horses, on the western fringe of the Gobi Desert. Like the Tarpan it has been hunted to near-extinction, and its biggest chance of survival lies in European and American zoos; and like the Tarpan it is an Ice Age relic. It lives in a rigorous climate with little food of any quality, and its savage attitude to outsiders must have something to do with its continuity of form. In its wild state stallions

51

and even two-year-old colts will attack and kill invading males long before they get within reach of the mares, and run away domestic mares who attempt to join the band are usually insufficiently hardy to withstand the extreme conditions in which the Asiatic Wild Horse lives.

Herds of semi-wild horses still continue to endure, running loose in the great remudas (remount herds) of Russia, the Americas and eastern Europe, but most of these horses are already broken to the saddle. At the very least they have parents who are broken in, and when their own turn arrives will be rounded up and trained as needed. It is sometimes convenient to let the horses fend for themselves, but as agriculture encroaches all the time on common land the areas in which horses can run without doing damage become increasingly limited. Small private herds on large private estates, such as the Dülmen ponies which run semi-wild on a reserve in Westphalia, are becoming more the natural way of life. On common ground throughout the world, horses and ponies will continue to roam at will—that is, until their masters catch them up and work them. But time, as well as masters, catch them up. The day of the wild horse is done, succumbing like so many independent creatures of the demands of domesticity.

The North American Mustang performs its traditional role of bucking bronco. This hasty method of breaking a wild horse by strapping a saddle on its back and sitting there until it had bucked itself into exhaustion was originally used because most working cowboys hadn't time to spare to train vast quantities of animals gently. It survives today in the sporting attraction of the rodeo bronc. The best of these have been ridden many times unsuccessfully, bucking through a powerful instinct to dislodge any rider and sometimes impelled to great jumps and pitches by a cinch strapped uncomfortably round the tender skin of their bellies.

Drinkers of the Wind

Allah said to the South Wind: "Become solid flesh, for I will make a new creature of thee, to the honour of
My Holy One, and the abasement of Mine enemies, and for a servant to them that are subject to Me."
And the South Wind said: "Lord, do Thou so."
Then Allah took a handful of the South Wind and he breathed thereon, creating the horse and saying:
"Thy name shall be Arabian, and virtue bound into the hair of thy forelock, and plunder on thy back. I have
preferred thee above all beasts of burden, inasmuch as I have made thy master thy friend. I have given thee
the power of light without wings, be it in onslaught or in retreat. I will set men on thy back, that shall honor
and praise Me and sing Hallelujah to My Name."

Bedouin legend.

The Arabian has been selectively bred for more than 1,000 years
longer than any other breed of horse, and there are those who claim
that he has run wild in the deserts of Arabia for many millennia.
Others disagree on the grounds that no prehistoric horse bones
have ever been found in the desert, and they are supported
by the fact that the Arab was not one of the twelve breeds mentioned
by the Romans; nor is there any mention of him in pre-Roman
history. The Mohammedans believed, literally, that Allah created
him out of a handful of the south wind, but very probably they were
barking up the wrong genealogical tree. A more likely source
of origin, at least in part, is the ancient race of Turkoman,
or Turkmene, horses of the steppe and desert regions of central Asia.

Selective breeding of the Arab by the Bedouin has been going on
since at least the time of Mohammed (seventh century AD),
and there is evidence to suggest that it was practised for as long as
a thousand years before that. The Bedouins' ruthless attention
to purity of line—so absolute that unless a horse was known
to be *asil* (pure) he could never be bred into the *asil* line no matter
how perfect his conformation—and the exceptional hardships

Below: Standing among the devout at prayer the holy Arab, having
brought his master to the mosque, is a natural part of the religious scene.
Right: Bedouin in Morocco. "The Evil One dare not enter into a tent
in which a pure-bred horse is kept" is an injunction in the Koran.

A breed of horse, though pure in blood-line, varies with the climate in which it lives and the richness of its pasture. The Polish Arabs (*above and right*) and the Moroccan Arab (*top right*) are noticeably finer-drawn than their luxuriant cousins (*top, center*) which are brought up on the deep grassland of southern England.

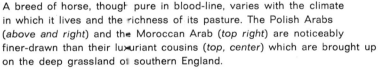

of the desert climate are the two factors that have produced this fine animal, the most graceful and individual horse in the world. Food was scarce in the desert. Grass grew only in winter and early spring, and for the rest of the year the horses lived off camel's milk, dried dates, locusts, and dried camel's meat. Only the strong could endure it. So convinced was Mohammed of the military importance of these tough desert horses, which he bought from the wandering tribes and paid for with human slaves, that he wrote into the Koran an irresistible injunction to men to feed their horses well: "As many grains of barley as thou givest thy horse, so many sins shall be forgiven thee."
Religious commandment reinforced by an extraordinary passion for their horses led the Bedouin into a man-to-horse relationship unequalled to this day. It was to last for thirteen centuries. Not only did a man share his food with his horse, but he even slept with it; and this, too, was on the instruction of Mohammed. (Or maybe it wasn't so much an instruction as a roundabout threat. What Mohammed put about through the agency of the Koran was this: "The Evil One dare not enter into a tent in which a pure-bred horse is kept.")
The mares, and not the stallions, were the animals most highly prized, and were the mounts that were used for war and plunder, the stallions being relegated to a role more similar to that of the

drone bee. Purity of blood line was treated with fanatical seriousness, and horses were generally inbred to reinforce good qualities— an entirely foreign concept to the Western breeder, whose school of thought has it that inbreeding produces congenital weaknesses. The several hundred "families" of the Arabian horse were divided into three main types, which are still to be seen today. They are: *Kehylan,* the masculine type, symbol of power and endurance; *Seglawi,* the feminine type, symbol of beauty and elegance, and *Munigi,* the angular type, symbol of speed and racing. The breeding of one Arabian type with another is not always desirable, since the offspring is sometimes of lesser quality than either parent.
Arabs were probably first introduced into Europe during the Moorish invasions of the western Mediterranean. Incidental breeding with local mares must have occurred, but there is little evidence to suggest that in those early times the Arab was thought of in Europe as anything more than perhaps a decorative parade mount. During the Crusades, captured Arab horses seem again to have acquired some stature as fit mounts for kings and princes on state occasions, though as cavalry chargers they never entered into consideration because the heavy armor of the times required horses of enormous size and power to carry it. Light arms and armor changed all that. From the Renaissance through the Napoleonic wars the superiority of the Turkish mounts, in fleetness of foot and movement and in endurance, was obvious, and the demand for Arab blood began to grow in Europe. Following the disastrous retreat from Moscow in the bitter winter of 1812, Napoleon's aide-de-camp wrote to his superior officer:

"The Arab horse withstood the exertions and privations better than the European horse. After the cruel campaign in Russia almost all the horses the Emperor had left were his Arabs. General Hubert ... was only able to bring back to France one horse out of his five, and that was an Arab. Captain Simonneau, of the General Staff, had only his Arab left at the end, and so it was with me also."

Given such proofs as these, Arabians were wanted wherever courage and stamina were at a premium, and so it came about that during the Crimean War vital news of the Russian defeat was entrusted to an Arab-mounted messenger. The bay stallion Omar Pasha galloped the 93 miles from Silistra to Varna in one day. His rider fell dead of exhaustion, but Omar Pasha seemed fresh as ever ... Arab horses are sometimes known as Drinkers of the Wind.

Above: A rare use of the Arab in Ethiopia. The Gougs Game, a contest with lances not unlike the mediaeval sport of jousting, is now seen only in remote areas. It is held in December, and contests may last several days with as many as 200 participants.

Right: The natural vitality of a young English Arab stallion.

Today the Arabian is bred in many countries, showing slight differences of type according to national preference, and variations in height and build according to the climate and the terrain (obviously a horse bred on rich temperate-zone pasture will be bigger and softer than his dry, desertbred cousin). Though his cavalry days are over, his dash and spirit as a riding horse ensure his future, and his prepotency as a sire will endure, as in so many cases in the past, wherever a new breed of quality and fire is evolved.

The Competitors

The origins of competitive show jumping are in all probability Irish. The earliest "leaping" contests to have been recorded were held at the Royal Dublin Society's annual horse show in 1865, where the "high leap" (three bars standing 4 feet 10 in) and the "wide leap" (a pair of parallel hurdles) were introduced as part of the test of a good hunter. Horses who had got over the high leap successfully were automatically qualified for a crack at the championship leap on the last day of the show, which was competed for over a 5 ft 10 in stone wall.

Leaping was not to be treated as a serious sport until many decades had passed, and so the records of its beginnings are woolly. It seems to have broken out fairly spontaneously in British agricultural shows of the 1870's, and to have occurred in North America at much the same time. It must have become popular in Europe soon after, as three jumping competitions were held at the Paris Olympics of 1900, two of them won by Belgium and one by France.

In 1902 a North American hunter named Heatherbloom cleared 8′ 3″ before witnesses on his owner's farm, though 7 ft 10½ in was the highest he ever managed in the show ring. Heatherbloom's 8 ft 3 in is not official in the sense that it is not recognized by the governing body of equestrian sports, the Brussels-based Fédération Equestre Internationale (hardly surprising, since the F.E.I. was not formed until 1921). The official F.E.I. records are as follows:

High jump 8 ft 3 in (2.47 m), held by Captain Alberto Larraguibel Morales of Chile, riding Huasó in a contest at Vina del Mar, Santiago, Chile on February 5th 1949;

Long jump over water 27 ft 2¾ in (8.30 m), held by Lieutenant-Colonel Lopez del Hierro of Spain, riding Amado Mió at Barcelona on July 1st 1951.

During the first half of the twentieth century show jumping was dominated by army officers. The two greatest men to influence the sport were Captain Federico Caprilli of the Italian Cavalry, who developed the forward seat in jumping and spent almost all his short life (he was killed in a fall when he was 39) studying and improving on jumping techniques, and the dedicated Colonel Paul Rodzianko of the Russian Imperial Guard, who after the Revolution became a director of the Cavalry School in Dublin and the trainer of the Irish team.

The army, which did so much for competitive show jumping between the wars, lost its grip a bit after World War II. Certainly there were many officers who still stayed in the game—recent history rings with famous names such as those of Italy's great d'Inzeo brothers, Captain Raimondo and Colonel Piero, England's Colonel Mike Ansell and Wales's Colonel Harry Llewellyn— but the civilian foot was in the stirrup and its grip is becoming stronger all the time. Most of the great international names nowadays belong to private people, a steady stream of farmers, businessmen and lady riders from countries throughout the world. Supreme among these are the consistently-good German riders, whose brilliant international performances, both as individual and team members, make them the most formidable competitors in the world. Names such as Hartwig Steenken, Men's World Champion 1974 on his great Hanoverian mare Simona, Alwin Schockemöhle with his bold grey Rex the Robber (so all-conquering at Britain's Royal International Horse Show in 1975 that some called it "Schockemöhle's benefit week") and his almost equally famous brother, Paul Schockemöhle, tend to dominate the sport.

Show jumpers come in all shapes and heights, ranging from Marion Mould (née Coakes)'s tiny Stroller, who, though only 14.1½ hands high, won the Women's World Championship in 1965 (when his rider was only 17) and competed for the British team in the 1968 Mexico Olympics, to horses standing well over 17 hands high. Most are mongrels, though the odd ex-racehorse, Anglo-Arab or other purebred is seen from time to time. There are no hard and fast laws about show jumpers excepting one: the horse must be a natural jumper, fond of jumping and brave-hearted, usually showing early in life by the enthusiasm and spring in him that he has the aptitude and the inborn wish to clear a fence. It helps also if he is handy, quick to collect himself and sharp to turn; but these things can be taught him by a good rider. The prices paid for show jumpers are so far in excess of the money they can win in prizes that show jumping has become a rich man's hobby, or, in many cases, a sport requiring the backing of a sponsor. A green horse showing jumping potential is worth £ 4,000 and up. A top-class international performer is beyond price, though a realistic guess for someone who wants to buy one might be between £ 80,000—£ 100,000. These horses have no worth at stud, and are only valuable in terms of the pleasure they may bring to their owners.

Much the same sort of generalization applies to the event horse, though he usually contains a large proportion of thoroughbred blood because he must be fast if he is to succeed in the cross-country and steeplechase sections of the game. A top three-day eventer is an outstanding all-rounder, possessed of courage and endurance as well as versatility. He is judged on his discipline at dressage, his speed over a steeplechase course, his endurance on roads and tracks, his adaptability and bravery over a tough cross-country course, and finally on his ability over show jumps. Three-day eventing is the supreme test of discipline and guts in horse and rider, requiring years of training and hard work and the sacrifice of almost all other interests to the pursuit of perfection.

Unlike racing, eventing is open to both sexes without prejudice, and it is here that equality in equestrianism for men and women is most freely able to prove itself. In the 1975 European Three-Day Event Championships, held at Luhmühlen, West Germany, first and

Alwin Schockemöhle on his famous show jumper Rex the Robber, winner of the Grand Prix at Britain's Royal International Horse Show in 1975.

second individual places went to women riders, both British: Lucinda Prior-Palmer riding her own Be Fair, and H.R.H. The Princess Anne on Goodwill; though the team event, a compilation of the best three scores put up by four competitors named as competing for any one nation, went to the all-male Russian team. Dressage, the supreme art form of equestrianism, is designed to improve the natural balance and movement of the horse. It is a developed form of artistry which began centuries ago with the need for manoeuvrability and unquestioned discipline in the war horse, and which has been refined into such seemingly-impossible feats

A well-designed show jumping course will test the all-round ability of horse and rider.

Top: A wide parallel needs speed and scope.

Above: A wall with pole, narrower and usually taller than a parallel, requires more vertical thrust, less forward impulsion.

Right: The great Schockemöhle and Rex the Robber move into a triple bar. The rider balances his weight so that it lies over the center of gravity of his horse.

as a controlled leap into the air from a standstill or the ability
to canter backwards on three legs. From the military point of view
the advantages are huge: a horse that would move sideways or
backwards as readily as it would move forwards; one that would turn
on its own axis, no matter whether the front or rear was used
as a pivot; one that would leap over a fallen horse or rear up
to confront an enemy, would move from a standing start straight
into a gallop—advantages such as these makes the horse a fighting
force that is far ahead of the armored car in every aspect except
vulnerability.

Unfortunately, vulnerability being at a premium and hand-to-hand
fighting not much the fashion any more, the horse has lost its place
in warfare and dressage has been relegated to an act of love
and dedication confined to those few who will give up their lives
to horsemanship for the sake of itself.

The highest form of dressage, *haute école,* is that in which the horse
moves freely and lightly in perfect balance, responding so directly
to his rider's invisible commands that he seems to be moving
of his own immaculate volition. This form of riding has been made
world famous by the amazing Spanish Riding School, which was
founded at Vienna some three or four centuries ago (the date of origin
has never been clarified) and was called "Spanish" because
the horses used by it originate from Spain. The horses of the
Spanish riding school are grays of the Lipizzaner breed, taken from

Left and below: Varied obstacles, often from rising or falling ground,
test all-round ability in the cross-country phase of a three-day event.

A difference in sty e: In the show jumping phase of eventing (*top left*), the all-round rider sits centred on a long rein over a comparatively small fence which her horse clears with the urnecessarily-big leap of the non-specialist. Tackling the big spread of a birch oxer (*above*), the experience and economy of top-class show jumping are evident in the low-slung forward seat of the rider. Though she maintains her balance to use her weight to her horse's best advantage, experience has taught her that the short distances between show jumping fences w ll not give her time to "slip" her reins midway in the air and shorten them again before she reaches the next fence.

The cross-country rider (*top left*) lands into the water on the typically-long rein of one who has ample time to readjust his position before the next obstacle is reached.

A show jumping rider (*left*) who has approached his cbstacle more slowly lands all set to take on the next jump.

the former Imperial stud farm at Lipizza, founded by Archduke Charles in 1580 on Andalusian stock with perhaps a sprinkling of Barb and Arab blood. Stallions only are used in the school, and after three or four years of training learn most of the basics of *haute école,* which is also known as "airs on the ground." The really talented horse may then go on to the "airs above the ground," the leaps and manoeuvres practised in the air during the sixteenth to eighteenth centuries and that now, exceeding Olympic dressage standards by a long way, are the exclusive prerogative of the Spanish Riding School. To illustrate the difficulty involved, it takes

Supreme control of the horse in a fairly advanced dressage manoeuver. The rider, Josef Neckerman on Mariano, sits immobile, his signals so slight that they are not noticeable.

four to six years for a rider to become proficient in these airs on a fully-trained horse and it will be two to four years more before he is capable of training a novice horse to this standard. Closely related to the Lipizzaner is the famous Kladruby Grey of Czechoslovakia, developed over the last three hundred years as the royal (now State) coach horse. Kladrubers have been known to draw a coach with up to sixteen horses in the traces, and have a pride and uniformity of movement which is the epitome of team-horse driving.

Driving as an art, as opposed to directing a carthorse or pony for an elementary function, is slightly less than 200 years old. It stems from the four-in-hands which used to pull stage coaches on the post roads, once the roads were made even enough to sustain a coach, and from the English fashion (much used by ladies at the turn of the eighteenth and nineteenth centuries) of taking the air in phaetons with a well-matched pair of elegant horses.

Like dressage, it has nowadays become an art form, with the high-stepping hackney of the past predominant. It is a great attraction at horse shows throughout the world, and in its own right provides pleasure and a demanding skill for the driver.

All of these sports require an amateur to make them work; and "amateur" does not mean unprofessional, but loving.

Dressage is a field in which women excel as much as men.

Above left: Jennifer Loriston-Clarke, a superb British performer, bows to the judges during an indoor performance.

Above: The famous Spanish Riding School of Vienna (men only; both human and horse) performs a quadrille at home.

Left: A dressage contest for the not-quite-so-highly-advanced demonstrates some of the difficulties which can only be overcome by many years of practice. In this picture, the wishes of the riders can be seen from the way in which each sits his horse.

71

Some of the arts of driving are demonstrated in the varying types of pictures here.

Above left: Scurry racing requires a good deal of effort and precise judgement to manipulate a pair of cantering horses round a number of sharp turns.

Above: The hackney carriage driver concentrates her efforts on displaying her horse to best advantage.

Right: A Hungarian four-in-hand.

Left: Lippizaners, at the Piber Stud in Austria, are the perfect type of carriage horse, strong-bodied and elegant with a proud carriage. Although these are used exclusively by the Spanish Riding School, their first cousins, the Kladruby Greys of Czechoslovakia, provide the finest ceremonial coach team in the world.

Drums and Trumpets

Near the end of World War II the horse was used for the last time on the battlefield. Its active military career ended much as it had started, roughly 5,000 years before, with a Russian raid on an immobilized enemy. What had begun with hordes of Central Asian bowmen, on their rough steppe ponies, attacking horseless tribes finished with Russian cavalry divisions, also mounted on rough steppe ponies, demolishing the frozen-solid tanks of Germany with hand grenades, galloping away across the snow and leaving an enemy powerless to pursue.

In the five millennia between, horses had dominated warfare in many different ways. Much of the early fighting was done from chariots, giving the swordsman mobility and speed as well as a crudely protected fighting platform from which to swing down at his enemy's head. Drawn by two excited horses, in themselves enough to knock a foot soldier aside, many of these chariots carried built-in lethal weapons such as sharp knives embedded in the wheels which could cut an opponent's legs off.

It was not until the fourth century A.D. that the Romans replaced the primitive horsecloth with the padded saddle, adopted from the east, giving some security and physical comfort to archers and to mounted spearmen. But even before the development of the saddle, and indeed long after it—the North American Indian was fighting without a saddle until comparativily recently— hordes of skirmishing bowmen stayed on board successfully purely through balance and the strength of their leg muscles.

The invention of the stirrup, although known in Asia some 1,600 years ago, was not fully appreciated in Europe until the time of Charlemagne. Its adoption changed the course of warfare in two devastating ways. First, by providing a footboard against which the rider could brace his legs, the spear automatically became a lance —a thing to be aimed and held securely, with the full weight of the galloping horse behind it. Secondly, because the rider was to some extent artificially held in place by the harness of the horse he was able to wear cumbersome protective clothing which shielded him against he weapons of the enemy.

The Medieval Great Horse, famous forerunner of the carthorse of today, demonstrated more clearly than any horse has done before or since the ultimate benefit of the stirrup and the strong-built saddle. Knights in shining armor, jousting for fair ladies during peacetime and demolishing the heathen when the days of fun were over, not only wore so much protective armor that they had to be lifted on and off their horses but also carried behind their lances the thrust of the heaviest horse then known to man.

Meanwhile more clever and more psychological uses of horses

Left: British Household Cavalry drum horse Hercules of the Blues and Royals Regiment.

Right: The Blues and Royals (formerly known as the Horse Guards) line up for early morning Watering Order. The name derives from the old picket line practice of taking horses to water three times a day. Nowadays, since the horse is no longer used in battle, "Watering Order" has become synonymous with morning exercise. Interspersed with the ceremonial "Cavalry Blacks" are the Trumpeters' Greys of the regimental band.

were going forward. Genghis Khan's bloodthirsty raids into the Western world were based not on heavy armor but on a vast remuda of horses herded along with him, so that fresh mounts were always available to outdistance the enemy. (They also provided fresh meat and milk to keep his men in shape.) The victories of Cortés against the highly-civilized Aztecs came about very largely because the horse was then unknown in America. Man and horse were taken as one being (the centaur myth again) and an unknown race appearing out of the sea became the conquerors of the land. Only when the lance became redundant with the development of fire-power did the course of cavalry change again forever. Heavy armor was useless if a pistol ball could pierce it at close range; what mattered was physical freedom of movement, versatility, speed of horse to stop and start and turn away. From the early eighteenth century onwards light cavalry became the rule and the

Above left: A Household Cavalry Black loads up nervously in London. He is travelling to Edinburgh to form part of Queen Elizabeth's escort to greet the King of Sweden on a State Visit.

Above: The Life Guards march past to take part in the annual ceremony known as Trooping the Color, an historic spectacle in which, in the presence of Her Majesty the Queen, the regimental color is displayed so that a soldier lost on the battlefield knows which flag to come to.

Left: Ceremony carries on regardless of the weather. The Life Guards in the rain.

Top left: Royal Buzkashi, Afghanistan.
Center: Argentinian Military Guard.
Above: Mounted salute to celebrate the end of Ramadan, Katsina, Nigeria.
Bottom far left: Emir's Procession, Nigeria.
Left: Red Cavalry of Senegal.

amazing arts of horsemanship exemplified by the Spanish Riding
School of Vienna came into their own.

All art forms pass, or fossilize into arts *per se.* The cavalry is
universally redundant, outweighed by new inventions that nullify
the horse's versatility and make his vulnerable mortality a hazard.
Yet, while hydrogen bombs may drop from 30,000 feet, the ceremonial
use of the warhorse, with its beauty and dignity, persists throughout
the world wherever grandeur and the continuity of tradition
are appreciated.

Both military and civil occasions will often feature mounted parades,
and horse soldiers play an important ceremonial role under very
different regimes: ancient monarchies, people's republics and
newly emergent states. They add color to daily life and often,
like those who draw the sightseers in London's streets, form an
important tourist attraction. Indeed, for some British state ceremonies
it is just as well that Elizabeth II is a capable horsewoman.

The British cavalry horse is very carefully selected and trained.
He will, most likely, be bought as a youngster from an Irish field;
chosen for his size and color by a buying commission made up
from officers of the British Army Veterinary Corps, the Household
Cavalry and the King's Troop Royal Horse Artillery who work
through selected agents and dealers who understand the Household
Cavalry's requirements.

Sent from Eire to Melton Mowbray in Leicestershire, the young
cavalry blacks are rested and grown for a week or a year until
a veterinary inspection clears them to move on to Windsor barracks,
where a toss of a coin decides whether they are destined for the
Horse Guards or the Life Guards. Once chosen, the number of the
new squadron they belong to is stamped on their hooves
(300 near-identical horses are difficult to tell apart, even to the most

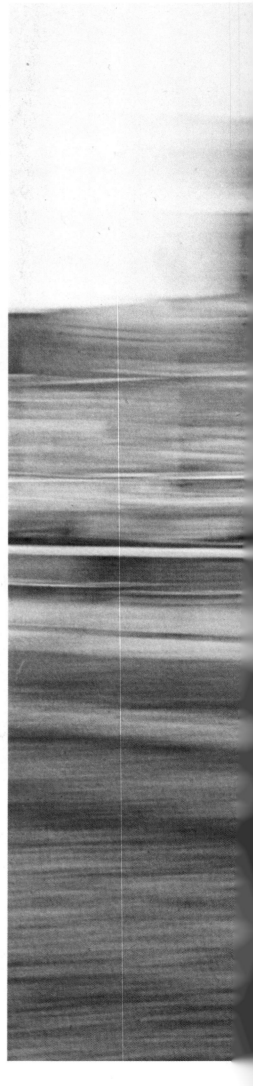

experienced horseman), and they are broken in and schooled on
for three months or so until their basic training period is considered
satisfactorily accomplished and they are shipped on to the barracks
in London for more instruction in their future jobs. Nine out of ten
of them develop into horses that will withstand the ebb and flow
of ceremonial life, which says much for the men who bought them
as youngsters, and the pick of these become officers' "chargers"—
the most conspicuous on parade, and often as a sideline the best
hunters or eventers or show jumpers that the cavalry can present.
They lead a life that could make a film star quail, travelling from
place to place, from country to country, to take part immaculately
in British state occasions. When they retire—through old age
or infirmity—they are often bought and cared for by a trooper
who has come to love them. Otherwise, provided they are not in pain,
they go out to grass to lead the easy, uneventful life of all
respected old-age-pensioned warhorses.

Above: Royal Horse Artillery
Wheelers pulling a light-
weight gun carriage.

Below: Pageantry at a
country show.

Right: Jousting, once a
leading entertainment of the
nobility, is coming back
as a public spectacle.

The Hireling

Not so long ago, in one of the great American cities, I went riding. Friends, who were not themselves riders, had told me of a place where I could "go horseback riding" in much the same tones as they had earlier told me where I could rent a bicycle. This made me apprehensive that I was about to visit one of those establishments that can best be described as Rent-a-Horse.

Sure enough. "Ever been horseback riding before?" they asked me at the stable. I said I had and asked for a look round the yard, which they sent me off to do unaccompanied. I picked out the best two of the hundred or so horses, which seemed to surprise them. The owner said, "OK, you can take the gray," and without any more checking on my credentials saddled her up and sent me out on her without any supervision into some of the most dangerous streets in the world and from there into a park so small that you could ride twice round it in your $5-hour.

The gray was a nice little thing, sweet and fresh. I learned later that she had been bought by the stable less than a week before, which must have accounted for the fact that going round and round the same old park still interested her. From time to time untutored enthusiasts passed us on their hirelings. None of them was supervised by an instructor, and most were hanging on by the reins and banging up and down in the saddle. Two of them came by at a gallop on the street leading back to the stable.

I got back to the stable precisely on the hour, and as soon as I dismounted someone else got up on the gray mare and hauled her back to circle round the park. She did not know it then, but Rent-a-Horse had got her.

Six weeks later I went back to the same stable and asked for the gray mare. Her ears were back and her face was sour, and she tried to bite me when I patted her. She rode with an iron mouth and unresponsive sides, trying to duck out of going round the park and bolt back to the stable. Some months afterwards, when a kind of miserable curiosity impelled me to find out what had happened to her, I learned after a bit of digging that she had become unrideable and had been shot. She had been only six years old.

All over the world there are riding stables, dude ranches and pony trekking centers that are in the game only to make the maximum amount of money out of a horse in the shortest possible time.

Ninety-nine per cent of their clients are people who genuinely want to learn how to ride, and who have no idea of the damage they do to the animals they ride. These novice riders are in no way to blame for the harm that is done through their agency. They, like the horses they hire, are the victims of profiteers who think of a horse as $5 an hour, 6 hours a day, 7 days a week, or $10,000 a year for as long as the horse can stick it.

Mercifully, the good riding establishments outnumber the bad. There is no better place to learn to ride than in a good riding school under a qualified instructor. A responsible riding school owner,

having a number of horses in his charge, can choose one that will suit the size and ability of the pupil and can bring the novice rider on by degrees on a diversity of mounts, each of which will teach him something new.

Most countries have some sort of organized body, such as a horse society, which approves, or fails to approve, stables which offer horses for hire. Many of these will give out lists of approved schools on request. If the world's novice riders knew about these lists and took the advice given on them, Rent-a-Horse would go out of business. It cannot happen soon enough.

Horses at Work

Once upon a very recent time the economy of nations depended upon the strength and versatility of the horse. There were horses for carrying you about, horses upon which the morning post depended, horses for defending your country or for acquiring another one, horses for turning the ground for the young spring wheat, and horses for taking you to church on Sunday. If any of these horses broke down, the consequences were serious. If you weren't rich enough to own a horse you were stuck in your own backyard for the rest of your life. Most of the world was in that position, and the few who kept a horse for pleasure—that is, purely because they enjoyed riding about on it—must universally have been oddities.

In most parts of the world, despite a backdrop of almost universal automisation, the horse can still be found in use. There is the milk-float or the small trader's horse, pattering through some city streets in early morning, so much a part of everyday life that no one seems to notice him; the junk dealer, recognized by his cry, whose cart is pony-drawn and forms a regular and welcome change to the sound of changing gears; the hackney pair, pulling a smart carriage up a central thoroughfare, jangling above the rumble of the city traffic and usually used as much as an advertisement as for making deliveries. Those who look about them for a horse will always see one, standing perhaps as a genuine taxi service in Rome or at the south end of Central Park in Manhattan as a joy ride to escape the rush of modern city life.

Police horses patrol the streets of many cities, looking picturesque enough until the hysteria of a mob provokes their gentle firmness. I once stood in the path of 100 police horses sent in to control

Farm horses are still employed in France (*right*) and England (*below*).

30,000 demonstrators who were protesting against the Vietnam war. I simply wanted to see how the horse and the cop would handle me and had no political motive. The rider swung his truncheon at me, failing it score because it wasn't long enough to reach beyond his horse's head. What the well-trained horse did was very curious: it moved its front feet, gently but firmly, *under* my shoes and not on top, stuck its nose against my chest, and quietly but irresistably forced me backwards. This horse had just moved out from a line which were having firecrackers thrown at them.

In many high-altitude areas, where cold or a tortuous pathway render any sort of motor vehicle unusable, the horse performs its age-old function of packing home the groceries, delivering the homestead produce into the valley market; and adds to this a thriving tourist business such as getting down the side of the Grand Canyon in Arizona, which is far beyond the capability of the jeep or Range-Rover.

Ecologically, the plough horse has seemed to be redundant. But with the rising cost of motor fuel and the limits of fuel supplies that are pushing prices up beyond the profit of running the machine he is beginning to come back into his own. What for a brief period

Left: Roping a steer in the United States.

Below: Australian cowboy

Right: Royal Canadian Mounted Police present a display.

of time has been forgotten is that the horse lives off the land he works, eating its produce, enriching it with his manure, and meanwhile expending his energy without charge into an agricultural economy that is severely set back by the much-faster depreciation rate of each new tractor bought and worked. Repair bills for a horse are minimal compared with complications to a combine harvester, and the owner is not nearly so dependent on the interplay of public services. Any speculator of the future is bound about with supposition. No matter: my own bet, failing the widespread use of self-generating electric batteries or some such cheap invention, is that with the exhaustion of world fuel supplies the self-generating horse will come back into his own.

Alternatively, it may be the mule (offspring of a male donkey

Left top: Picadors in the bull ring at Palma de Mallorca. The horses are protected (at least, to some extent) by padded blankets reaching almost to the ground.

Left: An Arab working in a circus. Dressage displays are popular with the crowd.

Right: The polo pony is a thriving reminder of an ancient game: polo was played in China and Mongolia many centuries ago. Today most of the world's polo ponies are bred in Argentina, which has about three times as many polo players as any other country. Since they need to be 15 hands high, or a little taller, they are not strictly speaking ponies at all.

and a mare) which holds the premium. This is an animal which has never reached redundancy, being excessively cheap to maintain, extraordinarily enduring, and possessed of so deep an ability to hang around indefinitely that the word "mulish" has become part of the universal tongue. It is seen throughout the Mediterranean countries, dragging a plough through the dried-out soil of Moorish terraces or standing patiently beneath the almond trees waiting for the ripening crop to fall into its panniers, but it cannot be produced without the horse.

Working horses endure in the present as they have throughout the past. Where would Indonesia be without the strength of its Sumba or Sumbawa ponies, or most of mid- and eastern-Asia without its Mongolian strains? All modern horses work, in the sense that riding for pleasure is a concept of the passenger and not of the means of locomotion. Even the most expensive racehorse works long before he reaches puberty, and at stud in later years is never pensioned off until his/her working value it proven to have disappeared.

Horses exist, and will continue to exist, only as long as they have value to man. It is in the way of things—in the way of a dominant species on a small planet that is part of a limited universe—that existence should depend on such precarious factors.

The horse's working use is still diverse.

Above left: Pack horse in Yugoslavia.

Above centre: Threshing wheat in Greece.

Above: Drawing a festive fiacre in Vienna.

Far right: Ploughing in Germany.

Right: The Roman carrozza is now largely a tourist attraction.

Below, left and center: It is often the only means of transport in Nepal and Afghanistan (respectively).

Below: The winter taxi in Zermatt is often a necessity in heavy weather.

Top left: Anything goes in the shafts in China, provided it will work.

Top centre: Mountain sleigh in Bavaria.

Top right: Horses in Yugoslavia.

Above: A fisherman's cart collecting cockles on the beach in Lancashire, England.

Right center: Mules are a common sight in all Mediterranean countries. These are in Andalusia, Spain.

Right: A farm horse in Turkey.

Below centre: These mules are Greek.

Below right: German dray horses.

End of the Day

Therefore my age is as the lusty winter
Frosty, but kindly.

> William Shakespeare:
> *As You Like It*

The oldest horse on record, Old Billy, a barge horse who used
to pull the barges on the waterways of England when shipment
by canal was very much the thing and the railways had not taken over,
died at the age of 62. Four years of a horse's life are said to equal
one year for a human, so Old Billy survived to the equivalent of 248,
which would make a tortoise feel like a babe-in-arms.
Horses, averagely, live to about 25 years. There are some curious
similes about a horse's age which have become part of the language
of man: if they get "much longer in the tooth" (horses' teeth
continue growing, humans' don't) they go to "fresh fields and
pastures new." One of the most common ways of achieving this
is by being put down, sometimes because they have outlived their
usefulness but more often because they develop geriatric complaints
such as arthritis or not being able to masticate properly because their
teeth are too long and angled out to chew their food. Putting an end
to it may be a whole lot better than protracting their discomfort.

Certainly, in natural circumstances, they would lose contact
with the herd through sheer inability to keep up, probably dying
by human standards rather nastily over a period of several days.
The difficulty of applying human standards is that they are
only human. There comes a point in every healthy horse's life
when a human decides that he is too old to work. At this point
he is either put down or retired; and since a good many years
may remain to him to enjoy, it is pleasing when he is given
the opportunity to revert to a natural (but protected) way of life.
Throughout the world, though limited by finance, homes for
old horses exist in which the herd instinct that wants company
is automatically satisfied and in addition there is shelter against
rough weather, extra food when the grass dies down, and
medical attention.
Under such circumstances the ripening years provoke a kind
of reverence. Old Billy must have drawn the admiration of all who saw
him for the last quarter-century of his life, but it is hardly likely
that he guessed at what it was they wondered.

The ultimate luxury for the old horse. A retirement home gives rest
and care to horses and ponies of all types.

Acknowledgements

The publisher would like to thank the following for supplying
the photographs reproduced in this book:
Anne Cumbers page 11t, 15b, 20t, 20bl, 21t, 24bl, 25c, 25bl, 68t, 84;
Robert Estall page 12-13, 14, 16t, 21b, 25t, 26l, 28-29, 30b, 36, 37,
38-39, 45c, 50b, 52t, 52-53, 63, 65, 71t, 73t, 74, 82, 85, 87, 96;
Paul Forrester page 38, 39, 59b, 61, 75, 76t; Robert Harding
Associates page 75b, 78t, 90bl, 90br, 92t, 93bl, 95b; Alan Hutchison
page 31b, 56, 78a, 79r, 92b; Ed Lacey page 44t, 45t; John Moss
page 19, 26c, 26r 60, 83t; Picturepoint page 7l, 7r, 8; Spectrum Colour
Library page 1, 2-3, 4-5, 10, 11b, 20br, 27, 30t, 33, 34t, 34b, 35b,
40t, 42-43, 45b, 30t, 80b, 81, 91b, 92c, 93c, 94, 95t; Sally-Anne

Thompson page 16b, 25br, 31t, 58l, 58r, 64t, 66t, 66b, 67t, 67b, 72t;
ZEFA page 6, 9b, 15t, 17, 18, 22t, 22-23, 24t, 24br, 32, 35t, 40c,
40-41, 44b, 46-47, 48b, 49, 50t, 51, 54-55, 57, 59t, 64b, 68b,
69b, 70, 71b, 73b, 77, 78-79t, 78-79b, 83b, 86b, 88t, 90tl, 90tr, 90c,
91t, 91c, 93tl, 93tr, 93br; ZEFA/Photri page 68t.

The publishers have attempted to observe the legal requirements
with respect to the rights of the suppliers of photographic materials.
Nevertheless, persons who have claims are invited to apply
to the Publishers.

KONOLULU
is an island

Outrigger Canoe Club's Molokai race champions.

'Ama'uma'u fern, Kahana Valley State Park.

Honolulu has its own fragrance.

B. J. Feldman
Former Miss Hawaii

Torch ginger, Kawailoa Plantation camp.

Puʻu Kanehoalani, Kualoa: The mountain ridge on windward Oahu named after a male ancestor of volcano goddess Pele; his female companion is said to "be" Kapapa islet in nearby Kaneʻohe Bay. Kualoa, now a city park, in ancient times was considered one of the most sacred places on Oahu. When *aliʻi* were in residence, passing canoes lowered their sails in recognition of his sacredness. It was also a place of refuge and is claimed by some to be the first landing place of early Polynesians on Oahu.

I think everybody is a human being no matter what land they go to. It doesn't matter. And I think if they want to come here to live, it's fine with me. And people here want to go to the mainland, which they are doing. That's fine with me. I feel that the land is created for all, even if it's said that it's only for the Hawaiians or only for the haoles or whatever. I think there's room for everybody on this land.

Mercy Kane Harvey
Fish merchant, Waianae

Condominium and columbarium constructed in the architectural style of two overseas cultures, share space in lower Nu'uanu Valley.

On King Kamehameha's birthday anniversary celebration, the proud descendants of former *ali'i* dress in the colors of royalty.

Everybody is a minority here. We've learned to live, work and play together like no other place in the world . . . Honolulu gives hope to civilization that someday all of the nations on this globe will probably emulate what we have here, like tolerance of one to the other, and to me that means peace. Here, everyone is beautiful.

Frank Fasi, Mayor
Honolulu

An early morning *mauka* shower drifts *makai* across the city, from Ko'olau mountain ridges to the sea at Waikiki (overleaf).

Kalaniana'ole Highway curves along Oahu's south shore, carrying early morning commuter traffic from Hawaii Kai to downtown.

HONO
is

Photographs and Text by
ROBERT WENKAM

OLULU
an island

 RAND McNALLY & COMPANY CHICAGO • NEW YORK • SAN FRANCISCO

Acknowledgement...

I wish to thank the many Honolulu residents who contributed quotations about the city they like best. Their personal comments are an important contribution. The extensive taped interviews necessary to obtain these quotations and the research, photography and writing, was made possible by financial grants from Pacific Resources, Inc., of Honolulu. This large-format, all-color book was sponsored by Pacific Resources as part of their continuing desire to present Honolulu to the world as a progressive island city and home of corporate leadership in the Pacific.

Other Books by Robert Wenkam

Hawaii The Big Island
    Photographs and text by R. Wenkam

New England
    Photographs and text by R. Wenkam

Hawaii
    Photographs and text by R. Wenkam

Micronesia: Island Wilderness
    Photographs by R. Wenkam, text by K. Brower

Maui: The Last Hawaiian Place
    Photographs and text by R. Wenkam

Micronesia: Breadfruit Revolution
    Photographs by R. Wenkam, text by B. Baker

Kauai and the Park Country of Hawaii
    Photographs and text by R. Wenkam

Editor • Herb Luthin, Chicago
Interviews for quotations • Rex Wills III, Hilo
Research • Sherry O'Sullivan, Honolulu
Design • Tom Rixford, Robert Wenkam, Honolulu
Printing and separations • R.R. Donnelley, Crawfordsville
Compositor • Boyer and Brass, San Diego
Photographs • Canon AE-1, Kodachrome 64
Production • Wenkam/Candere Publishers, Honolulu

A corner power pole near Fernandez Village posts directions to three Saturday afternoon parties on Ewa Plantation.

Contents

Introduction To An Island • 14

Hawaiian Glossary • 19

The City Is An Island • 20

We Did It Ourselves • 27

Trees Are A Soft Green • 37

Kalakaua Boulevard Is Waikiki • 43

We Did It First • 53

Everybody's Beautiful • 60

The Islands At War • 71

We Made It A Good Town • 87

The Surf Is Up • 97

The People Who Made It So • 101

Only In Honolulu • 110

Honolulu Is Many Kinds Of Living Places • 122

The Aloha Spirit Is Not A Myth • 126

Introduction To An Island

Honolulu is possibly the world's most livable city on the most beautiful island anywhere. By federal declaration Honolulu s the cleanest, most pollution-free city of its size in the United States. A cultural and economic crossroads of the Pacific, Honolulu is the home of people of every ethnic group from everywhere and the headquarters of major international corporations. Waikiki, along with the rest of Hawaii, is by any poll the nation's most desired vacation destination. It is my favorite place to live.

We banned roadside advertising billboards 40 years ago. Hawaii has pioneered in state-wide land use laws to help preserve agricultural lands and open space. There are no unincorporated ci ies in Hawaii — only counties and islands — therefore we hold to a minimum wasteful economic and political competition between the legal children of the state.

Honolulu is a family place, despite the large numbers of young people who have adopted swinging contemporary lifestyles in a climate most appropriate for T-shirts, bikinis, and bare feet. It's good weather for retirement, albeit expensive, and old Asian traditions of respect for elders has been combined with the new generation's desire for independence.

We are a city of high- ise apartments and hotels that multiply at an appalling rate. It is as if they clone, because once you see two buildings, within a few years there will always be more, gradually covering the flat space between the ocean and the hills. Some have said our population density equals Hong Kong. If so, it may explain our special vitality in what is ordinarily described as the languid tropics. We are doers on a grand scale, and take full advantage of the opportunities created by city concentrations of people and conveniently located Waikiki, which free-spending tourists have created for us. Honolulu affords a symphony, great art collections, a magnificent Pacific museum, community theaters, and a concert hall, where popular entertainers regularly stop off on their way to somewhere else.

We created our urban environment, and it satisfies our personal needs very well; therefore, is it not exactly what we want? Some say that urban design is a political art form, that our city was created in the political arena. Not so. Our politicians merely responded to the most powerful and influential economic pressures — the landowners and the businessmen that in contemporary Honolulu seem to have consistently acted in concert with the long-range best interests of the community. Even when their profit-motivated actions took priority, the end result was positive. The importation of foreign plantation workers and the expansion of monopolistic corporate land holdings are probably more responsible for the Honolulu of today than any other factor.

We created an urban package within our island state and added political appendages that further enhanced its livability. There are no separate school districts in Hawaii, or expensive property assessments to support them — all students, rich and poor, receive education funds on an equal basis from state funds. There is no state police (despite the myth of "Hawaii Five-O"), but there are excellent state library and hospital systems. Honolulu and Hawaii, by any measure a racially and economically divided community 20 years ago, solved most of its social problems before the federal civil rights act became the law of the land — and before Hawaii became the fiftieth state.

Honolulu is also a fragile city. Resting lightly between pleasantly green hills and the incredibly blue ocean, floating beneath a sky never dulled by smog (not yet), the island environment is easily damaged by too many people — residents or visitors. The danger is not just rhetoric by environmentalists. It is official government policy to be concerned about Hawaii's growth rate and population. The governor said so in his state of the state message. The legislature has passed a general plan policy statement that addresses itself to the problem of too many people on too small an island. Legislators have

I started out in Kalihi, when I was a youngster. Then I growed up in Kapahulu near Waikiki. In those days Waikiki was a nice place, back in the fifties, when I was a teenager, you know. There's too much building there now. The way the buildings went up overnight, yeah? Although I'm a construction worker myself, I hope this doesn't happen to the other islands — like Waikiki and stuff like that, huh? . . . And a lot of transients, yeah? Y'know Waikiki doesn't have the feeling of old Hawaii, but the young local people there are trying to bring it back I believe. I think they're getting successful now, because there's more Hawaiians and local people that are taking interest in their culture now. And that's important. You gotta hang onto some of the past because you gotta identify where you come from, eh?

Keala Brown
Bulldozer operator, Kaneohe

also requested the state Department of Transportation to determine how many automobiles can drive around the island at any one time.

The state Department of Planning and Economic Development has also tried to determine how many people is too many, again without success. Environmental groups generally agree there are too many already. Even the tourist industry has agreed on the maximum number of rooms Waikiki can absorb and still be a nice place for tourists; it encouraged passing of city ordinances that offer certain combinations of density and setback, and which would eventually limit rooms in Waikiki to about 29,000 — only 6,000 more than today's count.

Continued growth of Honolulu is a statistical nightmare. Computer projections, based on the last ten years of tourist growth rate, forecast very good business for the tourist industry 100 years from today, when 60 trillion, 450 billion tourists will arrive at the airport every hour! Perhaps such projections are absurb, but if so, the reckless economic philosophy of growth ad infinitum must be seriously questioned.

The Hawaii Visitors Bureau estimates that almost four million tourists visited Hawaii in 1978, most of them spending all of their vacation in Honolulu and leaving behind for the Hawaii economy over a billion dollars in circulating cash. Most tourists returned home satisfied with happy memories, but many remained because they liked living here better than at home. Many more flew over to work in fancy resorts and live like others dream. Some deplaned at the Honolulu airport and next day rode TheBus to the downtown welfare office — when they learned it is difficult to hold a job while surfing all day.

Most island residents are well aware there is no legal way to restrict immigration, as there is implied in Governor Ariyoshi's declared concern over population. As Herbert Cornuelle, president of Dillingham Corporation, says, "It would have been very nice to be able to pull up the drawbridge just after I arrived in Honolulu in 1953, but that's not possible."

"I can see what the governor is talking about, but I can't be against immigration," asserts Cornuelle. "The essence of everything the U.S. and Hawaii is — is based on people coming here from everywhere. And here is the one place that certainly epitomizes that you've been wel-

On Kalakaua Boulevard in Waikiki, the surf is up.

come, rich or poor, no matter what color, and I don't want to change that. I like that idea and I don't see why we would want to pull up the drawbridge."

Mainlanders, sick of street crime, prejudice, and pollution of their air and water, clamor for escape to Hawaii. The island paradise created by travel pundits is still the end of the rainbow despite a few tarnished hues. Never mind that Aloha Week is celebrated with plastic leis from Hong Kong and that the "fresh" *mahimahi* on hotel menus is mostly shipped frozen from Taiwan. So what if the Polynesian pageantry is fake and ancient torches burn propane. The rainbows and flowers and surf are real. The clean sky is real. So is the scenery, the beautiful people, and the soft landscape seemingly ever green. The sun is interrupted only momentarily by passing showers. Every day is a sleepy Sunday, and even the winter week is a shirt-sleeved summer. Is it any wonder the world wants to drop by and stay? ■

If you can't say anything good about anybody don't say anything at all.

Yvonne Elliman
Honolulu born vocalist

Spearfishing

Hukilau

Surfing, Makaha

Ilima, Flower of Oahu

KAHUKU PT

Kawela Bay Kawela
Waialee   Kii Res
                              5
83   Hawaii
                   Infantry
                   Training   Kahuku
                   Camp   MAKA
Sunset Beach   Malaek
Ehukai Beach Park   17   St. Pk
                 Paumalu Str
                        KAUNALA RIDGE
Puu O Mahuka Heiau   Ojo
St Hist Site   PUPUKEA PAUMALU FOREST RESERVE   Laie Temple
Pupukea Beach Park Waimea Camp Pupukea   Polynesian
Waimea Bay Camp Pupukea   KAWAILOA   Cultural Cen
Kupupolo   Waimea Bay Beach Park
Heiau   Kamananui Falls
         Kawailoa Beach Waihee Falls (Waimea Falls)
                     Kamananui Str   KOOLAULOA
KAWAILOA BEACH   Waimea Camp Kawiikoale   FOREST
PUAENA PT   Kawailoa   KAIPAPALI
Haleiwa Beach Park   Puu Kapu   FOREST
  Waialua   Haleiwa   Anahulu   1350 Puu Kainapuaa RESERVE
Kaiake St.   Bay   River   Kawainui
Rec. Area Waialua   Opaeula Res Kawaiiki
  WAIALUA BEACH Kaiaka Bay Helemano   Opaeula Res Kawaiiki Str
Mokuleia Beach Park   2 Opaeula   KOOLAU
Mokuleia Mokuleia   North Res   Opaeula   Str   RANGE
930 Polo Field Mokuleia Waialua Poamoho 99 Str
DILLINGHAM Kemoo Namooloa W A I A L U A RESERVE
A F B   Camps 930   99
KAENA PT Military Dillingham Str 8 10 Helemano
Coast Guard Reservation Ranch Kaukonahua Str MILITARY RES Str
Station   Upper   EWA Str Str
KUAOKALA Kaupakuhale Str Helemano Poamoho Puu Pa
FOREST 1567 Poamoho Res   FOREST
RESERVE 22 Puu Iki Str 803 Pomoho NAVAL RES RESERVE
              1146 801 Whitmore 804 North Fork Kaukonahua
Military MAKUA MOKULEIA Puu Pane Wahiawa SCHOFIELD BARRACKS MILITARY RESERV
Reservation WAIANAE FOREST Kaala 4040 Dam 80 (EAST RANGE)
Makua Str (Highest Pk SCHOFIELD 99 Ku Str
Barking Sands RESERVE on Oahu) BARRACKS Wahiawa Tree
930 KANEANA Waianae Kai SCHOFIELD BARRACKS Botanical Res Kaukonahua
CAVE FOREST Puu Kawiwi MILITARY RESERVATION Gardens South Fork Str
Kaeau Beach Park Puu Keaau Kaheaki 2975 78 Schofield WHEELER Mil Res
         2650 Hiu Str Puu Kalena 17 Barracks AIR FORCE Mil Res
         Heiau   3350 Kalakole   BASE Kipapa Puu Kamana
KEPUHI PT Puu FOREST FOREST Pass Maunauna   1472
MAKAHA BEACH Kepauola RESERVE RESERVE 1769 750 Waipio
(SURFING) 2678 Kauaopuu Puu Hapapa Maunauna Acres H2
Makaha Puu 1054 2883   Kunia Mililani Military
         Kapaileunu   Puu   Waikele Town Reservation
Mauna-lahilahi 1085 Puu Kanehoa NAVAL Str Military
Beach Park Military 2728   Reservation
Pokai Bay Beach Park Res Puu Kaua 9
Pokai Bay Waianae Kaupuni PAHEEHEE 3127 Mil Res Pacific
KANEILIO PT Lualualei Str RIDGE RESERVATION (CLOSED) Palisades
Lualualei Beach Park Puu Mailiilii Pohakea Pass Naval Pearl City
         723   2170 Reservation Waipahu
Maili Mailiilii RADIO Palikea Peak E   Pearl City ONE
         NAVAL STATION 3098 Pass 750 Peninsula
Military Res Gov't Waikele Naval Res
MAILI PT Res Puu 780 Puu Mauna Kapu Mil Res West Middle Aiea Bay
Maili Beach Park Puu o Hulu Uka Heleakala 2776 Loch Loch Naval
         856 1890 NANAKULI Honouliuli U S Air Sta Arizona
93 Naval FOREST Navy Pearl Mem
         Res Puu RESERVE Str LAULAUNUI I Harbor FORD SE Loch
Nanakuli Manawahua Puu Kuua H1   ISLAND 90
Kalanianaole Beach Park 2401 1548 Lower NAVAL HICKAM
         Mil Puu Kapuai Village Reservation AIR FORCE
Kahe Pt Res 1047 Puu   Pearl Harbor BASE
Kahe Beach Park 277 Makakilo Honouliuli West Entrance
         922 Makakilo Loch Government City Fernandez Village KEAHI PT FT KAMEHAMEHA
Reservation Tenney Village Ewa NAVAL Ewa Beach Park MILITARY RES
Campbell Industrial 764 RESERVATION Ewa Beach
Park 901 760 Honolulu NIMITZ BEACH
USC & GS BARBERS Observatory Oneula Beach
Observatory PT   Park
Coast Guard Res NAVAL AIR STATION
Barbers Point NIMITZ BEACH
BARBERS PT Beach Park

M A M A L A

N

HONOLULU
HAWAII

INTERCHANGE	(UC)-UNDER CONSTRUCTION	(PROP) PROPOSED	Multi-lane Divided Expressways
COMPLETE		(U.C.)	Other Divided Highways (paved)
			Wider than 2 Lanes (paved)
HARD SURFACED	IMPROVED	UNIMPROVED	Principal Highways (heavy to medium usage)
			Secondary Highways (light usage)
			Other Roads (surfacing not indicated)
			Trails (inquire before attempting)

(H1) Interstate Highways (25) State Highways Airports: ✈ International, ✈ Commercial, ✈ Military 1493 Elevations shown in feet

Distances shown in miles (red figures are distances between red pointers /; others are between towns and junctions).

Scale of Miles
0   1   2

Coral Gardens

State Tree: Kukui

State Bird: Nene

Hula dancer

Lei vendor

Outrigger, Waikiki

"We are still unique — we are still ourselves — we are still Polynesia."
Commentary at Polynesian Cultural Center, La'ie.

Hawaiian Glossary

The earliest known list of Hawaiian words is in Captain Cook's account of his explorations compiled in 1778, the year of Cook's discovery of the Sandwich Islands. Two hundred years later we have compiled another list, the shortest of all lists, to enable readers to better understand Hawaiian words not defined in the text.

Reverend Lorenzo Lyons wrote in 1878 that the Hawaiian language "is one of the oldest living languages of the earth, as some conjecture, and may well be classed among the best . . . The thought to displace it, or doom it to oblivion by substituting the English language, ought not for a moment be indulged." We agree and we prefer not to substitute where Hawaiian words have become part of our vocabulary. It is for this reason that anyone can quickly recognize a *kama'aina*, for their English will be well sprinkled with Hawaiian words fondly adopted over the years.

The Hawaiian language, first compiled by the missionaries after their arrival in 1820, has changed little, but dictionaries and the printed form have changed from time to time, and in this book we have used the presentation that most clearly reveals the correct spelling and proper way to pronounce even the most complex words. Glottal stop marks are used throughout; but for reasons of clarity in reading, we have dropped the hyphen, and I hope the linguists will forgive us. All that we know is derived from the *Hawaiian-English Dictionary* by Mary Kawena Pukui and Samuel H. Ebert (University of Hawaii Press).

I cannot explain how to pronounce Hawaiian, except to suggest the reader try to pronounce words the way they are spelled (I understand a knowledge of Latin helps). Pronounce each vowel as a separate syllable, with accent on the next to last syllable. Vowels are pronounced like *a* in above, *e* in bet, *i* in city, *o* in sole, and *u* like in moon. Don't worry too much about *w*. Most of the time, give it a very slight *v* sound. To further aid in pronouncing words with multiple vowels, we have included the glottal stop, which is similar to the sound between the *ch's* in English *oh-oh*.

Now practice on *Ka'a'awa*, a small community on Oahu's windward shore. Being able to pronounce Hawaiian the way it sounds greatly enhances the pleasure of reading about Hawaii. ∎

Ahupua'a · Land division
Akua · Powerful god
Ala Moana · Road by the sea
Ala Wai · Canal
Ali'i · Royalty
Aloha · Love, greeting
Aumakua · Family Gods
Hale · House
Hana · Work
Haole · White person
Hau'oli · Happiness
Heiau · Pre-Christian place of worship
Ho'omalimali · To flatter
Hulihuli · Turning repeatedly
Iki · Small
Kama'aina · Born in Hawaii
Kanaka · Hawaiian, person
Kane · Man
Kapakahi · Crooked
Kapu · Forbidden
Kaukau · Food
Kepani · Japanese
Kihapai · Garden patch
Kuhina nui · Prime minister
Lanai · Porch
Lani · Sky
Lei · Flower garland
Lililili · Extreme jealousy
Limu · Seaweed
Lua · Outhouse

Luau · Hawaiian feast
Luna · Supervisor
Mahalo · Thank you
Makahiki · Year, festival
Makai · Toward the sea
Make · Dead
Malihini · Newcomer
Mana · Supernatural power
Mauka · Toward the mountains
Mauna · Mountain
Mele · Chant
Menehune · Hawaiian gnome
Moana · Ocean
Mu'umu'u · Loose covering dress
Nui · Large
'Ono · Delicious
Pake · Chinese
Pali · Cliff
Papale · Hat
Pau · Ended
Piko · Navel
Pilikia · Trouble
Pua'a · Pig
Puka · Hole
Pukiki · Portuguese
Pupule · Crazy
Pu'u · Mountain peak
'Ukulele · Leaping flea
Wahine · Woman
Wikiwiki · Quick

The City Is An Island

At dawn a faint glow appears. Flying over Oahu, two miles above the sleeping city, the first light is without any color. Next, the glow is pink, laid below a fuzzy purple band against the gray darkness next to the black sky overhead. At this early hour only the stars give dimension to space beyond, a space gradually evolving to deep blue as the sun appears, at one point matching the ocean's perpetual blue when the sea blends into the sky and the horizon disappears.

At sea level, when the ocean accepts the dark blue of the sky at daylight, the dawn is dark gray at first, gradually changing into warm magenta hues, then pink and orange as the earth spins eastward and the ocean waves approaching the island reflect a first glimmer of light into Waikiki hotel rooms to leeward.

The day begins earlier for windward dwellers on the east side of Oahu, where the sun rises from beneath the ocean and shines directly into panoramic-view windows of suburban homes perched on low hills below the *pali* and above the sea. It is breakfast time for windward people.

Across the island, on the other side, away from the rising sun in the morning shadow of Ko'olau peaks, gray rain clouds spread outward over the still drowsy city, sprinkling streets with brief rain showers drifting *makai*. The air is sweet and still moist in the cool of early morning. It is twilight at dawn until the sun is high enough to burn back the clouds before sweeping downward onto the leeward shore, drying wet streets now gradually filling with mixed clutches of trucks, cars and the mayor's yellow buses (TheBus), all pouring together into downtown like colored sand draining from a glass funnel. It is not until later in the morning before the sun rises full over the city. Leeward people never see a sunrise in bed.

Honolulu is a skinny city, stretched out like some lazy hound dog relaxing on the beach with his paws in the water at Waikiki and long ears flopped against the green hills that in valley and ridge repeat the curves of the shoreline. The tail wags in Hawaii Kai and the tongue laps Pearl Harbor. Urban planners say it is the perfect kind of city for a fixed-guideway mass transit system.

Urban Honolulu has no main street that can be clearly identified. The town just rambles on all over. The old cow paths that eventually became boulevards apparently went only as far as the feeding trough. Kalakaua, Kapiolani, and Fort streets seem to end before they really get anywhere. Only Lunalilo Freeway squirms boldly through Honolulu between old residential areas and new condominiums, from its beginning in Kahala to its grand slam finish at Aloha Stadium, where it disperses rapidly into a maze of interstate interchanges.

Honolulu was not platted in square blocks like San Francisco or provided with wide boulevards like Paris. Nothing seems planned nor premeditated. The whole thing just grew, and continues to expand in the same unorganized pattern that somehow reflects the informality of its lifestyle. It defies the traffic engineer's logic. Improving traffic flow is like diverting a freeway through an ant hill, and as automobiles have steadily increased in this long, narrow city, conversion of many streets into one-way routes became the only solution. Driving home at times is best accomplished by continuing straight ahead around the island. Honolulu may be the only city where any direction is the way home.

The island is small. Kamehameha Highway, the only round-the-island road, is just 94 miles from the beginning and back. At the narrow part a two-hour hike to summit ridges offers a view of both sides of the island at once. It is difficult to believe that Oahu boasts 52 miles of the U.S. Interstate Highway System, with only one gap between Honolulu and the nearest stub in southern California. Eighty-two percent of the state's population of over 800,000 live in Honolulu, and these 656,000 people drive over 300,000 automobiles!

Half an hour from downtown by interstate freeway, north beyond Pearl Harbor, the city flattens out into a soft carpet of green sugarcane covering fertile plains between the Ko'olau and Wai'anae mountains. The twin mountain ranges, extending northwesterly, effectively interrupt trade wind patterns and force most of Oahu's rain to fall on windward slopes, leaving leeward shores sunny and dry. Honolulu and Waikiki seldom experience heavy rain — it is mostly "liquid sunshine," as defined in tourist advertising; mostly a misty drizzle falling lazily from broken cumulus sailing with the wind as the clouds break away from clinging hills. It is a rain that reflects rainbows across the city, and why there is a greater difference in rainfall between windward and leeward sides of the island than between summer and

The ocean path of the setting sun intercepts a schooner in Mamala Bay off Honolulu Harbor. Mamala was a shark woman in Hawaiian lore who lived at the entrance to Honolulu Harbor and often played *konane,* an ancient game resembling checkers.

winter. When the city forgets to pick up after itself, a night rain washes the dust away.

Honolulu is basic green, blue, and white — the colors of the mountains, the sea, and the sky. The space surrounding the green hills is blue. It is delineated by the highest ridge and softened by *mauka* showers moving slowly across the city. The rain falls from white cumulus clouds that define wind direction and strength, breaking away from the mountaintops in long clusters that cling to the hills briefly before letting go and bringing to the city moisture, shade, and coolness.

White buildings dominate the skyline like a sharp, serrated knife on edge, hugging the surf line like a crownflower *lei* thrown into the sea, and having floated back to shore, is caught in the ceaseless sweep of waves upon the land.

Only a close look reveals other colors. They appear on people and flowers, seldom on homes and buildings, but they blend well into the Hawaii landscape. Only the blue, green and white have always been here. Everything else is an immigrant from another continent, brought here by birds, waves, and early travelers to become a botanical Pandora's box that in this case is a pleasure to open.

The city is trimmed in white, the hue of almost everything man has made. No cold season interrupts the perpetual spring to change the basic color of things. All year the hills behind the city are green, washed clean by the evening rain. The city is as if built upon a magnificent natural stage, with the evergreen mountains its contrasting, never-wilting backdrop. The clouds are a proscenium arch bridging the sky, bringing mountain summits to the sea in one unbroken spatial grasp, giving visual unity to the city, and locating it stage center. Onstage, and outlining the green mountain shape with the random heights of urban shapes, are angular buildings and small white houses scattered among the high-rise apartments where man encroaches upon nature. The director is creating another scene.

Early Hawaiians had words for all these spaces, shapes, and places. The circle of sky extending from the horizon they called *kahiki-ku*. The space overhead was *luna-a'e*; the space between the heavens and the earth was sometimes called *kalewa*. Where the birds fly is *lewa-nu'u*.

The Hawaiian's close relationship to and dependence upon the physical world — land, sea, and sky — evolved into a language that reflected this relationship. With an unwritten vocabulary, and with word nuances perfectly suited to island needs, they understood the spiritual significance of the shape of spaces, and they defined spaces that have no equivalent in English. Who else has defined the space below where a person would swing from a tree with his feet clear of the ground? The space is *lewa ho'omakua*. And the space beneath where we stand — *lalo*.

Perhaps the island lifestyle and the easy-going human relationships are indeed inherited from our Hawaiian ancestors on some cultural bridge. To some extent, we are indebted to their keen understanding of the spaces around us and how it affects our daily lives. It is well known that we determine what we build and in turn are shaped by the World we build. Are we island people the way we are because we are on an island, and are conscious of the space around us that extends beyond where we can see?

Hawaiians called this space *kukulu-o-kahonua*, the compass of the earth. When it is understood that our physical world has its limits, when we can see both sides of the island that is our home, it may be easier to satisfy human relationships that clearly cannot be escaped.

Honolulu has experienced a cultural, economic, and social revolution since the end of World War II that has substantially changed the people, the land, and the economy. Yet in many ways Honolulu has not changed at all. With all the attributes of a big city, it is still much like a small town, with all the pleasant things a small town has to offer. Honolulu has made the quantum leap from an oligarchic plantation town into a sophisticated contemporary city with little pain and discomfort, without becoming hard and selfish. Somehow, the better characteristics of a small place were retained while adapting the economic advantages and cultural wealth of a big city.

Our pleasant, permissive weather obviously helped to keep dress styles informal; but positive humanitarian values also prevailed, even when opposing sides both had a battle to win. Under similar circumstances elsewhere, violence was often the answer to difficult controversy. Exceptions can be found, but in the years that Hawaii rapidly grew into a democratic community, creating in the process a prosperous middle class where none existed before, the incidents of violent confrontation scarcely rate a mention when measured against the major accomplishments that are the result of compromise and evenhanded judgement.

Somehow we grew up without fighting each other — without the remnants of hate and bitterness that plague so many world communities. Is it because we live upon an island? ■

In the hills above Oahu's urban tangle, a tropical forest surrounds Sunday afternoon hikers on a Hawaiian Trail & Mountain Club hike on the Honouliuli trail, Wai'anae Mountains.

Kamehameha's conquering army pushed Oahu's warriors over the *pali* in upper Nu'uanu Valley. The scenic view was later saved from subdividers by Hawaii's unique land use law (overleaf).

We Did It Ourselves

It required over seven centuries for the people of Hawaii to make these islands the place they are today — for the early Polynesians to find Hawaii and begin changing the landscape. They first investigated New Zealand to the south in voyages from the Tahiti area before sailing northward and settling into the several islands they called Hawaii. They apparently liked Hawaii and decided to stay here because there is no evidence they sailed any further to investigate the mainland, although these early sailors did have the necessary navigational skills and seaworthy double-hulled canoes to explore colder waters should anyone have desired. They adapted Polynesian living styles to their newly discovered home and settled down permanently to create the Hawaiian nation.

Women stepped ashore with the men, carrying seeds of edible fruits and medicinal plants, coconuts, breadfruit, taro, and sugarcane, bringing pigs and dogs, along with a spoken language, warriors, and ali'i — the cultural grafts for the new civilization that began in Hawaii about 700 years ago. Within 500 years their highest ali'i, Kamehameha, with the help of Western cannon and gunpowder, conquered all the islands and crowned himself king. Hawaii was possibly the last place on earth to be discovered and settled, although conquering is still going on elsewhere.

British Captain Cook followed long after the first Polynesian arrivals, navigating with sailing instructions given the explorer by the king of Tahiti. Cook sailed straight northward to Hawaii after leaving Tahiti, with only one stop enroute at Christmas Island over the holidays, where his ships were restocked with water and coconuts. Missionaries arrived in Hawaii some 50 years later, and they were appropriate precursors to the whalers and later merchant shippers, who introduced agricultural crops for export and established a plantation system that required the import of indentured labor from around the world. The land was fertile, with ample water, plentiful fish, and abundant natural resources; but if all this bounty was to last — to feed, house, and clothe a growing population — the land must be properly cared for.

The ruling Hawaiian ali'i called his unique land subdivisions ahupua'a, and specifically located boundaries to include differing land uses, thereby providing for all his people's needs within his own feudal domain, and incidentally making it much easier to collect taxes.

Feathers, canoe logs, and spears came from the mountains; taro, bananas, and sweet potatoes from the lowlands; fish and seaweed from the sea. Waters outside coral reefs were assigned to commoners; those between reefs and beach, to ali'i. The beach was unassigned and available to all. To this day, the beach between the high-water mark and the sea remains public.

It is said that in ancient times whenever a canoe log was cut in the high forest the ground was prepared for another tree to be planted in its place. And that collectors of feathers for the magnificent royal capes took only individual feathers and let the bird fly free. Even in later years a land lease granted by King Kamehameha's commissioner of public lands included the admonishment not to "permit or suffer to be done, any willful or voluntary waste, spoil or destruction. . . ." Conservation is indeed a tradition in Hawaii, a tradition adopted in kind by immigrants from other lands as their political and economic influence gradually become effective. The plantation manager, taro farmer, and resort developer all seemed to possess some kind of innate concern for preservation and protection of the land.

Cruel scars on the landscape, a legacy of 200 years of

Of all the cities in the United States as measured by five polluting elements being monitored in the atmosphere by government agencies, Honolulu is the only major city with a clean bill of health. Every other city is deficient in at least one category of pollution. Honolulu is the cleanest city of its size in the nation.

I've been involved in the kind of life in the last few years where I've had to be gone a great deal, and it gets a little frustrating because all I want to do is spend more time in Hawaii. When the plane lands at Honolulu airport (and it's usually midnight or one o'clock in the morning) and they open that door and that soft Hawaiian air comes in — it's one of the greatest feelings in the world.

James F. Gary, President
Pacific Resources, Inc.

Bertram Street on hilly St. Louis Heights, glistens in passing showers, bringing a rainbow to Waikiki, far below in the wet sunlight.

Sixty thousand people can sleep overnight in Waikiki. Only a few hundred will find room on crowded Waikiki Beach during daylight hours, but there will always be room for yellow bikinis.

intensive use since Cook sailed into Kealakekua Bay, are ample evidence that Hawaii has been sometimes treated roughly; but these scars seem less an overall indictment than a way of measuring the great beauty still remaining, even on Oahu where urbanization seems overwhelming. One of the problems in identifying environmental progress is that success may be vacant lots or farmland everyone takes for granted — as if it had always been there and always will be there. Defeat is a concrete high-rise monument we face every day.

It is difficult to imagine the streets of 60 years ago, when billboards hawking catsup, tamales, and whiskey blocked the view of Diamond Head. A giant green pickle was appliquéd across the *pali*, and on the slopes of Punchbowl white letters ten feet high advertised soap. Prime scenic areas were tacky with mammoth signs promoting everything from Bull Durham "roll your own" to patent medicines and chewing gum.

Forty advertisers were effectively blotting out choice portions of the scenery when a determined group of Honolulu women organized the Outdoor Circle to promote civic betterment, and specifically "to rid the city of billboards."

When it was learned their club treasury did not have sufficient moneys to buy the billboard companies, the women launched a city-wide boycott, urging the public not to use advertised goods, and directly challenged downtown merchants to stop advertising. They were the first to enlist the Honolulu Chamber of Commerce in a conservation campaign. The new Hawaii "tourist" bureau unanimously endorsed the women's campaign and the old Honolulu Board of Supervisors voted its support. It was the beginning of cooperation among environmentalists, businessmen, and politicians to keep Hawaii beautiful.

After 14 years of boycott and refusal to compromise on decorative smaller signs, only chewing gum and cigarettes remained on the billboards. Local firms had long since canceled their advertising, and there was little business left for the single remaining company; it agreed to sell when the women again offered to buy the last billboards. They successfully raised the money and for one week became the only conservation organization in the outdoor advertising business. Outstanding contracts were quickly canceled and the termite-infested boards dismantled and burned. Diamond Head could be seen again from Honolulu's open-air streetcars crossing the McCully Street Bridge. The next year, legislation was enacted outlawing billboards in Hawaii.

Struggles between development, economic growth, and environmental protection raged constantly in every state legislative session, in every meeting of the Board of Supervisors, and more recently in the Honolulu City Council as well. But as the battles raged, protagonists on the side of preserving Hawaii's natural scenic resources, open space, and the island environment gathered together unusual allies that did not occur elsewhere. In the confrontation over saving Diamond Head — to halt construction of high-rise hotels on the famous landmark — Honolulu councilmen advocating "growth and progress" and more hotels, were opposed by the Sierra Club, Chamber of Commerce, Conservation Council of Hawaii, AFL construction trade unions, and the Oahu Development Conference, a planning group sponsored by the largest corporations in Honolulu. Diamond Head won.

Environmental controversies extended over many years, even during the time of the Republic of Hawaii and territorial days. When sugar and pineapple interests generally prevailed over all else, concern over the land and its proper use was always given serious consideration at all government levels. Many compromises were made, many unfortunate plans were approved, and permanent scars were imposed upon the land, like Interstate TH-3 cutting the heart out of Pu'u Papa'a on its spear-straight route to Kaneohe; but overall, most of the decisions

Article VIII
PUBLIC SIGHTLINESS AND GOOD ORDER SECTION 5.
The State shall have power to conserve and develop its natural beauty, objects and places of historic or cultural interest, sightliness and physical good order, and for that purpose private property shall be subject to reasonable regulation.
The Constitution of the State of Hawaii

seemed to be the correct ones. Somehow we saved more than we lost, and what we did save was the most important.

Probably the most significant legislation passed by any state is Hawaii's progressive land use law, which provides for state zoning and management of all public and private lands in the state. Supported by another unusual coalition of citizen conservationists, businessmen, and large landowners, the unique law was enacted to slow down urban sprawl, to halt rising farmland taxes, and to end speculative manipulation of agricultural lands. Like any law, implementation by appointed administrators has determined how effective it is; but much of the natural beauty and open space of today's Hawaii is a testimonial to the land use law's effectiveness, despite attempts to repeal made in every legislative session by county governments demanding a return to "home rule."

The late Governor John Burns fully supported the law and also urged the use of the legislation to protect scenic beauty, as well as sugar and pineapple lands, arguing that both are of equal importance to the state's economy and deserve equal protection. In a talk before the Conservation Council of Hawaii, he said, "We have the basic land use law on our books to protect and enhance Hawaii's resources of scenic beauty and open spaces. . . . Ownership of land does not carry with it the right to deface its natural beauty in the name of progress." I had written that speech for the governor, along with many others on conservation that were given during his successful campaign.

In his first month of office, Governor Burns appointed me a State Land Use Commissioner. My first thought was to take whatever action necessary to reverse the usual priorities that favored development over everything else. As for me, "conservation" zoning was far more important to the future of these islands than expansion of urban land uses. One-half of all land in Hawaii is now zoned "conservation" and given the state's strongest protection against unwise short-term uses and destructive development. It's not permanent protection, but it's better than any other state offers. The ancient *ali'i* had actually taken the preparatory action hundreds of years before when they divided their *ahupua'a* into primitive land use districts. We just updated the old Hawaiian system.

Protection of the land is the law of the land in Hawaii. A total ban on billboards, state-wide land zoning, a restrictive business sign ordinance for Honolulu, a protective coastal zone act, creation of a general plan for the state, and even establishment of specific tourist destination areas backed up by the land use law, all are demonstra-

Dole pineapple, Wahiawa Plantation.

tive of the people's determination to grow and prosper while conserving the island environment. The people of Hawaii, through their elected representatives and appointed commissioners, have been able to play a role in creating the Hawaii seen today.

As in any working democratic relationship, compromise has been the name of the political game. Political corruption is not unknown. The ownership of land still carries most of the traditional constitutional rights of development, speculation, and profit. But the history of Hawaii and Honolulu — and of the scenic beauty around us — is surely ample evidence of the fact that concern for our land and the island environment is an integral part of our island lifestyle.

Most of Hawaii's politicians hold to the usual free-enterprise economic thinking: that growth is good and that development is to be encouraged, "to make jobs" and "to provide a larger tax base for the city;" but their final votes, even after checking with campaign con-

31

tributors, generally seem to be tempered by thoughts of how their decisions will affect our environment. If elected legislators are a bit slow in recognizing this concern, a veritable army of active citizen environmentalists reminds them. During the campaign to stop high-rise hotel construction on the front profile of Diamond Head, over 35 community organizations joined together to convince wavering city councilmen that their political future was in jeopardy if the famed landmark's profile was to be desecrated with hotels. The candidate for mayor who thought it proper to build a few hotels on Diamond Head was defeated. Frank Fasi, who won, appointed a conservationist chairman of his Advisory Committee to Save Diamond Head. No hotels were built and the land was up-zoned to park and to open space.

There have been a few losses. Developers filled in Salt Lake, the only large natural lake on Oahu, to build a golf course. Twenty years ago we tried to convert Kalakaua Boulevard into a pedestrian mall, but Waikiki property owners were able to convince city politicians otherwise. We haven't been able to stop the continuing urbanization of caneland around Pearl Harbor, nor strip development of Kamehameha Highway on the north shore; but we did stop the rampaging transportation planners from going ahead with ill-advised schemes for freeways on offshore reefs, for a double-decked interstate *makai* freeway to cover Ala Moana Boulevard and the waterfront, and for another spur of the interstate through beautiful and historical Moanalua Valley — the TH-3 to Kane'ohe.

Hotels planned for Magic Island and Ala Moana Park were never built. I remember walking to then-Governor Burn's office and being shown several elaborate color renderings of hotels to be built in the park, "to help pay for the park." I took one look at the plans and assured the governor that every citizens group in the city would oppose this scheme, and that he would be well advised to have nothing to do with hotels on Magic Island. After a short discussion he agreed and stacked the drawings against the wall behind his desk. They were never released to the press, and the hotels were never built.

When Standard Oil of California came to town a few years back, announcing plans to construct a major oil refinery on Sand Island in Honolulu Harbor, within one mile of downtown Fort Street, the general public was outraged. Especially when Standard insisted that Sand Island was the only possible site and threatened to cancel the project, with all its promised jobs, if they were not granted permission to build where it wanted to build — in Honolulu Harbor. Full-page ads financed by philan-

thropist and Bishop Estate Trustee Atherton Richards helped convince Standard Oil that the industrial park at Barbers Point on Campbell Estate lands would be a better location.

When I joined the state Land Use Commission, the privately owned Castle Ranch lands below the Nu'uanu Pali viewpoint were already subdivided on paper. Engineering drawings were completed, streets named, and preliminary subdivision approval granted by the city. I immediately went to work to stop the subdivision that would destroy forever one of Hawaii's famed scenic views. Land use conservation district regulations prohibited subdivisions, so it was my intent to have the land zoned "conservation," to make it possible for existing dairy pasture and banana farms to remain and benefit from lower property tax assessments.

I traded votes wherever necessary with my fellow commissioners to obtain a unanimous vote to zone all the *pali*-view lands as "conservation." There are controversial subdivisions on all the outside islands that benefitted from my "yes" votes to obtain a "no" vote for subdividing Castle Ranch lands. It was a practical example of legislative democracy at work, to achieve a community goal that benefitted the long-range best interests of everyone.

Hawaii didn't get to be the "most beautiful islands anchored in any ocean" by accident. We did it this way quite deliberately — from the very beginning. We learned from everywhere. From the early German forester who carried water on mules into the Wai'anaes to water his seedlings, planted by hand. A stroll on the Honouliuli trail proves his effort at reforestation was quite worthwhile. When sugar planters overthrew the monarchy to assure their valuable crop entry into the profitable American market, they also established a state forest reserve system on private lands to protect their watershed. It thrives to this day — there are no federal forest lands in Hawaii.

Even the monopolistic plantations and large estates, which together own and control most of the land in Hawaii, played a role in preserving, intact, extensive agricultural lands — it was not necessary for them to sell off bits and pieces like smaller property owners. The great unbroken expanses of cane and pineapple growing on the uplands of Oahu still preserve visual open space between the mountains and the sea that continue to make a drive to the north shore from downtown an unusual spiritual experience. Crossing Oahu to the other side is to verify again the limits of our island home, and to confirm that this finite geography is what probably gave us the concern for its care and protection. Our immigrants from everywhere gave us the skills to do so. ■

People are happy here because of comparisons. We may get a little worse over the years, but compared to every other place we're better. The gap between us and the rest of the world, if anything, has widened. We're better compared to them.

Herbert Cornuelle, President
Dillingham Corporation

Young *keiki* from Kapi'olani Butterworth's Hula Studio dance for Sunday visitors and residents at the vast Ala Moana Shopping Center.

Honolulu is one of the prettiest cities in the world. I have been to 67 countries in my life and I have never seen a city that has as attractive downtown area as this one, and it's continuously improving. Going back 30 or 40 years I can remember the downtown areas and the city was not pretty. Somehow, gradually, with the redevelopment that has taken place in downtown, with the big, broad highways that go up through the valleys, which I think add to the beauty of the city because people can enjoy the beauty of the city, because people can enjoy the beauty from the Pali Highway, from Likelike Highway — Honolulu has indeed become a very beautiful city.

The aloha spirit obviously gets diluted as we get more and more mainland people here. The core of Hawaiians and old-time residents obviously is smaller in proportion to the total population, but Honolulu does have a spirit. It does have a feeling all of its own. And I think that people who come here and stay for a time become imbued with that feeling. Of course, there are exceptions, but I know all sorts of people who've moved here from far away and have taken Hawaii as their own. And I think that's very definitely true with Honolulu, and one of the reasons that Hawaii is a nice place to live. Some of these people have built the Honolulu we know today.

I think that all the companies in Hawaii, for obvious reasons, are searching out competent women, are searching out competent personnel from minority races. I don't think a double standard is really a problem here, because in the first place we don't really have any minority races. However, in the old days there was unquestionable bias against Orientals. That has long since passed. Some of the more competent people, perhaps some of the most competent people in this company, are Orientals. Some of the most competent people I know of in Hawaiian business are Orientals. The old days of bias have not only passed, but are well past. . . . I'm very proud of the fact that I actually made the motion to admit the first citizen of Japanese ancestry into the Pacific Club some years ago. That is all in the past and it's a good thing.

Honolulu is more than just a place — it's a state of mind. It's a particularly beautiful place and state of mind combined. It's beautiful because it is racially harmonic — as racially harmonic as a place in this "state of change" can be. It has this happiness halfway between the Orient and the West. It has the mixture of Polynesia, of Asia, of the Europeans — all put together in one location. And I think that makes a super mixture. A super kind of place that only happens once in the world and it's happened here.

Henry A. Walker, Jr., Chairman
Amfac, Inc.

The financial center of downtown Honolulu surrounds Bishop Street, named after Charles Reed Bishop, early financier and public official who married Princess Bernice Pauahi and established the Bishop Museum in her honor. Bishop Street was cut through their old home site.

Trees Are A Soft Green

Trees are green. Lots of them are a distinguishing feature of Honolulu where shaded tunnels on residential streets are nostalgic reminders of another era when the horse and carriage always traveled a tree-lined path. Today new apartment towers stand high above the blanket of green softly covering older sections of the city, gracefully wrapping urban space between the mountains and the sea.

It is quite evident from viewing old photographs that Hawaii has many more trees than say, a hundred years ago, but it might be debatable whether we have more trees today than twenty years ago. For awhile, during the post-statehood building boom, we may have been cutting urban trees faster than they grew. The community did object, as they always have been very protective of trees in Honolulu, but the economic pressures of "growth and progress" often overwhelmed even the best intentioned city official. A previous administration actually sent out workers in pre-dawn raids to cut down more controversial trees, so it would be too late for conservationists to seriously object after the denuded streets were discovered.

In the days before accountants kept tabs on expenses, plantation managers would on occasion divert a few field hands from sugar growing to tree planting. The magnificent exotic trees shading Kemo'o Road to Waialua are part of this heritage. Wives of these same sugar executives joined downtown women in organizing the Outdoor Circle 65 years ago to augment rural planting and bring some greenery into the city. Half a century ago, Honolulu hillsides were bare and dry, with more cactus than grass, much of the desolation due to overgrazing by goats and a general die-back of sensitive native plants and grasses.

Writing in the *Historic Hawaii News*, Dorothy Hargreaves tells of the first planting by Outdoor Circle women in A'ala Park, Honolulu's earliest public playground. The women planted 28 monkeypod trees, which now offer a continuous shaded canopy surrounding the grassed play area. The Circle women also planted coconut palms along Kalakaua Avenue in Waikiki; the rows of mahogany trees between Beretania and Kapi'olani; and miles of colorful shower trees on highways and residential streets. These trees have all grown into mature specimens that in some cases have spread across the street from curb to curb, creating great gothic arches of green that considerably enhance the city. The more than 280 ironwood trees *(casuarina equisetifolia)* in Kapi'olani Park were planted in 1890 by A. S. Cleghorn, father of Princess Kaiulani.

Several trees over 100 years old grow on the Castle Ranch behind Olomanu. Here is a large Norfolk Island pine *(Araucaria),* where Queen Lilioukalani is said to have composed "Aloha Oe," and a double row of 30 royal palms still lining the old carriage road used by royalty in the days of the kingdom. One of the oldest monkeypod trees in Honolulu covers the entire front yard at Borthwick's home on Wyllie Street. A Moreton Bay fig *(ficus macrophylla)* about 125 years old grows in Queen Emma Square. It was planted in the old Royal Gardens established on this site by King Kamehameha IV.

We began to lose some of our older, now extraordinary, trees in the sixties. One of the trees on the American Forestry Association's "Social Register of Big Trees," a sandbox *(hura crepitans)* in Moanalua Gardens, was felled for a state highway interchange. A number of other large trees were lost at the same time, but one of the largest monkeypods in Honolulu still struggles for survival between steel protective railings in the median strip of the H-1 freeway. An earlier successful fight by Outdoor Circle supporter Alice Spalding Bowen saved the tremendous Indian banyan growing at 'Iolani Palace, but then a dozen of the mahogany trees on Kalakaua were cut to make a left-hand turning lane that was never used. The state tried the old carnival shell game on Dillingham Boulevard, trucking in coconut palms from Wai'anae and replanting them along the airport entrance road to appease the Outdoor Circle; then later the state uprooted the palms when construction commenced on the airport freeway and replanted them God knows where.

In the old days people were much more happier, I think. Now we have more people and more people are interested in making more money, money, than like the old style, very leisurely, less traffic, less people . . . Now buildings unbelivable, unbelievable. Especially on Fort Street. Never expect these tall buildings compared to the low six stories. Old time Aloha Tower was the tallest building. Young Hotel wasn't too tall. Now the buildings are more twice the size . . . I have one kid very happy in San Mateo. One is happy over here. The one here is more of a money-making man. All he does is try to make money, working very hard. But that's like Honolulu now.

Robert Lum
Retired Grayline driver

The yellow shower, one of many varieties of flowering trees that brighten every Honolulu street, drops most of its green leaves to produce a golden glow.

The city attempted to remove the rows of giant ironwoods along Kalakaua extension in Kapi'olani Park, claiming they were full of termites and might fall down on tourists; but vociferous opposition stopped the chain saws. Traffic engineers, supported by the City Council and the mayor widened Ke'eaumoku and King Streets, removing a beautiful 100-year-old banyan with a canopy so large it extended clear across the intersection. Community opposition to destruction of the Ke'eaumoku Street banyan reached a climax on the Sunday morning scheduled for cutting, when I helped organize "memorial services" for the tree. Artists arranged for a "paint-in" and photographers took their last pictures. The mayor announced plans to perpetuate the now-famous tree by dismembering it and planting its limbs in various parks around the city. After the remains had been removed by city workers, someone placed a small white cross in the scarred earth, reminding the drivers on Ke'eaumoku that something old was missing from Honolulu.

Killing of the banyan caused a strong public reaction and undoubtedly led to the chain-sawing, very early one morning, of the graceful circle of royal palms that once surrounded King Kamehameha's monument in downtown Honolulu. The palms had been planted many years ago, with proper dedicatory services, in front of the Judiciary Building, one of Honolulu's most significant historical sites, and it was incredible that anyone would destroy them; but the local tree-trimming crew *luna* claimed the state ordered them removed. When pressed he said he had no copy of the work order, but the man who authorized him to cut down the palms said his name was Albert Camus.

While enraged state officials continued to denounce what they described as a meaningless prank pulled by a "screwball," a University professor thought he saw a meaningful message in the act. The choice of the name Albert Camus could be no coincidence when viewed against Honolulu's recent record of sacrificing historic and aged trees for highways and subdivisions.

Albert Camus stressed in his writings man's need to carry out a personal responsibility in the fight against social evil. Camus, a member of the French Resistance during World War II, wrote, "considered as artists, we perhaps have no need to interfere in the affairs of the world. But considered as men, yes . . . I have written so much and perhaps too much, only because I cannot keep from being drawn toward everyday life, toward those, whoever they may be, who are humiliated and debased. It seems to me impossible to endure that idea, nor can he who cannot endure it lie down to sleep in his tower." The royal palms were never replaced.

In 1925 the city authorities had tried their best to extend Hotel Street through the center of historical Thomas Square, a park opposite the Honolulu Academy of Arts, and were stopped by the state legislature, which at the urging of the Outdoor Circle, passed a resolution asking the city to cease and desist. Fifty years later the State followed up by passing Hawaii's Exceptional Tree Act in 1975. The same year Mayor Fasi appointed Honolulu's first County Arborist Advisory Committee. It's been a running battle to outwit the city and state, but we may yet win the war. ∎

The young people of Hawaii do consider Honolulu as a gathering place. They like a bit of the big town atmosphere and yet like to relax away from downtown, and because of the good roads and cars they're willing to ride away from downtown and enjoy themselves 10 or 15 minutes away from downtown, but still in Honolulu. And the kids who are trying to make a living look forward to living on a neighbor island, perhaps, but still working in Honolulu because it is the gathering place. With new people coming in from the east, west and south, it makes it very much the crossroads of the Pacific we always talk about. It's a nice place to gather, and well, "do your thing," you might say. It shows so much diversity. Almost anything you want to do you can do in Honolulu.

William S. Richardson, Chief Justice
State of Hawaii

This is still one of the least expensive places to come to and one of the safest places to come to in the world.

J. Akuhead Pupule
KGMB early morning disc jockey

It is Aloha Friday in Honolulu and the island mu'umu'u, *in every color and design, decorates the city. Overleaf, urban Honolulu covers the land between the mountains and the sea. Diamond Head and Waikiki lie beyond.*

Kalakaua Boulevard Is Waikiki

Waikiki is one of the world's great walking places. Not along the narrow beach, for there is no Boardwalk like in Atlantic City, but along the sidewalks of Kalakaua Boulevard. It's Hawaii's version of the Ginza in Japan, of Michigan Avenue in Chicago, of Fifth Avenue in New York. Kalakaua is not the ritzy "seen and be seen" street of Rodeo Drive in Beverly Hills, nor is there the history and romance of Paris's Avenue des Champs-Elysêes; but to the visitor, Kalakaua has much of the excitement of all these streets contained within the two-mile central Waikiki core. It's slightly dingy, almost risque, and promises more than it delivers, but it's where "the action is," where something seems to be about to happen at any moment.

Kalakaua in Waikiki begins at Ft. DeRussy, where servicemen on leave from every branch of the military first blend with vacationing civilians and are drawn toward Diamond Head hidden somewhere behind the solid phalanx of hotels, condominiums, and office buildings. Slender coconut palms soften the concrete hulks facing each other across the wide boulevard that is never empty of traffic.

Kalakaua begins totally undistinguished and actually quite seedy, with garish islands of honky-tonk before it settles down into a consistent style and flavor. In the first block, discount gift shops, adult movies, and gift bazaars compete for customers and offer little evidence of anything worthy. Canlis and Chez Michel, two of Honolulu's best restaurants, squeeze in where each would be least expected.

One of Waikiki's two McDonald's is well-disguised within the elegant blue-tiled Gumps Building across from the likes of "The Pearl Factory," "Garment Factory to You," and the "World's Fastest Overnight Film Processing." Here is Woolworth in a bank and office building, and the "Deli–coffee Shop — Kosher Style" next to the new Waikiki Shopping Plaza. Hardly a distinguished collection of shops for any worthy street, but Kalakaua combines this frothy mix in just the right proportions to satisfy the insatiable street appetites of perhaps 70,000 tourists, night and day.

Kalakaua Boulevard, Waikiki, 1941.

I came to Waikiki alone one month ago. For me, each new day has been a miracle. I have welcomed each new dawn — in awe and humility . . . Regretfully and sadly I leave. I take with me beautiful memories and many intangible gifts from your people — Smiles, the touch of a hand and caring. Where else in the world does one see picnic benches carved with hearts and love instead of filth? Where else does one find a sidewalk full of soapsuds or windows being washed early in the morning? Where else can one learn the hula and quilt making only for the asking? Is this what the critics call commercialism? . . . I'm going home a richer, healthier, happier person because I have been to your enchanted haven of Honolulu — and I shall return.

Viola Ulberg, tourist
Helena, Montana

Kalakaua Boulevard, Waikiki, 1978.

There are also McDonald's in Hawaii — 28 of them, with the notable difference that in addition to green shakes and quarter-pounders, they serve up heaping plates of hot rice oriental saimin, and spicy Portuguese sausage with eggs.

Bright splashes of *aloha* shirts and missionary-styled *mu'umu'u* covering everything from neck to toe invite casual shopping in window-front stores, which need to offer little in choice of stock when many of the first tourist purchases are matching shirt and *mu'umu'u* in the most garish designs imaginable. They are suitable for nowhere else on earth, but none is intended for back home.

Waikiki is the place where changes in identities and philosophies are subtle and sometimes irreversible, for here is the place of escape. Arriving from stuffy mainland cities in coats and ties, plain slacks and bouses, the hotel room is only a brief stop to strip away mainland encumbrances and step into the brand-new world of Hawaii. The warm, humid air of fabled Waikiki is absolute proof that paradise exists. A stroll down Kalakaua is a symbolic release of lifetime conventions and unsuspected inhibitions. For many, Kalakaua is a discovery of living, and the realization that with even a simple change of clothes almost anything is possible. The discovery of new people and a new self adds dimension and excitement to the Kalakaua scene, making the experience itself an encounter of a new kind.

Open shirts, string bikinis, and short shorts are street dress on Kalakaua. They mix comfortably with yellow city buses, red cycle rickshaws, and the steady stream of automobiles also sightseeing through Waikiki, dodging surfboards on bicycles and brown sunbathers with straw beach mats and airline flight bags. It's warm here, and next to nothing is the fashion from early morning until late night, with visitors walking from off-beach hotels to the ocean and from on-beach hotels across the street to stand in line for breakfast at Minute Chef or to wait for their round-the-island tour bus to arrive, coupons and camera at the ready. The buses creep around back streets searching out their hotel stops,

Changes in Honolulu over the years have been awesome, astounding. The superlatives never stop, particularly for those of us that date back a little while. As we look around, the profile of Diamond Head is harder and harder to single out. When I started there were about 5000 hotel rooms on the island of Oahu. Now we have approximately 30,000 rooms in high rise hotels all around us. Our hotel is the only one that has stayed the same like in the old days.

Honolulu is the cultural center. It's the center of finance, the center of fine arts . . . the island is large enough so that it encourages people to speculate in motion, movement, sightseeing. There is a great deal of life and vibrancy, a great deal of jubilation . . . It is difficult to envision something like this being duplicated on the neighbor islands. The neighbor islands have their own aura, and I think everyone agrees that you don't want to repeat many of the things that have happened in Waikiki. But, nevertheless, it is still the gathering place and for the foreseeable future there will be little that can deter the movement of people to Honolulu.

Randy Lee, Manager
Halekulani Hotel

traveling close behind each other like multicolored caterpillars. They park together, and travel together, picking up and disgorging loads of tourists together, as if afraid to be separated in the wilds of Waikiki.

At the Royal Hawaiian Hotel entrance, Kalakaua Boulevard straightens out and coconut palms shrink in size as high-rise hotels grow higher. Only a glimpse of Diamond Head's profile can be seen between hotel towers. They loom high — above the eyebrows at International Market Place, the only space still open to the sky along Kalakaua, before Kuhio Beach Park where the solid concrete wall is broken, permitting fresh ocean smells to blow across the street. A large banyan tree grows here, surrounded by unusual benches with roofs attached. The sign overhead says "Warning: Beware Bird Droppings." It's a favorite nesting place for mynah birds and local residents.

Across the street is Hyatt's Regency Hotel, built on the site where Peter Canlis invented the steak and lobster combination in 1947. The first Canlis restaurant was installed inside an old wood residence converted by Peter's architect friends, Pete Wimberly and Howard Cook, into the first steak and lobster house in the world. Postwar strollers on Kalakaua remember the great clouds of billowing spicy smoke produced by Peter's new charcoal broiler. It could be smelled on yachts a mile at sea. Thirty years ago there were only seven items on the menu, and lobster was $4.50. Today the Canlis restaurant at the other end of Waikiki has 30 items on the menu, and lobster is over $16.

Canlis has an astonishing employee record. The headwaitress, Kuni Kawachi, began working at the original Waikiki location in 1947. She and her sister, cocktail waitress Skoshi Uyemura, have worked for Canlis 31 years.

Tahiti's South Seas Spectacular rocks the Beachcomber Hotel's Bora Bora Room in Waikiki. Afficionados who have "watched the hands" in Waikiki hula shows over many years have noted that *ti* leaf hula shirt lengths go up and down with contemporary mainland fashion.

I think that growth on this island should come virtually to a stop . . . I hope that growth here certainly from the tourism standpoint will come to an end pretty soon, particularly when they reach the limit of rooms in Waikiki . . . One of the problems you face with government is it takes an awfully long time to get things done. The Governor's Travel Industry Congress of 1970 recommended a limit on the number of hotel and condo rooms, apartments, in the Waikiki area. It wasn't until 1976 that we finally got action by the City and County of Honolulu to actually put those limits into law. If I recall correctly it's about 26,000 hotel rooms and about 3000 apartments . . . We're getting very close to that. Probably another year or so and it should see us at the limit. It's not going to hurt. People will not be refused the opportunity of coming here, because there's very simple things that happen in tourism. We've been experiencing this for a long time — the change in the length of stays. People used to stay here for weeks. Now, we've gotten to where the average length of stay is about ten days or so . . . What can very easily happen if you have a limit on the number of rooms and the tour operator wants to send more people here, is to change his packages to decrease the length of stay in Waikiki and take them to the other islands for the rest of their Hawaii visit.

John Simpson, President
Hawaii Visitors Bureau

Japanese tourists may eat at Marushin, Americans at Canlis and at Bagwells. Tourists on a budget split hamburgers at McDonalds, and royalty dines in the Kahala Hilton's Maile Room. Eighteen different ethnic restaurants serve their national dishes in Waikiki, including Thai, Moroccan, and Greek. Eating out in Waikiki is indeed a tour of the world.

Kuhio Beach begins its crescent curve where Kalakaua bends seaward — still without revealing the famed profile of Diamond Head. Hundreds of surfboards are stacked in beachside lockers, near where pretty girls bake like lobsters in the tropical sun, white mainland skin barely hidden behind skimpy bikinis. Sailboats meander aimlessly on the horizon, beyond the gentle waves inshore where surfers rent a wave for a day.

Kalakaua gradually becomes seedy again opposite Kuhio, where "factory to you" outlets outnumber U-Drive car stands and whirling postcard racks. The silly pots of bougainvillea struggling to grow on lamp posts are discarded when Kapahulu Avenue begins at Kapi'olani Park — where the full profile of Diamond Head is finally and suddenly spread across the sky. Kalakaua emerges from the tourist crowds of Waikiki and quickly transforms itself into a stately drive through the park.

Waikiki Beach is narrow and small compared to its reputation; but the first morning swim in its tepid, clear water and an outrigger canoe ride to shore on the crest of a wave that seems to last forever, evoke emotions that keep "sand in the toe," as locals put it. It's ocean spray in the face; a sky always clear; cool breezes on a hot, humid day; and shimmers of the setting sun reflecting across smooth waters inside the reef. It is the rainbows floating overhead on afternoon showers. It is drinking a mai-tai in the short twilight when day quickly becomes night and hotel *lu'au* torches are lit. No garish neon advertising signs gouge out the night sky; but never-ceasing traffic noise from Kalakaua is constant accompaniment for tin-can Tahitian drums in noisy Polynesian nightclub acts, and for more gentle Hawaiian melodies played on the guitar in contemporary slack-key. Joined together with the brass of dance bands and raucous rock, the sounds mix in a caterwauling tribute to Waikiki mania.

Nighttime entertainment mirrors the varied choices and contrasts of Waikiki, in local rescreenings of a late-late show arranged by tour packagers, and in commercially oriented nightclub operators catering to the music, dress, food, and living modes that are new here but old elsewhere. Hawaii has always adopted strange imports quickly, and the newest Hollywood aberration joins old flowers and people to augment further the Hawaiian mélange.

So, Honolulu and Kalakaua thrive, in a gently simmering *poi* bowl of island-flavored lifestyles stirred together with people, flowers, and cultures still arriving from overseas. No wonder the mainland visitors love the place. ■

I have an idea called Aina Malama — preservation of the land. I would like to see certain lands which are important to Hawaii's quality of life placed under the protection of the state Constitution — beyond the reach of the legislature, the Land Use Commission, county councils, and zoning boards. The people of the state should decide by vote which lands will be used for conservation, recreation, preservation of historical sites, and agriculture. Those lands should be placed in the Constitution and placed beyond the reach of those agencies. We will then have taken meaningful steps to protect those lands so that they can help maintain and sustain a quality of life for a long time to come.

I think I made a speech once where I said maybe the county government ought to be abolished. I have a feeling if we could sit down and have the neighborhoods come in — the people of the neighborhoods to effectively give input — we may be able to operate only with a state government. They get money from the county and state, and a lot of money from the federal government. Many of the services provided by the county can easily be assumed by the state. The county and city governments as we know them may not be necessary.

I do not think we should rest and be comfortable just because our crime rate is lower than some cities. I'm not going to compare Honolulu with others. I think what we have here now is not enough. Not good enough in terms of what we are and what we can become. Honolulu still has its attractions. It's better than New York. Better than Chicago. But so what? What is New York? It's failing. What is Chicago? It's not an example to look up to. It's like the people in the press and TV. Most of them here today are people from the mainland and that's the attitude they have. They think, well, this is better than New York or Chicago or Los Angeles, so it must be pretty good. But that's not good enough for me. I was born and raised here in Hawaii and I know what Hawaii was, and I want Hawaii to be what it can be.

Nelson K. Doi, Lt. Governor
State of Hawaii

Young Hawaiians at a Kapi'olani Park festival recapture their ancient Polynesian heritage while Waikiki at twilight (overleaf) reflects the excitement of a thriving resort on what was once a royal bathing beach. Only Diamond Head remains unchanged.

46

Certainly our growth is too fast and it needs to be slowed; but on the other hand, it's like plants. Either you grow or die. So, I would hope we continue to grow, but with a more planned pace and with a more sensitive attention to public facilities which are a necessary part of growth. . . . I hope that we can slow our growth to the point that we will not pass that divide which carries us from a small town to a metropolitan monster like New York, which has developed to the point where people are not received, judged, and communicated with quite as people. . . . This I hope Honolulu never comes to. It's one of my apprehensions of building a high-capacity transit system for Honolulu, because such a system stimulates growth because it's an attractive system to use, and growth around the stations can become just as dense as New York City or any other. And when you get that kind of thing, you lose the personal touch. Like when you stop speaking to people in elevators, then you're over the hill.

I love the mix of individuals. Not just in their ethnic background, but in their thinking. There is such a wide variety of approach to civic and business problems, and this is particularly stimulating. I came here from Charleston, South Carolina, and there the thinking is pretty much routine and there's not much difference between the groove and the rut. I like the individual thinking here and the differences of opinion on many issues.

Honolulu is still a small town and it thinks like a small town. The intimate acquaintance of people and their communications is still as it was when I remember it in the early fifties, and I think it's one of its beauties. The fastest way to get word around in this town is by word of mouth. . . . And as in many small towns, I think people seem to hear what they seek to hear according to their background. This happens here as well, and it still has that beautiful flavor of a small town, which I hope we never lose.

In the many times that I have to travel, particularly to the mainland, I squeeze that round trip ticket because I know that in returning to this Aloha Land I will be with people with whom I can communicate and with people who are worldly and understanding. I love them.

E. Alvey Wright, Former Director
State Department of Transportation

The *puka* through the *pali* was pushed through the Ko'olau Mountains in 1956, moving cars and people across the island to booming suburbs in Kailua and Kane'ohe.

We Did It First

Oahu is a small island, but if you include the ocean around us it's a very big place, and living in Honolulu definitely extends beyond the shoreline (where we swim and sail), to the horizon (where we look) and above the clouds (where we fly). By this measure Honolulu is indeed a big place.

Honolulu is also a long place — the longest city in the world, measured from Makapu'u Point on the Molokai Channel to Kure Atoll at the northernmost boundary beyond Midway, about 1,400 miles and eight islands, depending on what size you call an island. The city charter includes all the leeward islands (except Midway), and this places all of Honolulu (except Oahu and Kure) in the Hawaiian Islands National Wildlife Refuge, an unusual distinction for any city, although some wags have suggested that Waikiki at times has sufficient wildlife to be included.

Honolulu has long been a collecting place as well as a gathering place. It has been a testing laboratory for new ideas brought in by travelers, who continue rediscovering Hawaii as if no one else had arrived before them — as if they were the first to learn of the island's unique lifestyle. And these "visitors" had always been missing the boat home (now they miss airliners and lose flight schedules), and many never do return where they came from. It is part of the local problem, an acquired affliction of *malihinis,* for the island environment seems to excite the dreamer, and we eagerly continue to hold out a *poi* bowl to stir innovative ideas and old traditions, for experiments with new visions. We have always been a place for original research in people relationships, which is rapidly leading to a completely new and original society.

And as the visitors came from different continents, so did the flowers, birds, and trees collected by early immigrants to live with them on their tropical landscape. The exotic botanical introductions thrived, as did the people, and soon most of the native living plants were crowded out and smothered by new arrivals, just as were the native Hawaiians. It was not possible to resist new introductions — the island plants and birds disappeared as rapidly as the Hawaiian culture and language. What remains is a dazzling botanical mosaic for the eyes, and a new societal treasure for the soul.

Imposed sometimes roughly upon this island foundation were economic and technological support systems also imported by pioneering merchants, traders, and planters intent upon transforming these isolated islands into a profitable enterprise. The island development occurred swiftly, with every problem, political and economic, quickly becoming a bold bridge to another goal.

Growers developed new varieties of sugarcane and pineapple to facilitate use of mechanical harvesting machines, to overcome disease, and to permit intensive use of herbicides and chemicals to control plant growth and sugar content. Eventually computers determined the optimum time to irrigate and fertilize, and when to harvest. Soon, the plantation manager just carried the message, making few decisions himself, and Hawaii continued to gain a reputation for getting things done better and more profitably.

Hawaii is a somnolent lifestyle gathered on a string of semitropical islands floating in just the right place. Not too far south in the Pacific, where humidity is a bother, nor too far north, where sweaters are needed, yet not too far west, where the wind blows hard. But Hawaii is far enough west to be that "different" place to visit and to do business where English is spoken, yet still a destination for escape from smog, city crime, snow, foods, hot summers, and cold winters. (With no seasons and ideal climate the Hawaiians had no word for weather.) It was only a matter of time before busi-

Honolulu is the smallest large city in which I've ever lived and it is the smallest in which I ever intend to live. I like the things that go with big cities — the cultural and business affairs, the transportation facilities to move internationally. Honolulu has it all, combined with the liveability of a small city. It's the only city its size in this country that has such easy access to everywhere. Honolulu is the international crossroads for the world's decision makers. Heads of state, advisors, cabinet members, principal military people, are easily accessible to us. It makes a very stimulating situation and one that is unique, I think, to Honolulu. It provides one of the elements for successful corporate leadership and is a characteristic which will help Honolulu as a future headquarters for international corporations.

James F. Gary, President
Pacific Resources, Inc.

Night-blooming cereus on the stone wall surrounding exclusive Punahou School, blooms for one night only. It is wilted and dead by first sunlight.

nessmen and tourists found the islands and began to use them like home. In short order, local residents objected and, as rapidly as promoters and salesmen introduced mainland routine that changed the island way of doing things, residents responded with restrictive laws intended to keep the islands just the way they were. Some laws succeeded, some didn't, but in most cases Honolulu is still a beautiful island because we deliberately decided to keep it that way.

When the business visitors erected advertising billboards, the territory soon passed a law banning billboards (the first in the nation and still the only state law totally banning them). When new businessmen began using revolving signs and flashing neon to advertise their business, Honolulu became the first city of its size in the nation to prohibit all off-premise advertising signs and anything with words that shook, moved, or flashed. And in opposition to all principles of advertising display, laws require the sign must be small, so its message cannot be seen very far away! Electioneering politicians with squawking speakers were driven from the streets, and outside political display posters banned. Only bumper stickers, pedicabs and taxis remain as moving advertising space.

When it became evident all the island land was taken for one use or another — military, transportation, agriculture, urban buildings, hotels, or forest — and no existing use could be expanded without encroaching upon another, the state legislature decided in its wisdom to assume all zoning powers, and Hawaii's state land use law was enacted. With the counties being legal children of the state, it was quite proper to take away most of their zoning rights in the best long-range interests of all the citizens in the state. Hawaii was the first state to do so, and is still the only state with state-wide zoning. We were the first state to give farmers the right to dedicate their land exclusively to farming and pay lower taxes

accordingly, even when their farms adjoined higher-taxed urban lands.

When too many hotels appeared on beachfront property, a shoreline protection law was enacted to keep them back. When excessive spear fishing began to deplete the once abundant sealife in Hanauma Bay, legislators created the first underwater marine preserve in the nation. When it was noticed that street improvements were in occasional conflict with trees, the first Exceptional Tree Act in the nation was drafted, giving the oldest, largest, and most beautiful trees equal rights with road builders. When office building and hotel owners protested high taxes on landscaped property, taxes were reduced to zero on gardens used by the public. And just to be sure nothing was overlooked, an environmental policy director with cabinet-level status was placed in the governor's office.

Honolulu cannot boast of a great "think tank" or a large industry to spur important inventions; but our isolation and relatively sudden thrust into the competitive business world has caused us to do much by ourselves, and to build major international corporate enterprises in the process.

Amfac's president, Henry Walker, is Honolulu born and his firm, selling under many different names, is one of the largest retailers in the West. Not only is it possible to stay in Amfac hotels on every main island in Hawaii, but also in Los Angeles, Las Vegas, on the rim of the Grand Canyon, and in Death Valley. Castle & Cook, with headquarters a block away from Amfac in downtown Honolulu, is the nation's fifth largest food processor, growing pineapple in the Philippines, bananas in Central America, sugar in Hawaii, and canning tuna in Oregon. Dillingham Corporation, whose founder built Oahu Railway, the first railroad in Hawaii, digs coal in Canada, barged most of the oil pipeline supplies to Alaska, and sells liquified gas in almost every state of the Union. Pacific Resources

Honolulu is going to be a bright star in the future of our country and the Pacific, where all the action is going to be, where two out of every three people in the world live in countries abutting Pacific-Asian waters. I think Honolulu has a destiny and the people living in Honolulu are beginning to realize how important Honolulu is to world peace, to our country and to the friends and neighbors who live in the Pacific-Asian area.

Frank Fasi, Mayor
Honolulu

Elaborate harvesting machines mechanize pineapple picking on the world's largest pineapple plantations surrounding Wahiawa. On the other side of the island, 30 minutes from downtown Honolulu, the lava rock shore and coral sand beaches extend to the horizon from Makapu'u (overleaf).

Flower *leis* of plumeria, orchids, carnations, and what is available that morning are strung for *kama'ainas* and tourists at airport *lei* stands.

operates oil tankers on every ocean and ranks number one in the nation in average sales growth over the past five years, a performance attributed mostly to an unusual activity for a Honolulu corporation — refining oil.

As a result of this business growth, Honolulu has many "firsts" to boast of, some not very important, but all ample evidence of our vitality as an island city. We used the first city-wide dial telephone system; we built the first revolving restaurant (Le Ronde, atop Dillingham's Ala Moana Building); we invented the condominium apartment, both vertical and horizontal regimes (the first one built under Hawaii's original law is at 3019 Kalakaua); we were first to establish legal limitations on the number of hotel rooms that can be built in a resort (about 29,000 for Waikiki, where there are now 23,000 rooms); and we had the first bottomless male waiters in the U.S. (at the Dunes Restaurant).

The first domestic scheduled hydrofoil passenger service started in Honolulu (Sea Flite), as did the first scheduled air cargo service (Hawaiian Airlines holds CAB Certificate No. 1). The two local airlines flying out of Honolulu (Aloha and Hawaiian) are the only scheduled airlines in America that have not had a fatal accident. Henry Kaiser built the first aluminum geodesic dome at his Hawaiian Village Hotel; we have the first movable bleacher sports stadium, convertible from baseball to football at the flick of a switch; and we enjoyed the first radio broadcasts west of the Rockies. Honolulu International was the first U.S. airport to service a commercial jet airliner (BOAC's De Haviland Comet III) on its first flight around the world.

Honolulu is a small kind of place where things vibrate more individually. It's also a small town where problems are temporary obstacles still solved by friendly cooperation. Even the usual governmental bureaucracy is easier to overcome when 82 percent of the state lives in one city, and when city hall is across the street from the capitol. It all fits neatly into Honolulu's sunny day, where the means to an end have always been the beginning. ■

Continuing to rely on tourism as the state's most important industry can be a self-fulfilling prophesy, as little effort will be made to diversify the economy. We could be looking into more light manufacturing, making more of the things we consume here. We can become exporters of energy, and self-sufficient in our foodstuffs, but all we are offered is more tourists. Must we become a vast collection of servants? Can't we be more like normal communities, engaging in a wide variety of healthy enterprises, supplying our needs with local manufacturing talent?

Dennis Callan
Life of the Land

Honolulu International Airport is a flying crossroads of the Pacific for 15 domestic and foreign airlines.

Everybody's Beautiful

Hawaii's Chinese (damn *pakes*) are all wealthy and spend 20 hours a day scheming how to get richer.

Hawaii's Japanese (damn budda-heads) are too big for their britches and spend 24 hours a day trying to control the state legislature.

Hawaii's Filipinos (damn flips) are pushy, dress in funny colors, and are getting rich on fighting cocks.

Hawaii's English and Scots (damn *haoles*) are arrogant no-goods who think they're better than everyone else and own everything.

Hawaii's Hawaiians (damn *kanakas*) don't like to work and are trying to take back their islands.

The stereotypes are everywhere — perpetuated by best-selling authors, and repeated without qualification by travel writers producing superficial froth simmering endlessly in racial melting pots. But the facts are simple. We found out long ago that what makes the living great in Hawaii is the differences, and nobody was a minority long enough to give anybody real trouble. Honolulu may be the only community anywhere with state funds being used to sponsor ethnic festivals like Chinese New Year and Japanese Cherry Blossom Week. We still have a separate Chinese and Japanese Chamber of Commerce, and another one where they speak English. It is the style of Hawaii to perpetuate the differences while we enjoy the differences. With keen competition for limited jobs and exploitation of favored positions in the economic and political communities, some rough edges will undoubtedly be ruffled; and if the street kids don't start a rumble on occasion, unrelated frayed tempers will. But long before the federal civil rights act, we had abolished our segregated "English Standard" school system and began living together on both sides of the street. There are no ethnic neighborhoods in Honolulu — everybody is all mixed up.

Of course, it all began with the Hawaiians, who had a very loose immigration policy — they let anybody in. When Captain Cook arrived, the anxious Hawaiian girls greeted his crew in their own flamboyant style and the mixed Hawaiian race was born. The missionaries (somewhat reluctantly), whalers, and proper merchants carried on the old traditions, giving birth to the Aloha Spirit, the neo-Hawaiian race, and the concept that everyone is beautiful.

Despite colonial attitudes of early businessmen who organized the great sugar factories, many did marry Hawaiian women — both commoners and members of royal families. Their descendents became social and economic arbiters of the islands and, in the case of merchant wives like Princess Bernice Pauahi Bishop, founder of the Bishop Estate, they had a continuing influence over the economic life of Honolulu.

The pattern was set long before Chinese and Japanese arrived to work sugar and pineapple plantations, with hopes of arranging for "picture brides" to be sent from home. For many sugar workers it was more convenient to marry the "native girl" at hand. It may be that the apparent acceptability of interracial marriages in Hawaii, and the children born of them, is partly because men have always outnumbered women in the islands. It was plantation policy to only contract for single men, and for many men far from home with little prospect of returning, marrying a part-Hawaiian girl was not only practical, but desirable. They were very beautiful women.

The Portuguese in turn made their cultural and physical contribution to the islands — soon there were Hawaiian-American-Chinese-Portuguese people. Portuguese immigrants also brought with them hot *malasada* doughnuts and *pao duce* to eat and the ukelele and guitar, both instruments adding considerably to the pleasure of

I went to the English-Standard School. It wasn't fair — wasn't fair. Haoles all went to the English-Standard, but there was a few taken — like a few Hawaiian and I was part-Hawaiian. They did give you a little test before you entered. I recall it very clearly, well, they showed you an apple and an orange. They wanted to hear you say the words. I looked quite Hawaiian and my German grandmother went with me. I can remember that, and they wouldn't dare to turn her down. So, there I was. But I spoke proper English, so there wasn't really any problem, but I suspect that others with no one to talk with them — one look and — so, sorry. We did have a few Chinese, but mostly a haole school. See, we were not very conscious of all that. In fact, we weren't conscious at all until we got quite a bit older. I don't think it was very necessary to separate the races, because even if I had gone to the so-called local school which was Kawananakoa I don't think I would have changed. The kids who went there didn't really speak the proper English, but how were they ever going to learn if they weren't associated with the kids who did speak properly?

Emilie Lemke Williams
Honolulu

Kahana Bay State Park.

How is the fishing out here in Haleiwa?
It was good at one time, but not anymore because of population. Too much netting, diving. I believe for my type of fishing divers have destroyed most of the holes. I prefer line fishing with a boat. Go out — bottom fishing.
What for?
Used to be menpachi, but there's no menpachi now, so you have to go a little deeper for opakapaka, uku, ulua.
When do you go fishing?
Night is the best. That's for mostly akule and opelu. That's the main type of fish that we go for. It's the akule and opelu. We market right here.
What kind of price does fish get?
Oh, akule and opelu hasn't gone up in the last 15 years, but your exotic fish, y'know, the red ones, they've gone up — tripled. Like red snapper.
You're living kind of a retired life now?
Yeah. I just fish when I want to and I don't care too much for the commercial fishing. It's mostly for table use — family use. That way I don't have to spend a lot for groceries anyway.
Do you ever go crabbing?
We used to go. We used to get good Kona crab out here, but the law is too weak on crabbing. Now, they close crabbing for the summer, but it doesn't help.
What's the biggest fish you ever caught?
That's a marlin, 208 pounds. I marketed it. Marlin makes good smoke fish. Marlin is good for everything, steaks.
What kind of fish do you prefer?
For small fish, opelu. For sashimi fish, uku.
Are you always going to live here?
Downtown Honolulu is all business. Waikiki is all entertainment. The rest of the island is all mixed up with sugar and pineapple. It's more relaxing and I like it that way . . . Sugar out here is going to fade out eventually, because the zonings don't hold up. They're always changing it, so there's going to be more buildings. My home and lot is in a park zone. It was made park zone about ten years ago — can't even build a new home, can't do anything here. For a small man like me I can't do nothing.
Living is changing in the country then?
In the old days in Haleiwa we knew each other, knew everyone. We had no problem. We had no thefts. We had doors open day and night — closed, maybe, but unlocked. We had no trouble 'til a few years back. Then we started getting newcomers around. Things happened. You can't live around here now without a dog. It's not locals, it's all the newcomers.
Do you go downtown much?
I hardly go downtown unless I gotta go see a specialist. I never go for shows or parties or restaurants. I rather stay out here in the country. My life is full enough out here. Full of relaxation. Right? Relax with my beer. I hope life continues this way without too much encroachment by high rises or residential areas . . . You feel very tight downtown, and, well, you drive more carefully in town. We're not used to that type of traffic. Well, I guess maybe we wait too long to make a turn. There's more courtesy in the country than in downtown Honolulu. When you come home you just relaxed. The first thing you go for is a bottle of beer. When you come out of Wahiawa and down the hill you in third base, then almost home.

George Niimi
Fisherman, Haleiwa

Hale'iwa town on the north shore.

Hawaiian music. *Kama'ainas* still will joke about the Portuguese having been made *haoles* by act of the legislature, to make racial statistics look better to Southern congressmen in the struggle for statehood. Keeping racial statistics has always been a problem in Hawaii, where nothing matches up with mainland bureaucratic definitions, and where many interracial couples refuse to refer to themselves or their children as anything but American.

The final plantation immigrants were Filipinos, who are still barely represented in politics and business. Their numbers increase as new arrivals report home favorably on the democratic political weather.

Latest to arrive in large numbers among Pacific ethnic groups are Samoans, very much aware of their status as lowest on the totem pole in Hawaii's intricately woven tapestry of people. Still somewhat culturally isolated by age-old family relationships brought intact from their home islands, they have yet to join the mainstream of island life, and their cultural contributions are still to be felt.

In some ways, prejudice, or lack of it, can be measured by the degree that members of one group can enjoy a joke told on them by another. Like the story of the Portuguese who was raging about "damn *kanakas*," and after listing in great detail all the outrages committed by this particular Hawaiian, added, "And I tell you one ting! Dat damn *kanaka* — he sure can play one ukulele!"

What fighting there is in Hawaii may be mostly a family fight or the usual differences between the "haves" and "have-nots." Perhaps those who arrive in Honolulu with a chip on their shoulder, or who dislike the differences, would be better off in some state where everyone is alike. Hawaii's feelings may have been expressed quite aptly in a newspaper advertisement the day statehood was granted. The headline read: "Statehood For Hawaii — We're all haoles now."

Hawaii's epic story has too often been retold by magazine apologists emulating waves on the shore. Like the ocean surf they sweep words onto the beach and cover every disturbance in the sand. The waves quickly recede into the sea, smoothing out any irregularities remaining — erasing every trace of past events. They have glossed over the most exciting and controversial aspects of Hawaii's historical past, lessening the importance of our contributions to society by concealing the fact that we did trip and fall while growing up to statehood. Hawaii's renowned diversity and harmony, reluctantly resolved over the years, was born of severe economic and social struggle by immigrants from East and West who had no idea they were creating a completely new and original society, a cosmopolitan gathering place famed for its racial harmony. By the beauty of our differences and of our pride in shared responsibilities, we may well serve as an example to the world. After all, we did it ourselves.

What most of the rest of the world strives for is, in a real sense, what Hawaii already is. It is important to understand, however, that we did fight for the changes that removed Hawaii from yesterday — from cruel racism and alien worker exploitation. They were all shameful facts of a colonial outpost annexed by U.S. businessmen intent upon carrying out the biblical precept — multiply and subdue the earth.

The immigrants from Asia, North America, and Europe planted crops, built homes, started businesses, and imposed their special political and economic ideologies upon the islands. In the process they pushed the native Hawaiians aside, took their lands, and overthrew their kingdom. They corrupted Hawaiian dances and music. The soft Hawaiian language that missionaries had created in written form was virtually abandoned. In the process of joining a prosperous society, the Hawaiians lost everything — their land, language, and culture. Yet, in a way, they are still part of everything, racially and culturally, for every aspect of daily living in the islands reveals how much we owe our Hawaiian heritage. ∎

I've been here since January, 1971, when I came from the Philippines. I was supposed to go to New York and try my luck there, but I happened to stop over in Honolulu because I have relatives here and I fell in love with the place and I stayed here. I felt at home here.

A lot of Filipinos move here and stay for good, because over here in Hawaii you have a chance to go up as long as you're industrious. As long as you work hard you can go on top.

Lettie Tesoro Gaoing, Owner
Diplomat Tours and Travel

Hibiscus, state flower of Hawaii.

On strike I've lived together with local people. Ate three meals a day. I had to learn to use chopsticks. They have no inhibitions. Absolutely honest. No sham. If they liked you they made a point of letting you know they liked you. But the local people are changing. I think they're changing. I prefer the old days. . . . People are more greedy today than they were in the past. I don't think that it is because of the fight for higher wages. I think that the population has changed. A great influx of new immigrants from the Orient, Caucasians from the mainland, and people from the South Pacific, too. I don't know if Honolulu is losing its ability to assimilate people. After all, that's how Honolulu grew; but it appears to be more difficult living together now, than before. You're continually finding problems in the schools, which are in many instances based upon race. There was no "kill a haole day," 30 years ago.

Honolulu before the war was a place without any middle class — a bunch of haves and have-nots. You went out to Waikiki you didn't see a local boy, a local person in any of the hotels or the restaurants other than as menials — employees. As a matter of fact, it was the policy of most of the companies there not to hire Caucasians in certain jobs, because these jobs were considered to be jobs for non-Caucasians.

When Jack Hall and I organized the plantations the Oriental employees were frightened and intimidated. Remember when the plantation workers wore "bango" numbers? . . . There was no such thing as going into a large downtown store and having a charge account for a sugar worker. He bought at the company store and he was "bango" number so and so, and he was "hey you" by his supervisors. Now he's mister and she's missus. Probably the greatest thing the ILWU did for these people was to give them human dignity.

Robert McElrath, Regional Director, ILWU
Sugar and Pineapple Workers Union

We've had some strife in our labor relations, but not as much as the mainland. Some plantations did have some violence, but it was wrong-doing by management, there's no question about it. I recently looked at an old contract where they brought people out from Scotland. Now, you talk about discrimination against Filipinos and the Chinese, and how they were worked so hard; well, that contract with the Scots was pretty bad, too. It really tied them up. It was a tough contract. But I do think that the employers did have too much of a hold on plantation people. When you bought anything you bought from the company store. You know the old song, "You owe your life to the company store." Well, that was true. You owed your life to the plantation and the sugar factory, and there was something that had to be done about it and it was done.

John Bellinger, President
First Hawaiian Bank

Harvesting sugar cane on Oahu Sugar Company lands in Kunia.

The Islands At War

I arrived in Honolulu on September 16, 1941, responding to a notice of civil engineering jobs available with the U. S. Army Corps of Engineers. I had sent them my educational résumé and within a week received a first-class ticket on Matson's *Lurline,* good one way to Hawaii. It was my first job.

I began work immediately, assigned to a drafting table in the converted top floor nightclub of the Alexander Young Hotel. The view from the top took in all of leeward Oahu from Diamond Head to the distant Wai'anae Mountains. Flat-topped Mt. Ka'ala dominated the far skyline and was the site of my first job assignment, to prepare construction drawings for a secret army radar installation atop the mountain. It would have clear electronic sight-lines in all directions to detect far in advance any enemy aircraft that might approach Pearl Harbor.

There was considerable military activity during the following weeks, but not until November did anything unusual occur. On Sunday morning, the last day of November, 1941, I awoke to the noise of army tanks clattering along School Street, snaking in long lines across town behind truckloads of armed, helmeted troops. Hawaiian Electric's waterfront power plant was ringed by extra guards with fixed bayonets, gas masks ready. The entire Oahu military establishment had been placed on "sabotage" alert, a reduction in classification from the previous weeks "attack" status.

Governor John Burns, then a young police captain working closely with army G-2 and the FBI on espionage investigations, had learned of a probable attack on the U.S. by Japanese forces several days before December 7. The Honolulu FBI office head, Robert Shivers, had informed him in a private meeting, "We're going to be attacked before the week is out." Burns was curious why the military did not alert itself to attack if the FBI knew what was about to happen; but he prepared for the worst, placing his own espionage unit on alert for possible illegal information gathering and transmittal by Japanese residents — something that never occurred.

On the first day of December 1941, 72-year-old Governor Joseph Poindexter's M-Day Advisory Council, assuming a more relaxed attitude, said its "report is being built around the entire wartime preparedness picture in Hawaii," and was to be submitted to the governor for recommendations "this week."

On Saturday, December 6, the army on Oahu had been on "general alert" for over a week, the public mostly ignoring the military preparations. They assumed the activity to be routine military maneuvers that had been going on for some time. While the British recalled troops to their posts in Singapore, and the Philippine cabinet ordered all nonessential citizens out of Manila, Honolulu seemed more in tune with U.S. Senator Ralph Brewster of Maine, who said, "The U.S. Navy can defeat the Japanese Navy any place and at any time." We didn't even consider the possibility of a Japanese attack on "impregnable" Pearl Harbor. Saturday evening, American soldiers and sailors purchased tickets at the Waikiki Theater to enjoy the movie, *Yank in the RAF,* starring Tyrone Power and Betty Grable. To everyone at the time, the movie was the closest Hawaii would get to war. Some people made plans to hear the Twenty-seventh Infantry Division Band giving a concert at the Iolani Palace bandstand at 4:30 p.m. the next day, Sunday, December 7, 1941.

The only person in Honolulu who may have sensed something might be about to happen was local columnist James Chun, writing in the *Honolulu Star-Bulletin* for December 6. He wrote, "America and Japan are nearer the brink of war today than at any time since relations were established between the two countries by Commodore Matthew Perry."

I was up at 7:00 on Sunday morning to join the

I'm Scotch, English, Spanish, Portuguese and Hawaiian. My children are marrying and there's no concern about race. I don't have any concern about race either — never have had. I think that makes our golden people. I've been exposed to the opposite having traveled and lived on the mainland. I do know that prejudice does exist, that people are concerned about races and culture. When I was first introduced to this it startled me. I think for many of us brought up in Hawaii it's a blessing in disguise because our ignorance is bliss. A lot of times it probably has gotten me in trouble because I didn't even know what they were talking about, but I'm glad I didn't know. And, you know even my children don't know.

B. J. Feldman
Former Miss Hawaii

Family picnic on the lawn, downtown main branch, Library of Hawaii. Overleaf, the back side of Honolulu reveals a fluted *pali* for Kane'ohe and Kailua residents, a wilderness only minutes from downtown.

National Memorial Cemetery of the Pacific, in Punchbowl Crater. Called Puowaina in the old days, the name means a hill for placing human sacrifices, for which this crater was famous before the *kapu* system was abolished.

Hawaiian Trail & Mountain Club's scheduled hike down the long ridge above Mokulei'a, from Makua to Ka'ena Point. We gathered early at our regular meeting place, the downtown Army-Navy YMCA, because of the long drive across the island, and were on our way before 8:00, approaching Pearl Harbor, when we noticed several unusual aircraft overhead. I recognized the Japanese red "meatball" insignia at the same time I saw billowing clouds of black smoke over Pearl Harbor. This was obviously no elaborate naval rehearsal, so I changed my schedule for the day to walk the streets of Honolulu and see what happened. I had brought my small folding Kodak Retina with me for pictures on the trail. Perhaps I might photograph the beginning of the war if I could get close enough.

I left the car behind and walked up into residential Alewa Heights until I was sufficiently high for an unobstructed view over Pearl Harbor. It was like opening a page of *Life* magazine in full color, three dimensions, and sound. Seeing the rumble of distant explosions, black smoke mixed with splashes of bright orange, and small airplanes darting swiftly about was like watching an old war movie. Silver planes occasionally dived toward the earth and as quickly returned, into a sky peppered with small splotches that suddenly appeared, as if artist Jackson Pollock was creating a giant landscape by throwing buckets of black paint against the sky. It was frightening to watch.

As I stood with my mouth agape, asking myself what happens now, I heard the sound of a faint whistle, becoming louder and louder as it obviously moved closer. I took it to be the sound of falling bombs whistling in the air as they fell. Puffs of gray smoke rising above nearby homes, followed by muffled explosions, verified that the neighborhood was under attack and that I should find shelter. I looked around me, not knowing quite what to do, then I saw the flash of an explosion in the next block. Quickly I rolled into the nearest gutter, lying as flat as possible, as the whistling grew uncomfortably loud, heading directly toward me. The bomb exploded with a sharp bang in the middle of the street a few yards away, shrapnel pieces whistling outward in every direction. I heard them pass within inches of my ears and watched in amazement as the white paint of the wood cottage behind me instantly acquired dozens of black holes, the shrapnel spraying through the house like someone shaking black pepper on a baked potato. I didn't know the exposure, but I took some pictures, anyway.

I waited until I heard no more whistling and stood up, shaking dust and dirt off my hiking clothes. In the street, a new 1941 Packard sedan had stopped, its engine still running, a strange hum in an eerie silence. I walked over, curious, noting that the automobile, too, was punctured everywhere with the same black holes. I looked inside. The passengers had red holes and the man nearest me was trying to hold his arm together, the bone protruding from torn flesh. There was no way I could help them

I finished the roll of film in my camera and walked back down the hill. Several friends were waiting for me on the front *lanai* of my apartment on Judd Street and asked what I had seen. I started to tell them, but I could only open my mouth. I could not utter a sound. I was in shock and it was several hours before I was able to talk coherently about the beginning of the war.

On Monday I delivered my film to Wadsworth's Camera Shop for processing, and on Tuesday U.S. Navy Intelligence confiscated my film. When the next issue of *The Saturday Evening Post* magazine arrived in Honolulu, I saw my pictures spread across four pages, with captions telling of the death and destruction by the Japanese bombing of Honolulu. They were not my captions, but they were my first published photographs.

Most of the other hikers tried to continue, but police turned them back before they reached Pearl Harbor. One group, which left early to meet friends in Wahiawa, was surprised when no one else arrived at the trailhead, then did the hike anyway, enjoying the trail by themselves, unaware that anything unusual had happened until they returned home to a curfew and blackout.

Newspapers and radio were a mixture of rumors and unverified reports of enemy landings and sabotage. Japanese parachutists were said to have made night

Hawaiian music will be around a long, long time. In many respects, it's all we have left. I live in Waikiki, and every time I look out my window and see all the high rises and buildings, it makes me sick. But when I sit down and start playing a song that's survived for 100 years or so, it makes me feel better.

Eddie Kamae, musician
Sons of Hawaii

Two opposing cultures meet in Waikiki at the corner of Kalakaua and Ohua.

landings and were waiting in hiding for a follow-up invasion expected at any time. The next morning, when planes from U.S. aircraft carriers flew in to land at Ford Island, jittery Pearl Harbor gunners opened fire again until calmer heads got things quieted down.

Monday morning I was notified to report with others to Kewalo Basin and help scuttle fishing sampans used by local Japanese fishermen — before their vessels could be used to refuel submarines reportedly cruising offshore. I thought the request was silly and refused to go. The request was typical of the strange behavior of otherwise reasonable adults that occurred often while the military slowly pulled itself together again.

Next day, in the early morning hours of Tuesday, one of my army engineer bosses, Colonel Theodore Wyman, started out with a truck convoy, headed for the University of Hawaii in lower Monoa Valley. His orders were to take over the university buildings to accommodate a rapidly expanding engineering staff (soon to triple in size). He drove out Wilder Street in the blackout, headed toward the Manoa campus, not quite sure where he was, looking for the identifying concrete gateposts at the university entrance. Nearing Manoa Valley, his car headlights reflected off the bronze plaques reading Oahu College.

Assured that he had arrived at the university, Wyman, who should have known better, pushed through the entrance gates, disregarding protestations of the night watchman, and took over the campus in the name of the Corps of Engineers. Not having keys, he broke open doors to buildings and moved out furniture and personal belongings, replacing school books with engineering manuals. The centrally located auditorium was divided by scaffolding into two floors, and my drafting table was removed from downtown to a high-level perch on the newly built second floor of Dillingham Hall.

When the faculty and students of Punahou School arrived in the morning, unaware their school had been occupied, they protested since it was clearly evident to them that the army had made a mistake in the dark and had occupied the wrong campus. The army steadfastly denied any error, but it was not until two days later that official notice was received by the Punahou president. Punahou students moved to the university and we stayed at Punahou for the duration of the war, until the Corps of Engineers constructed its own headquarters building at Fort Armstrong. The name of Oahu College had been changed to Punahou School seven years before, but unfortunately no one had gotten around to changing the entrance nameplates.

Kane'ohe Marine Corps Air Station.

On the first day of March 1942, two Japanese Nakajima four-engined long-range flying boats took off from Wotje Island in Micronesia, flying to French Frigate Shoals in the Hawaiian Leeward chain. Landing on the quiet lagoon, the aircraft taxied slowly to waiting Japanese submarines, where they were quietly refueled

I always think of the definition of Honolulu — fairhaven. In the days when we were growing up with the steamers, and now, of course, the planes taking the place of the steamers, it's still fairhaven. In spite of all the growth and the modern buildings and all, I think that Honolulu still has a welcoming feeling to it, a warmth; that, perhaps, is taken care of by the sea, the sky and the mountains, regardless of what man has done to pollute the landscape.

R. Alex Anderson, Composer
Lovely Hula Hands, Mele Kalikimaka

Arizona Memorial, Pearl Harbor.

and loaded with 500-pound fragmentation bombs. The next evening they were again in the air, this time on a direct course to Honolulu.

On the same evening, March 4, four employees of the Corps of Engineers, including myself, who had together rented a single large house on Pacific Heights, were hosting a typical "curfew" party of the time. Since our war restrictions prohibited late night travel, it was common to hold all-night parties, because no one could go home anyway and it was unnecessary to limit liquor consumption. Liquor and gasoline were the only items rationed in Hawaii, but there was always plenty of wine and whiskey. The parties were often rambunctious affairs, and our house, with three floors of rooms, provided many opportunities for varied activities. Windows on the first two floors were blacked out with opaque paper because martial law's General Orders prohibited lights that could be seen from the street. Even lighted cigarettes and pipes were prohibited unless an actual attack was underway.

We kept our top floor, with its broad *lanais* and large sliding glass doors, clear and open, so we could always see the great panoramic view we enjoyed from Diamond Head to Pearl Harbor. The night of our party was no exception, and groups of laughing couples would, on occasion, venture up the stairs to dance a little or simply sit quietly holding hands, looking over the dark city spread below. The blacked-out city always held a fascination for me, as it lay stretched out in front of the house, sound asleep, with seldom a sign of activity or movement. The city was always very still, without night auto traffic, and it was fun to imagine what went on in the darkness. Only sporadic shafts of light from army searchlights trying to find something in the sky would interrupt the silent nights.

Every 15 minutes or so I would climb upstairs with my flash camera to photograph friends in our "open" room, not worrying too much about any possible blackout violation because, after all, the light wasn't on very long! As was the usual procedure, around midnight everyone gradually went to sleep, scattered here and there on every floor in the house. I flashed a few more photo-graphs of sleeping couples before finding my own bedroom.

At what seemed like only minutes later, we were awakened by loud pounding on every door in the house. Before we could reply, doors were broken open and army soldiers, holding rifles with bayonets, crowded into the house. Moving from top to bottom they quickly herded us together in the kitchen and an officer stepped forward. We were all half-asleep and irritated at being suddenly awakened. But our aggravation was partially relieved by the knowledge they were *our* soldiers.

The officer asked who was responsible for the "coded light signals being sent from this house." We pointed out that all of us were civilian employees of the Corps of Engineers and were not spies. None of us were sending signals. He said the command post atop Diamond Head had been recording light signals from our house for several hours. There was no mistake. I then remembered my flash photography. That was it! The intermittent use of flash could easily be interpreted as signals from a distance. I brought out my camera and explained what had happened. We were sorry, but none of us had any idea my flashes would be seen by someone who might try to decode them. (I've always wondered what the message was.) The army squad was convinced they had uncovered a nest of spies, and were disappointed on learning we were merely a bunch of drunk engineers. They took my camera to process the film for proof that I was indeed taking flash pictures, and departed, offering apologies for breaking the door. We all went back to bed again.

An hour later a trembling boom practically knocked me out of bed. I ran to open the door before anyone else broke it down, and saw a bright orange flash in Pauoa Valley below followed quickly by another boom that shook the house, then a third behind Punchbowl Ridge near Roosevelt High School. I knew what was down there in the dark — I had designed the sewer and water systems for two army camps in the area. Behind Punchbowl was a

I'm sorry we had to go to the high rise condominiums. So many of our people who always lived in houses with yards now have to live in apartments, especially the young people, but I understand that we just don't have that much land. For myself I just don't dig those 20 and 30 story things. I just can't imagine not being able to hang clothes on a clothesline and walk barefoot in the grass.

B. J. Feldman
Former Miss Hawaii

Kolekole Pass Road in the Wai'anaes, carries military traffic across the island between the Navy's Lualualei Ammunition Depot and the Army's Schofield Barracks.

light tank battalion, and in upper Pauoa Valley was a battery of 16-inch mortars. I'm sure the commanding officers of those units felt the Japanese bomber was right on target.

I heard a siren somewhere after searchlights came on, stabbing the dark sky, trying to locate the distant sound of a high-flying multi-engine aircraft overhead in the night. The entire house was now awake, rushing to the "open" too to see what was happening. Most of us were probably wondering how we would *now* explain our "flash signals" to army intelligence. The bombs were real and the bomber flew right over our house.

On the way to work in the morning I visited the Pauoa mortar battery. The bombs hadn't hit anything important, except the latrine I had designed. The commanding officer, unshaven and a little disheveled, had apparently been informed of the raid on our house just before the bombs fell and showed me fragments of the bomb with Japanese inscriptions. He implied quite strongly that it was probably all my fault. I hardly knew how to reply, but did mumble a sort of "I'm sorry." It's the only time I ever apologized for a bombing.

Our work intensified in the weeks ahead, with many overtime hours on top secret underground installations. Oahu was preparing to outlast an expected Japanese siege of many months, and all the necessary military hardware was being removed to vast underground tunnels. A complete three-story aircraft assembly plant, power units, long-range radio facilities, and millions of gallons of ship bunker oil and aircraft gasoline were placed underground in excavated caverns.

When we learned a Japanese battle fleet with troop transports was approaching Midway, it was evident the success of our work would be soon tested. The entire population was aware of the forthcoming battle, understood its significance, and watched with concern as soldiers and sailors disappeared from Waikiki and downtown brothels on River Street. It seemed that most of our aircraft flew north, and the public "grapevine" of battle information seemed to verify the fact that many did not return. Defense workers had finished repairing the carrier *Enterprise* in record time, and she left Pearl Harbor without fanfare, also headed north. No fighting ships of any consequence remained. Island activity stopped after the intensive effort of past weeks. We were almost all government employees, so even with censorship, the word passed quickly about battle progress. It was quite evident we had broken the Japanese code, because most of our Pacific Fleet fighting forces were waiting near Midway. For most of us there was little to do except wait. We had given the soldiers, sailors, and marines all we had. Now, it was up to them. The battle was joined.

It was Sunday in early June, during the last days of the Battle of Midway, when I joined the scheduled Hawaiian Trail & Mountain Club hike to Sacred Falls in the Koʻolaus back of Hauʻula. The trail begins at a narrow cleft in the hills, where a clear water stream exits from its underground mountain source. We hopped back and forth between boulders in the stream to keep our feet dry, gradually moving farther and farther into the mountain, where the black lava walls are close together, until the stream suddenly ended against a vertical cliff. The gulch there is only about a hundred feet wide, and a steady flow of water dropped from the *pali* above into a small, rocky pool. We lounged quietly for several hours, eating our lunches, occasionally looking straight overhead, where jagged upper edges of the gulch opened to the sky in a narrow crack that almost sealed us off from the rest of the world. Perhaps in a way we had escaped into the earth for a short respite; into ourselves where contemplation of the fierce battle raging outside was made easier to understand.

Walking into Sacred Falls we passed large boulders with piles of three smaller rocks atop each other. Beneath the smaller rocks were remains of old leaves, sometimes with only the dry-vein skeleton remaining. They were offerings to the pig god, *puaʻa*. We prepared our own offerings, placing three small pebbles atop an avocado leaf so the gods would not permit any rocks to fall on us from the *pali* overhead. None did.

It was a pleasant day inside the mountain, away from the world. But upon returning outside, with the windward hills already in late afternoon shade, we found an even better world waiting for us. The Battle of Midway was over and we had won. ■

Honolulu is a great place to live, everything's convenient. There's a lot of things going on too, but too much violence. The high buildings, okeh as it is now. They might just as well leave it like it is, but just stop building more and leave it like how it is now.

Matthew Tavares
Parking lot attendant

Tasseled sugarcane, Waipahu.

Hawaii Kai, 1978.

When Henry Kaiser first saw the old Hawaiian Kuapa fishponds, still being used for raising mullet in 1960, he could think of little else than progress: how to dredge, fill, and subdivide them into the Hawaii Kai of today. It was believed by some that *menehunes* built the pond, working only at night and connecting the pond by a tunnel to Ka'elepulu Pond near Kailua.

Hawaii Kai, 1960.

I was born in New York, but I traveled all around the country. Went through school in San Francisco. A guy on board a ship saw me on the street one day and asked me if I wanted to take a trip to Hawaii, and I said when? He said this afternoon. I said OK. So, I came over here. . . . I had been here several times on ships as a musician, and I enjoyed Honolulu. I wasn't doing anything and I thought it would be a great change for me to be warm. I figured if I was going to starve to death I might as well be warm, y'know. So, I came and I stayed. . . .

I always refer to the mainland on the air as "America." Honolulu isn't really like "America," even today, just because of the people who live here. A third are haoles, a third are Japanese and a third are all mixed up – in different colors. And the real thrill, even though maybe it's sublimal with the tourists, is to see all these different kinds of complexions working together, living together, studying together. And nobody has any real problems. Not like in "America."

When I first got here after the war, I think there were two restaurants in Waikiki. One was the old Moana Hotel restaurant that was out on the pier out over the ocean. It was run by Matson. It was a good place to eat. The food was good. And the other place was called the Waikiki Tavern. God help us. They had a cafeteria and they had two dishes — greasy mahimahi *and greasy liver and bacon. And that's all they ever served, except for beans, I guess. There were no street restaurants in Waikiki at the time. Now, of course, I think I could name off 50 magnificent restaurants. Any cuisine you like. You can spend as much or as little as you want. I go everywhere, from places like Bagwells, The Third Floor, Canlis, Michel's. I can't remember all the high-class joints. To places like Seikya's, where you get, y'know, the Japanese hamburgers, the* sushi, *and all that stuff across from Kaimuki High School. Or King's Bakery. Or Coco's — used to be Kau Kau Korner. Or the old days of the Smile Cafe or The New Eagle, which is still around. And today I still eat all the way from those high-class joints down to these kind of, well, hash houses, y'know, one-arm joints like Ono Hawaiian Food with six tables, but very good.*

J. Akuhead Pupule, disc jockey, KGMB
Self-proclaimed legend in his own time

Well, Honolulu it gotta change, yeah? Everyplace gotta change, yeah? So, everybody move with the tide — with the change, too.

Sam Kanehailua
Carpenter, Nanakuli

Waikiki Beach, summer 1978, the tourist years.

Waikiki Beach, spring 1942, the war years.

We Made It A Good Town

Growing up with Honolulu is an adventure story, replete with suspense, romance and excitement. The island changed considerably in the process, emerging from its tropical cocoon into the modern world, to grow rapidly into a mature city and state, yet somehow still retaining much of the gentle small town feeling first encountered upon my arrival, three months before the bombing of Pearl Harbor.

I had no premonition of the violent event soon to occur, nor was I aware at the time of the revolutionary social changes already begun by different individuals I was yet to meet, some of whom I would strongly oppose in days to come, and others — both *kama'ainas* and new immigrants like myself — whom I would join to help create a new social and physical environment on a group of islands that would eventually become the fiftieth state. The experience has been immensely satisfying, for I was able to actively be involved in the changes that directly affected the eventual character and physical appearance of Honolulu. I had always urged citizen participation, and while my part in most instances was probably a minor role — I was just pushing a little, with many others — it is clear in retrospect, and an exciting contemplation, that I may have made a difference in some cases.

It is always difficult to determine who has cast the deciding vote. Given the normal inertia of events, much might have happened anyway, but I see little that may have occurred without the urging by personalities who wanted it to happen. As a political advocate and an active environmentalist, it has been possible for me to experience the failures, where growing up resulted in painful dislocations, and, in my opinion, some unfortunate mistakes. I see them everywhere — a missing banyan tree, high-rise hotels where none should be, subdivisions in cane fields, and a lost lake. But I find few mistakes in the economic and social community that we created. I'm pleased with the results. Honolulu grew quickly from territorial status into statehood with few serious traumatic

incidents along the way, generally escaping the worst with only a few scratches. We made it a good town to live in.

Postwar Honolulu could be accurately described as a "plantation town." It bore none of the visual appearances ordinarily associated with traditional company towns; but its dependence on a single economic oligarchy was quite typical of the time.. It was called the "Big Five," and its corporate family control over sugar, pineapple, shipping, and politics was complete.

Many attempts had been made to organize the plantations in past years, but all failed, with the strikes generally being organized and broken along racial lines. It wasn't until union organizers from Harry Bridges, San Francisco-based longshoremen's union (ILWU) arrived in Hawaii, that organization of the sugar and pineapple plantations on an industry-wide base was accomplished after World War II. The first sugar strike called by the ILWU was, more than anything else, to achieve union recognition.

On the first morning of the strike, I drove the union's regional director, Jack Hall, across the island to Waialua, where he delivered an almost revolutionary speech to Waialua sugar workers. Hall was quite nearsighted and had difficulty driving, so I took "annual leave" from my government engineering job and volunteered to chauffeur him to three different plantation strike rallies. It was my first actual meeting of island plantation workers, and I was amazed with the offhanded way they had occupied sugar company property; the company gymnasium at Waipahu had been taken over as strike headquarters, without any apparent attempt by the company to evict them. Neither was there ever any serious move to reopen the sugar mills with strikebreakers. I was deeply impressed by this unusual relationship between employer and union, and could not help but compare the relative peacefulness of this Hawaiian strike with the

---

Anyone moving to Honolulu is moving into one of the best cities in the United States — maybe the world. His children will have an equal educational opportunity in this state which he may not have on the mainland. Our school money is appropriated by the legislature and is not collected from property in a ghetto area which might be very low or in a wealthy Beverly Hills. Here we allocate our money equally irrespective of the income in a school district . . . Honolulu is the example I hope someday all America will follow . . . It's the Aloha spirit we have — no other place has it.

Charles Clark, Superintendent
State Department of Education

Legal secretary on her lunch hour, Fort Street, downtown Honolulu. Overleaf, Halona Cove on a quiet Sunday afternoon. One of the last volcanic eruptions on Oahu poured lava into the ocean from Koko Crater at Halona.

My parents born Japan. I'm second generation. We lived in Kipu, Kauai and in the morning they bakes, takes care of the bakery and work on the sugar plantation for Charlie Rice. In the morning they do the baking, early in the morning. Then go out and work on the plantation — take all the kids, and then come back and start selling the pastries that he baked. That's how he get enough money, y'know, to start his own business, a chop suey house on Fort Street. They hire one Chinese cook and they learned as they paying him, y'see. My wife and I, we started with four tables. I'm the cook and my wife is the waitress. My parents purchased this property. From there, just keep going, eh? I could see that catering was going to be a big type of business, so we started with one station wagon doing this international type of food. Today we sell all kinda food, like Filipino, Japanese, Chinese food, Hawaiian food, Portuguese food, and so forth. But you have to learn all those things from your friends. Like my father knew that if you know people they would teach you. So, Johnny Wilson, he used to be Mayor, the wife, from them we learn how to cook Hawaiian food. So, to learn things it takes friends.

But in all kinda food or culture or so forth, like the oriental, you are born with certain talent, so you learn the basic thing when you use your common sense. So, for example when you kalua a pig, 'cause I'm a Japanese they say I don't know how to kalua a pig. I say, look, brudda, the main thing is you make the stone hot and put 'em inside the pig stomach in the right place. Then you cook the pig. That's the main thing. That's the kind challenge I gotta go through.

Before when you make a luau you go to the mountain and get a pig. Go down the ocean and get the fish and the limu. You can get the flowers in the mountains, too. You can get this and you can get that. As time keep going they all keep coming in Honolulu, so in Honolulu they say, chee, we don't have this an we don't have that, because not too much island here and everyday people is going into the ocean. So, what we do, call Kauai, Maui, Molokai. You can't get the stuff in Honolulu so easy. So, now you gotta have friends on the different islands. Now people gotta get their own things, like opihi. They very expensive — one gallon about $100 it costs. But there's different type of opihi. You want the good one. That's the one that stay in the limu. The thing is orange. When you chew 'em the milk comes out. Same thing with squid. That's a seasonal thing. The legislature is trying to control those things like opihi because some people just goes and pick opihi and just throws the meat away and just sell the shell for jewelry business, and that's how we running out of opihi.

And like the pig. The Hawaiians, they kill the pig, they take the blood and they take a certain part and they feed that to the workers — the pipe, the intestines, na'au and loko. But the Federals say you cannot use that part. But they don't understand the culture and the food and so forth. Local people, wearing nice clothes, they get good job. They go down Ala Moana, eat plate lunch. They don't go fancy restaurant and sit down, all the linen and so forth, because they were born eating that certain kind food like stew and rice with a hot dog or maybe spare rib, 'eh? So, like when you go into real deep Hawaiian food, like crab, loko (that's that liver), other people say, we don't eat that stuff. They don't eat 'em. But then when you take all that raw stuff out — they eat 'em.

Tourists we cater to fit their mouths and their taste, because if you don't the crowds get less and less. Poi gotta be there, little bit. Now let's say a person go back home, it's say in Chicago, New York, Tokyo. Their friends ask did you eat that thing just like paste? Little story you see. But you have to feed them not too authentic. You have to make 50-50, half authentic and so much other kind. Let me see, before it used to be poi in the lau. Now in there we have ophi, haupia, luau chicken, laulau, baked banana, green onion, Hawaiian salt and limu. And we had sweet potato, lomi salmon, cake. But today we give 'em steak, one small piece mahimahi (gotta put fish inside there), fried rice, the poi, the salmon still there yet, the pineapple gotta be there, and the cake plus fried chicken — southern fried chicken. They love it. We make any kind food you want.

Ted Kaneda
Kaneda Catering

The "Hawaiian" garden by tradition is not too well organized, but a place where you stick something in the ground and stand back. Wai'anae.

End of the island, the westernmost point of land at Ka'ena, beyond paved roads and the last house.

history of police-enforced evictions and the widespread violence that surely would have occurred almost anywhere else.

Sugar employees lived in free company housing at the time; it was the kind of "perquisite" that union members wanted to eliminate in favor of independence and cash. On a subsequent trip to Ewa Plantation, Hall told me a story about company housing that had particularly aggravated the employees, and which emphasized the need to rent and own their own homes. He said company management thought it had satisfied a request for replacement of broken toilet seat covers by installing new seat covers in supervisors' homes and then repainting the used covers for replacement in the housing of union workers. It was not known who in management was responsible for this insensitivity, but union members were outraged. Hall said it was typical of the minor grievances that grew into major issues during the long, difficult strike, which eventually ended with management recognition of the new union and the signing of a contract for full cash wages. It ended the period of indentured laborers and ever-mounting debts at the company store.

At the time, I had been helping organize a downtown Honolulu department store where *haoles* and Orientals working at the same job were paid widely disparate wages. Hall decided it would make a dramatic gesture to have me join the ILWU contract-negotiating committee then in session at the American Factors old office building at the foot of Fort Street. I attended the meeting, and during a particularly tense period, Hall interrupted the company negotiator to introduce me, and to warn his opponent that it might be better to agree on a sugar contract soon, "before Wenkam began to organize the plantation company stores."

It is perhaps illustrative of Hawaii's unusual social environment that, many years later, having in the meantime gone into business for myself as an advertising photographer, American Factors (now Amfac) became one of my best customers, and I was busy producing illustrations for its annual corporate reports. On another occasion, when I encountered opposition in joining the Honolulu Chamber of Commerce because of my "leftist and pro-labor views," as claimed by a chamber officer, I

92

found my entry eased considerably by the new executive director, who said I was just the kind of community activist the chamber needed. The executive director was the retired manager of the department store I had tried to organize many years before.

I served on the Chamber of Commerce's Community Beautification Committee, along with Nancy Bannick, who personally saved many downtown historical buildings before Kukui redevelopment bulldozers flattened everything old; with George Walters, responsible through his landscaping for much of the appearance of Honolulu as we know the city today; and with Alfred Preis, who stopped designing buildings in his own architectural office to help determine the design and appearance of a city growing very rapidly and a bit out of control.

Before the days of environmental activist organizations like the Sierra Club and the Life of the Land, the Chamber of Commerce found itself, through its beautification committee, a strident vocal advocate of environmental preservation, an activity not ordinarily associated with a business-oriented organization. Our primary goal was to change the usual conservationist's "No, no, no" concerning unwanted projects. We developed constructive plans for the advancement of the city's growth in ways that would not harm the island's fragile natural beauty, yet would maintain opportunities for a prosperous business climate.

One of the more lasting ideas dreamed up in our committee was for the creation of an organization of major corporate businesses, with a professional planner at the head, a group that would know everything that was going on in town and would coordinate activities of influential decision-makers. If large corporations were to be making the important investment decisions, we thought they might as well do it on an informed basis and in communication with their peers. The idea thrives today as the Oahu Development Conference, with Aaron Levine as the professional planner.

We originated the proposal for a Nu'uanu Pali Regional Park, which resulted in banning of restaurant construction at the famed lookout and considerable improvement of public areas. We also wanted Kapi'olani Park expanded to the sea at Diamond Head. From the chamber's point of view, this translated into quite a controversial proposal when we urged that existing residential lots be rezoned to "parks and open space." They called it "down-zoning;" I called it "up-zoning." And we recommended that the chamber's Board of Directors adopt a resolution opposing construction of any high-rise buildings on the front slopes of Diamond Head. After considerable debate the resolution was approved by one vote. It was probably the first time anywhere a chamber of commerce had voted *not* to build anything!

Probably our most controversial activity was to help push through the Honolulu City Council a restrictive business sign ordinance to keep Oahu from turning into a playground for sign manufacturers. It was evident that most small merchants, and all the large ones, supported our efforts; but a minority threatened to resign from the chamber, feeling it was outrageous for the chamber to be indulging in such "anti-business" activities. Our entire beautification committee was called into a meeting with the membership committee to resolve the problem. They asked us not to ban the signs. We said "no" and continued to work in close collaboration with the Outdoor Circle. The ordinance was duly approved by the city council, but Holiday Inn had to miniaturize their garish logo to conform. McDonald's yellow arches never did appear in Honolulu.

In a year I can't remember now, I was subpoenaed by the Hawaii legislature's Senate-House Un-American Activities Committee. I had previously told the same kind of U.S. congressional committee, then on a junket to Honolulu, that I would be uncooperative and it canceled the subpoena. Now I was to appear at a closed hearing of a local version of political repression, and wasn't too excited over the idea.

The hearing room, on the second floor of the tax collector's building, was somber in color and poorly lighted, with the committee members arrayed evenly along each side of the table with note pads before them, waiting in anticipation for my testimony. The chairman questioned me

---

Agriculture plays a smaller and smaller role all the time. There's very little agriculture. I wouldn't be surprised to see it phase almost completely out — maybe in the next decade. Frankly, I would hate to see it happen, because I think from a visual standpoint it adds an awful lot to the beauty of the island. Just purely from that. But, if this island continues to grow in population you're going to have increasing pressure on that agricultural land which becomes more valuable for homesites.

John Simpson, President
Hawaii Visitors Bureau

directly and I gave my name, address and telephone number. Then he asked the first germane question, which I expected to be about my labor-organizing activities or friendliness with the ILWU. Instead, he asked quite seriously, "Are you an international Communist spy?"

I was absolutely shocked. I remember at the time thinking that it was a silly question, since if I were a spy I surely wouldn't tell him so. I told the entire committee they could "go to hell," saying I was insulted at the insinuation that I was a foreign spy, and refused to say another word, didn't plead the Fifth Amendment or anything, despite their assertions I would be held in contempt and imprisoned.

I was never jailed and never heard another word from the committee until several years later, at the time of state senate hearings on my confirmation to the state Land Use Commission. The governor's announcement of my appointment had already precipitated an uproar in the conservative community, complaints being made that "a Communist was being added to the governor's cabinet," and that if an environmentalist joined the commission "everyone would soon be living in tents!" Cartoons and editorials, pro and con, appeared in the daily newspapers, and I sat down to listen in on the public hearing with considerable interest.

All the testimony (except for Imua, the local anticommunist group) was in support of my appointment; but most surprising to me were the words of the state senator, now retired, whom I had personally challenged when he was chairman of the state "un-American" committee. He testified that I "was not a Communist, never had been, and would never be one." It was totally unexpected and I thanked him on the way out. In a few days I was confirmed by a majority vote of the state senate. The Democrats voted "yes," the Republicans voted "no," but then I was never much of a Republican.

Almost exactly one month after the voting in my first Land Use Commission meeting, the same senator telephoned me for a private appointment at my office. I should never have wondered, in my naive way, what was wanted. He brought a large map, which he unrolled on my desk, to locate the property of a client of his, pointing out how the conservation district boundaries seemed to encroach upon the adjacent land parcel. He asked if I didn't agree that all of his client's property shouldn't be zoned urban. "It was probably a mistake, wasn't it?" It was my first encounter with the wondrous convolutions of American democracy. In some ways, I guess, Hawaii politics are the same as everywhere else.

My years on the commission were constructive and eventful. I learned the basic principles of legislative democracy — how to trade votes — and was able personally to investigate stories told of political commissioners who are invited to elaborate dinner parties, complete with all you want to drink and girls for the evening — it's true. I think every developer and landowner in the state bought me a drink at one time or another. It was difficult to sit down at a hotel bar and pay my own check. Someone across the room always paid it first. It was, in a way, disappointing to me that no conservationist ever bought me dinner or a drink. A free drink never influenced my vote, but the friendships that developed were lopsided when they were all landowners. However, the lobbying didn't change my environmental goals, for after three and a half years on the commission, the acreage of conservation-zoned land had almost doubled.

When my first term on the commission expired, Governor Burns reappointed me for another, also requiring confirmation by the senate. Three days before senate adjournment, with no appearance on the senate floor of an appropriate resolution for my confirmation, I inquired among my legislator friends about what was happening. They informed me it probably was in the senate president's desk drawer. I asked the senator and he said it would stay there, and if I wanted it out to go ask my ILWU friends. I did, and they said I wasn't "playing the game properly." My name never came to a vote in the senate, where it undoubtedly would have received approval. I later learned that two subdivisions planned for agricultural and conservation land, which would require rezoning to urban, were never built because of my vote against them. Both projects were supported by the senate president and the clerk of the senate. It was apparent I had done my job too well. ■

What balance between good and evil our civilized ways will bring, we cannot now foretell; but experience shows that they destroy unprotected wilderness and wildlife with appalling ruthlessness; and that, unlike man's civilizations, destroyed nature cannot be rebuilt. Once violated it is gone forever, as is the ancient beauty of Waikiki beach.

Charles A. Lindbergh
Conservationist

Kuhio Beach, Kalakaua Boulevard, and St. Catherine's Church, Waikiki.

The Surf Is Up

Hawaiians were great navigators of the open sea, possessing considerable knowledge of wave patterns and currents, of the harmony and rhythm of wave sets, storm waves, and wind waves. Like so much in the Hawaiian lifestyle that is close to nature, riding these waves on a board and body surfing on the giant waves that broke upon the coral sand must have been the quintessential acts of an island people.

They were very much at home on the sea and spoke knowingly of the ocean in words that have no English equivalent. There are different words for the three waves in a set: *kakala* is the first "roller;" *pakaiea*, the second set; and *opu'u*, the third. Where the waves actually break, is *po'inakai. Kai-kohala* is the shoal water extending shoreward ahead of moving waves, indicative of good surfing conditions.

Hawaiians rode the first heavy *koa* planks on their bellies, in time developing the techniques of standing upon and maneuvering a board in the surf. Sacred grounds were dedicated to surfing, and special chants spoken to call up the surf and announce contests, which often lasted several days, providing personal enjoyment and testing of physical skills.

The sport virtually disappeared in the years after Captain Cook, when Hawaiian chiefs changed the islands from a subsistence economy to a money system. Commoners were taxed heavily in order to obtain goods to trade with foreigners. Complete families were sent into the mountains for sandalwood. Little time remained for water sports.

In the old days surfers were always nude, and when a man and woman found themselves riding the same long wave together they generally celebrated the ride upon reaching shore — making love on the sand, just beyond the sweep of the highest wave. The missionaries soon forbade the sport completely, and ancient skills were nearly nonexistent for over a hundred years until surfing experienced a revival in the early part of this century.

As old skills were sharpened, the heavy ten-foot wood boards with square tails became hollow, lighter, and shorter. Fiberglass and foam allowed new freedom of design, and boards were custom-built for wave height, surfer's weight, and surfing style. Young Californians helped rediscover the old surfing grounds, unused by tourists, on the west and north shores of Oahu, and they rapidly changed the sport from riding waves "just for fun" into the competitive events of old Hawaiian times. The Duke Kahanamoku Surfing Classic became an international event, first on the waves at Makaha in Waianae, then in later years on the "big ones" — tube riding at off-the-wall and Sunset Beach. Those were the days of "endless summer," and a new surfing vocabulary — off-the-lip, pipeline, velzyland — the years when Hawaiian waves gained their reputation of having a "punch" like no others.

Surfers now talk of 'radical aggression" and "clear-flowing" styles, the ascetics of surfing differing greatly from old Hawaiian attitudes. The sport of Hawaiian *ali'i* has spawned a new generation of fanatical devotees enveloped in a philosophy of life responsive only to the unrequited joy of riding a wave. Their entire experience is the personification of being free, with an accompanying social life that allows it.

The fleet of battered vans and bugs with board racks cluster along north shore beaches like ants at a picnic, their brown occupants watching the tide and counting sets, their women clustered behind and slightly to one side. Should the sea flatten or the afternoon winds ruffle the waves, the entourage will move on to check out other more promising reef systems, where hidden undersea contours may still produce a curl on the foaming crest and a tube to ride out of.

In ancient days the Sunset Beach surf was called Paumalu after the adjacent *ahupua'a*, and even in those times the waves had a reputation among *ali'i* as a fierce surf. When Chief Kahikilani of Kauai came to Oahu to surf, he was riding the giant waves at Paumalu when the legendary Bird Maiden saw him and immediately fell in love. She sent her messengers to give him an orange *lehua lei* and guide him to her cave, where he was considerably enamoured by her love. The chief stayed for many days until he heard the high surf one day and longed to ride the waves again.

The Bird Maiden allowed him to return to the surf if he vowed never to kiss another woman; but after surfing all day, he made love to a beautiful Oahu girl who rode together with him on the last wave and then placed an *'ilima lei* around his neck. The Bird Maiden's messengers saw Kahikilani break his vow, and told her what had happened. When she realized Kahikilani would never return, she turned him into stone and as a rock he remains today — on the hill above Sunset, watching the high surf at Paumalu. ∎

Along the Mokule'ia shore, high seas generated by a northern Pacific storm reach Oahu. The surf is up at "Avalanche".

High surf curls across the fringing reef at Pa'umalu (Sunset Beach).

The People Who Made It So

The city of Honolulu was too young to celebrate America's Bicentennial. Captain Cook had not yet discovered the Sandwich Islands (as he called them) for the British Crown at the time when Massachusetts minutemen returned the fire of British troops on Bunker Hill. Nor had the missionaries yet been ordained. Kamehameha was still a young warrior fighting with spears; his establishment of the kindom of Hawaii, after conquering the islands one by one, was an achievement still many years in the future.

Cook's flagship, the *Resolution,* was a refitted coal collier restored to service for his third voyage by a British admiralty with few available ships. King George III's newest vessels were being used to send replacement troops for the British armies in New England. In a letter to friends written prior to sailing, Cook lamented over the ill-advised British military intervention in the New World that deprived him of new vessels for what he considered the greater priority of Pacific exploration. Even the revolutionary American government considered Cook's Pacific voyages of great importance, for when the British government asked Ben Franklin, then American Commissioner to France, to provide safe passage for Cook on his return to England, it was promptly granted by American authorities. Cook was unable to avail himself of this courtesy, however, because he died in Hawaii on the shores of Kealakekua Bay.

Hawaii was possibly the last place on earth to be discovered and settled when the Polynesians opted for a change in political climate and sailed north, reaching landfall on the Big Island's South Cape only 700 years ago. Cook followed 500 years later, navigating with sailing instructions provided by the king of Tahiti and a well-informed local sailor named Tupaea, who had helped him explore nearby islands and undoubtedly told him about Hawaii. The two British ships sailed straight north to Hawaii with only one stop, over the holidays, at Christmas Island to replenish stores of water and fresh food. Cook appeared to know exactly where he was going.

Boston missionaries sailed to Hawaii years later by request of disgruntled Hawaiian commoners appalled at the continuing fighting between chiefs and a cruel *kapu* system that enforced the death penalty for anyone allowing his shadow to fall upon the *ali'i.* However, the archaic Hawaii *kapu* system and idol worship were abolished by the Hawaiians themselves before missionaries arrived to prepare the islands' political, moral, and economic environment for later planters and merchants.

The people who made a significant impact on the islands, and who determined the direction that Hawaii would move among nations, are relatively few in number and it is not difficult for historians to follow the trail of growth and development of the Hawaiian kingdom, republic, territory, and state — all occurring in less than 200 years, within the life span of the United States.

Much of what has occurred in Hawaii has been a

Hawaiian Independent Refinery, Inc., Campbell Industrial Park.

Twenty-two men and women selected by editors of the *Honolulu Star-Bulletin* as people of lasting significance in the history of Hawaii. Some are living legends, most are gone and still controversial, all have left their personal imprint on Honolulu, home of kings, site of the only royal palace in the U.S., and capital of Hawaii since 1893. Drawings by Ray Higuchi.

"palace revolution." Only in recent years has the general population become involved in the decision making process. A strong middle class, with influence at all levels of society — economic, social, and political — did not exist to any significant extent until post-World War II events forced major changes in the plantation system and mainland investors were able to enter the Hawaii market. Kresge and Sears were first to break the local merchants' monopoly before the war. Following union organization of sugar and pineapple plantations by Jack Hall and the longshoremen's union (ILWU), economic pressures were effectively combined with political action to create a new Democratic party. Joined in collaboration with young Japanese-Americans returning from the war, Hawaii changed rapidly into a democratic, sophisticated community.

Many people were involved in this growth and development; but over the seven centuries of Hawaii's short history, only a few individuals assumed leadership roles and were responsible for a significant impact on the economic and political life of Hawaii. It is these few who took the necessary bold steps, often facing considerable adversity, but always with subjective knowledge of the correct time to act, to move forward — a little ahead of when the people themselves were ready to accept changes begun in the best interest of Hawaii's future.

A list of these history makers, compiled by the editors of the *Honolulu Star-Bulletin,* is an excellent introduction to the history of Hawaii and Honolulu.

Senator Hiram Fong, first Republican U.S. senator from Hawaii, financier.
Captain James Cook, British explorer.
Chinn Ho, financier, developer of Ilikai and Makaha.
Governor John Burns, founder new Democratic Party of Hawaii, delegate to Congress during statehood campaign, second elected governor of Hawaii.
Father Damien, priest to the Molokai lepers.
Senator Dan Inuoye, U.S. Democrat senator, first U.S. Democrat representative from Hawaii.
Charles Bishop, sugar planter, royal minister.
Mayor Elmer Cravalho, Maui County, state Speaker of the House.
Riley Allen, editor *Honolulu Star-Bulletin.*
Henry Kaiser, industrialist, developer of Kaiser Hawaiian Village Hotel and Hawaii Kai.
Jack Hall, regional director of ILWU, union organizer.
Duke Kahanamoku, gold medal in Olympic swimming, father of modern surfing.

Prince Jonah Kuhio Kalanianaole, ten-term delegate to Congress, initiator of Hawaiian Homes Commission.
Senator Oren Long, territorial governor, first Democrat U.S. senator from Hawaii.
Walter Dillingham, organized Hawaiian Dredging Company, built first Pearl Harbor drydock and harbors throughout Hawaii.
King Kamehameha IV and his wife, Queen Emma, established schools and founded Queen's Hospital; royal palace given one of his Hawaiian names, 'Iolani.
Joe Farrington, newspaper publisher, delegate to congress at time of first moves for statehood.
President Sanford Dole, Republic of Hawaii, first governor of territory of Hawaii.
King Kamehameha I, conqueror of the islands, founder of the kingdom of Hawaii.
Queen Liliuokalani, last royal ruler, composer, "Aloha Oe."
Princess Bernice Pauahi Bishop, founder of the Bishop Estate and Kamehameha School, last of the Kamehamehas.

Two women who should be added to the list are Chieftess Kapi'olani, who successfully challenged the wrath of Pele, the volcano goddess, on the edge of erupting Halema'uma'u firepit, and Ka'ahumanu, the *kuhina nui,* who first advocated eating with men. Ka'ahumanu, the favorite wife of Kamehameha I, whose rule was something like a police state, decided before his death in 1819 that the *kapu* system must be abolished. She may have begun the women's movement in Hawaii over 150 years ago.

Not eating certain foods, according to Hawaiian historian Kamakau, was "a profound act of submission to the will of the gods." It was believed that for men and women to eat together was disrespectful. Ka'ahumanu was particularly anxious to break the eating *kapu* and enjoy pig and bananas along with the men, but she waited until the mourning period was over for Kamehameha I, before arranging a sit-down dinner with the men.

It apparently was quite an event, according to oral chroniclers of the time. The new king, Liholiho, was invited, but for two days he and his chiefs waited offshore of the dinner site in Kailua, drinking rum aboard his two-masted canoes. When the wind died down and the king's canoe was becalmed, Ka'ahumanu sent a double canoe to tow the reluctant monarch ashore for dinner. On this first night he ate some dog that had been previously available only to chieftesses, and several times entered the once-forbidden women's *lau hala* house. Men drank rum with women and smoked tobacco together. Those

Descendents of the varied people who made history in Honolulu visit King Kamehameha's *lei* shrouded memorial on his birthday celebration. Black gowned descendents of Hawaiian *ali'i*, trimmed with orange ilima flowers join an elderly Japanese-American representative of early plantation immigrants, contemporary young city women, and the ever-present mainland visitor—standing slightly apart and perhaps not fully understanding the significance of this unusual gathering of people in downtown Honolulu. Overleaf is the magnificent bowl of Hanauma Bay Beach Park on Oahu's south shore, site of the first underwater marine preserve in the nation.

Construction cranes, the "native bird" of the construction industry, raises condominiums to house Honolulu's slowly increasing population. They embellish the skyline dramatically along the Ala Wai Canal, dredged to drain the original swamps of Waikiki.

watching are said to have shouted, "The tabus are at an end! The gods are a lie!" Ka'ahumanu asked the king to "make eating free over the whole kingdom from Hawaii to Oahu," and it was done. Sacred images were burned, *heiau* torn down, and great feasts of *kapu*-free eating were enjoyed throughout the islands.

Under Kamehameha III, Honolulu became the capital city, with elaborate balls given by the king, who issued invitations printed on white satin. Operas and concerts were in vogue. And Hawaiian royalty traveled abroad to be received and entertained by the crowned heads of Europe.

While there was some interest by imperial powers in colonizing Hawaii, nothing of consequence happened until American sugar planters and merchants recognized the favorable business opportunities and began to agitate for annexation by the U.S. Once in 1843 the British flag flew over Honolulu, but five months later Queen Victoria sent word to Kamehameha III that it was a mistake. Upon raising the Hawaiian flag again, the king in appreciation said: *Ua mau ke ea o ka aina i ka pono* (The life of the land is perpetuated by righteousness). His words became the motto of Hawaii.

These, then, are the people who have made the difference. Others might also be included if we knew who they were. Some have been forgotten as new leaders followed with new accomplishments. Still more have never been recognized for their contributions, or their names were erased by a displeased establishment.

In years to come the list will surely include leaders in the tourist industry and even environmentalists, when we are able, in the light of history, to measure their special impact. I know that I would want to include the woman who first said we should have no billboards in Hawaii and decided to do something about it — and eventually did succeed in having them banned. There is Lorrin Thurston, who over considerable opposition pushed on until Congress approved establishment of Hawaii National Park (now divided into two great parks, Hawaii Volcanoes National Park and Haleakala National Park). Perhaps some would want to rate highly the very important skills of legislator and lawyer Tom Gill, who obtained the vital information necessary to stop construction of the proposed double-deck "interstate" freeway along Ala Moana. Gill was also a prime mover in pushing Hawaii's controversial land use law through the state legislature. He called it the "greenbelt" law to make the package more acceptable for opponents.

Two commoners, a missionary-educated Hawaiian scholar, and a mainland *haole* who settled in Honolulu in 1847, also warrant listing: Samuel Manaiakalani Kamakau, a graduate of Lahainaluna School, an active politician, and a prolific writer of Hawaiian history; and Abraham Fornander, who married a Hawaiian chiefess from Molokai, worked as a newspaper editor, and ultimately became a justice of the Hawaii Supreme Court.

Both of these men became proficient in the written Hawaiian language evolved by missionaries and were first to translate the oral history of Hawaii as passed down through the ages in chants and *mele*. Our appreciation of Hawaiian traditions and lore is possible because of their published work. The fragments of song, dance, mythology, and Polynesian lifestyle that have gradually become part of our own contemporary island lore, are the unusual benefits derived from Kamakau and Fornander, who transformed "legendary" chants and geneology into written history. Because of them we can better appreciate and adapt the unique gifts of Polynesia.

Aristotle wrote that, "Men come together in the city to live; they remain there in order to live the good life." Honolulu is the kind of city where many influential men and women have gathered together and stayed to enrich each other and future generations. The history of Hawaii must be why Honolulu is the place to live the good life. ∎

I went up to Oakland to train to fight professional. It was all right, but not like Hawaii. You know, people not as friendly over there as they are here. Like there, if you get sick, if you're in your house, you don't even know your neighbor. They don't even bother with you. You could be dead in your house for all they know, and they wouldn't even find you maybe for one or two weeks. Honolulu everybody help each other. If your neighbors need help, well, you help them. You have a kind of ohana *feeling.*

Gilbert Rivera
Driver for "da Bus"

Ohi'alehua blossoms in her hair. Lehua was the name given to the first warrior killed in battle.

Only In Honolulu

Several years passed before it was finally agreed whether the city or the state would clean up the seaweed covering Waikiki Beach after Kona storms. (The city). It still has not been definitely confirmed if it is legal for city lifeguards to work from state-controlled beach lands to rescue out-of-state tourists. Continuing jurisdictional struggles between the city and state had caused state grass-mowing crews to stop clearing weeds from city bridge approaches, until someone reasoned that when 82 percent of the state's population lives in one city, everyone using the highway must be from the same place. Many of us have also wondered where city streets become state roads and federal aid highways begin. We still call highways by name rather than by the arbitrary numbers that come with federal highway funds, and it has always been a mystery how Senator Dan Inouye was able to have Hawaii included as part of the interstate highway system, when Hawaii is 2,400 miles from the nearest state! It is matters of this import that keep any really clear analysis of Honolulu at arms length.

This is the place where a bumper sticker says "Honk if you Hula," where Sears offers a "mildew wash" service — possibly the only mildew removal specialists in the world — and where national TV advertising for antifreeze is totally wasted. In the Hawaii legislature a few years back, Senator Kazuhisa Abe actually introduced a bill abolishing Christmas after his fellow legislators stubbornly refused to declare Buddha's birthday a state holiday. Christmas won.

Meanwhile at City Hall, Councilman George "Scotty" Koga voiced his displeasure at the food dished up by Ala Moana Park concessionaires. "I wish they would improve the quality of their hot dogs. I was very, very disappointed," he said at a meeting of the council's Finance Committee. City business stopped while the size and price of hot dogs was considered before taking action on a resolution making the semiautonomous Honolulu Board of Water Supply a regular city department. The committee needed a performance audit of the water board.

The water board manager and chief engineer, Edward Hirata, gulped, then tried to explain why in the two months since the water board was trying to get everyone in Hawaii to reduce water use by 10 percent, the water board's own consumption climbed 14 percent. The water people increased their consumption by one and a half million gallons more in one month. Hirata explained that a new reservoir in Kuilima was landscaped and considerable irrigation was required. Then two other reservoirs in

Polynesian Cultural Center, La'ie.

For business, I like the growth, naturally, being a food broker. It's good for my business. I can sell the tourist hotels, restaurants, but I think personally I don't like the growth. I like it better the way it was in the old days. Where everything was open and you could go to the beach when you wanted to and you weren't afraid to walk out into the streets. I don't like the one-way streets, but this is progress. When you have the amount of tourists you have in Waikiki it does get to be a jungle.

Clifford Kramer
Meat broker, Kailua

Aiea were very leaky, accounting for a million gallons down the drain — and they were still trying to find out how the missing water leaked out of a St. Louis Heights tank. Hirata hoped "the public has enough confidence in our overall program so they won't let temporary problems cloud the issue." It was fortunate the council's performance audit request was delayed by the hot dogs at Ala Moana.

Then the garbage department had a serious problem to contend with over Christmas. It seems the trash collectors were concerned about the occasional cases of Primo beer left out for them by friendly residents. Would these gifts represent a violation of the code of ethics? It all depends. If the beer was intended to keep the trash collectors from roughing up their garbage cans, it was probably extortion or outright bribery, according to some legal briefs. The board of ethics will probably meet in executive session to provide an advisory opinion.

Following the victory of a new city law prohibiting dogs from barking, the Citizens Against Noise announced a new noise target: tour buses. "We can't afford to let tourism's noise problems generate hostility among residents," said William J. Atkinson, the organization's noise problems' committee chairman. He added, "When motors are left running to keep air conditioning going next to apartment buildings while tourists visit a park, have a meal, see a show; or when quiet residential streets become noisy so tour buses can avoid a traffic light, the 'aloha spirit' wears thin."

Citizens Against Noise proposed that the city council set up another task force just like it did to quiet the dogs. In the meantime, Mayor Frank Fasi signed the dog ordinance into law, providing a fine of up to $50 and a possible jail term of up to 30 days for the owner of a dog that barks too long or too loudly. Previously passed laws kept dogs on a leash and picked up after; now it is illegal to bark incessantly for 10 minutes or intermittently for 30.

At a public hearing prior to the law's passage, the Hawaiian Humane Society advised dog owners having difficulty with dogs barking to call the dog's name, shout "No," and douse it with water. One distressed owner replied that his dog is pedigreed and all pedigreed dogs are named Titcomb's Alfred Prince Snowfield of Sandringham Greystones, and "By the time I finished shouting Titcomb's Alfred Prince Snowfield of Sandringham Greystones, no!, the dog figured out he was going to get doused and he was halfway to Waimanalo — barking."

Each year, Bob Krauss, columnist for the *Honolulu Advertiser*, reviews the new telephone directory to uncover any important trends that may be underway. In the latest directory he noted that the "Smiths have overtaken the Chuns as Honolulu's fifth biggest family and pizza has swept past chop suey in the Yellow Pages."

Krauss considers the latest directory exciting but difficult to interpret, noting, "There's something stirring in there but I'm not sure what it is." As long as he can remember, chop suey has been undisputed champion of foods advertised in the yellow pages with around 3 pages. There are 3¼ pages of chop suey currently, a slight increase. But pizza has jumped from 2 pages to 4¼ in an unprecedented history-making shift in Honolulu taste or in number of fast food outlets. Hawaiian *luaus* have held steady at less than a page.

As far as ethnic groups are concerned, the conglomerate Lees (Chinese or Korean or Caucasian) continue to lead all other Honolulu families with 19 columns, closely followed by 17¼ columns of Wong numbers. Then come the Youngs (12 columns) and the Changs (11¼ columns).

Since Krauss began reviewing the telephone directory in the 1960s, the Changs and the Chuns have been in either fourth or fifth place in alternate years. This year the Smiths (who must like pizza) have overtaken the Chuns, 10¼ to 10 columns for fifth place. This drops the faltering Chuns, according to Krauss's research, to sixth place. Next comes the Chings (9½ columns), then the Nakamuras (9 columns), the Lums (8 columns) and the Yamamotos (only 7 columns). The Tanakas (6½ columns) dropped out of the top 10 and, as possibly indicative of the new Hawaiian society, the Browns, Millers, and

Well, I was born here, you see, and I'm going to spend the rest of my life here, so I guess that speaks enough for it. Honolulu is not, naturally, what it was fifty years ago or even longer. But that's progress, and I think comparing the old to the new is crazy, because there is nothing to be gained with comparing the old with the new. They say the old Honolulu didn't have the night clubs — something going on every night. Well, we didn't want it that way. Some of us don't even care for it now, but it's there to be taken for what it's worth.

Vernon "Red" McQueen
Sports writer

Williamses are now creeping into position to offer a challenge.

Then there was the great canoe snafu when the Outrigger Canoe Club won a 37-minute victory over the Tahitian team in the annual Molokai-to-Oahu canoe race during Aloha Week. Teiki Tamari, a paddler for the Tahitians, wanted a rematch because the Hawaii canoe, "Manu' Ula," he said, didn't meet Hawaiian design specifications — it was of Tahitian design and made of fiberglass. The Tahitians had won the year before in a Tahitian design made of wood.

And Leslie Okumura was absent from part of his trial because he was receiving treatment for a broken arm suffered while trying to escape the courthouse where he was being tried for escaping from Oahu Prison (where so many prisoners were escaping at one time that pundits suggested posting a sign for the street — "Danger, prisoners escaping"). He missed closing arguments and return of the guilty verdict, so the Hawaii Supreme Court reversed his conviction, saying the defendant wasn't present during part of the trial and ordered a new one.

Ocean waters between the islands making up Honolulu and the state are, by federal court decision, international waters, making the short 30-minute trip to Molokai Island an international excursion. Local airlines are not flying intrastate, but operate under CAB regulations like national carriers. Only recently enacted laws reserving fishing and resource rights within 200 miles around the islands limit foreign mining on the Molokai shoals. In past years elements of the Soviet's Pacific Fleet regularly cruised a zigzag route through the island chain, testing their right to sail in the international waters of Honolulu.

Honolulu politics, like most small-town politics, presents many twists and turns, mostly revolving around various personalities rather than political parties, and all of the involved machinations are of a kind that is very difficult if not impossible to describe to an outsider. Possibly the best way to offer an introduction to Honolulu politics is to provide a brief commentary on the most intriguing local political affair in recent years, an elaborate confrontation involving the governor and mayor: the Kukui Plaza Caper. This was a political redevelopment farce in many acts and with a surprise ending, taking place mostly in the Honlulu City Council chambers because everyone else in City Hall denied that anything took place.

Sources close to the Kukui Plaza affair said it was remarkably successful at its apparent purpose — to provide gainful employment for witnesses, jurors, reporters, lawyers, guards, city councilmen, and one lawyer from Los Angeles. The *Honolulu Advertiser* quoted a usually reliable source after proceedings had been underway for a year, that it might go on forever, and that the hearings and trial were "thought to be the fourth or fifth biggest industry in Hawaii." One economist, who asked not to be identified, said, "We ought to be thankful it will never end. If it ever did, the number of people thrown out of work could trigger a depression." It is estimated that participants on both sides spent over one million dollars on the event.

The council had been feuding with the mayor for some time, so the members took this opportunity to begin a public investigation of Kukui and the mayor. Using subpoenas combined with considerable fanfare and press conferences, they began by picking as chairman of their investigating committee a councilman who switched from Democrat to Republican to run against Fasi for mayor, an

Cartoon by Corky Trinidad, courtesy *Honolulu Star-Bulletin*.

Rough seas are no deterrent to a young Hawaiian swimmer at the Blowhole along Oahu's south shore.

Waikiki skyline, 1941.

Waikiki skyline, 1955.

Waikiki skyline, 1978.

Honolulu is a changing city in many ways, and the visual changes are dramatically revealed in the continuously changing skyline of Waikiki, built alongside the unchanging ocean, against the lower mountain slopes and craters, and below the trade wind clouds, all providing the natural environment for an island city. Overleaf is Waikiki from the air, the nation's most famous and most desired vacation destination.

arrangement that seemed imminently fair to councilmen at the time, although they eventually switched to another chairman who was still anti-Fasi but wasn't running for anything. Fasi described the televised hearings as a "kangaroo court" and an attempt at political intimidation.

As testimony continued under TV lights, threats were allegedly made on the life of some witnesses, so the council hired armed bodyguards to protect them on a 24-hour basis. It didn't seem to matter that the private guard company had no business license and the guards no permits to carry guns. The public hearings dragged on for several months until the council decided nothing to anyone's satisfaction, turned over its files to the governor, and returned to its normal activity of granting zoning variances.

In the meantime, Fasi won reelection for mayor by a landslide, beating the council chairman and everyone else, and made it obvious he would next run for governor. At this time the state decided to enter the fray and Attorney General Ronald Amemiya hauled the principals into court, charging Fasi. When asked about his interest in the action, Governor George Ariyoshi said he had nothing to do with this turn of events, claiming in numerous interviews that he had never talked to his attorney general about Fasi, and the fact that he might be running for reelection for governor against Fasi was just a coincidence. On the same day the state's indictment was returned, Fasi, never one to be upstaged, answered the charges by announcing his candidacy for the governorship.

The actual trial was many months in starting, because of numerous preliminary motions of one kind or another, and attempts to remove witnesses or to grant them immunity. Just selecting the jury took weeks. The state's private prosecutor, hired from Los Angeles to take the proceedings "out of politics," didn't like the idea of people being on the jury who voted for Fasi, which proved difficult since Fasi had already won two elections in a row. Most jurors said they liked Fasi, but would be "fair" anyway. Dispositions by the dozens were collected by opposing attorneys, and Fasi himself often appeared in court on "vacation" time to observe proceedings. With daily front-page press coverage, nobody could say they hadn't heard anything, and it took as much as eight hours to screen a single juror, who was then often thrown out on preemptive options argued by one lawyer or another. The trial began after jurors had already been sequestered for two months.

It was clear that some kind of payments had been made, but were they just "campaign contributions" as Fasi claimed? Circuit Judge Toshimi Sodetani dismissed everything and went home, and so did the lawyer from Los Angeles. So, after almost two years, the Kukui Plaza Caper ended — and without a single word from Jack Lord. ■

No place can touch Honolulu. It has a great diversity of races and I think it has more harmony with all our multicultural people than any other place I have been in.

I live in Kailua. I have never minded the drive from Kailua over the pali to Honolulu. I always enjoy coming over the top of the hill and looking at the city and seeing how much it has grown since I have been here. There's been a tremendous growth in the last thirty-two years . . . I think I kind of basically liked it when it wasn't quite as large as it is. I'm kind of spoiled. I liked the Honolulu of thirty years ago better than I do today. I don't tend to be a city dweller. Basically I like the country. We moved to Kailua 25 or 30 years ago because it was a rural area. Now it is no longer rural.

Charles Clark, Superintendent
State Department of Education

Honolulu is a place where the people want to see and feel what they have heard and read and talked so much about.

Eileen Lota, City Clerk
City and County of Honolulu

Honolulu's civic center, the new state capitol, and Iolani Palace. Overleaf, the Hawaiian sunset colors Waikiki long before the hotel lights go on.

Honolulu Is Many Kinds of Living Places

Halfway around Oahu, as far as you can go without turning back, is Kahuku, an old sugar town now growing mostly seed corn and watermelons. The refurbished sugar mill is open to tourists, with the usual curio shops arrayed alongside. A paved parking lot accommodates round-the-island tour buses, whose drivers allow their passengers only enough time for the rest room and the mill tour.

Within sight of the tour bus passengers is a town they never see — the old Kahuku Sugar Company plantation camp, one of the last remaining sugar camps on Oahu. The narrow streets are still unpaved, the small houses whitewashed, and the tiny backyard vegetable gardens instant identification of the owner's nationality — they plant the ethnic food they eat. Crowing, fighting cocks betray the homes of gamblers, and the pungent odor of yellow pickled turnip will identify a first generation Japanese. In the fall, Boys Day is celebrated with a colorful red and blue paper carp flying in the wind. Far back here the dusty streets twist and bend, then widen to allow parking space in front of Owan's General Store, still open and selling. In the back is Tsuru's Restaurant and across the street is Helen's Barber Shop, not far from a weathered, gray Buddhist temple.

Kahuku Camp is far away from Waikiki in time, distance, and standard of living — still another facet of the cosmopolitan flavor of Honolulu as a city and island. The city is like a skein of multicolored yarn, with unknown colors gradually being uncovered as the round-the-island bus passes remote beach resorts, strip developments crowding the road, plantation towns, military housing, and expensive residential neighborhoods creeping up narrow ridges into the hills. It is a kaleidoscope variety of places to live fitting every pocketbook and style.

Mililani town, probably Honolulu's newest neighborhood, sits squarely in the center of what were once Dole pineapple fields. Waipahu's new residential areas are old C & H sugar cane fields, and many *mauka* Kane'ohe subdivisions cover banana farms that were reluctantly given up by their owners. Only Makakilo above Barbers Point is built where nothing was before.

On the windward side long, strip communities fill in the narrow plots remaining between the *pali* and the beach. Some beach homes are perched clear of the ground on poles, permitting high waves to pass through without washing the house away. The posted warnings of "High Surf Area" and "Tsunami Evacuation Road" have particularly significant meaning along the shore at Ka'a'awa, Punalu'u and Hau'ula, where 30-foot-high "tidal waves" swept inland on April Fools' day in 1946.

Sea Life Park, Makapu'u.

Well, I've seen a lot of changes. A lot of people complain about all this brick and mortar, but, I don't know, it's still home to me. It means a lot to me. They talk about planning. I don't know. There is a certain amount of planning you've got to do, but there has to be some uniqueness to your local situation that makes something out of it. A good example of that is Kona — Kailua Kona. It probably has the least amount of planning and yet people like it and want to go there and it's growing. It's still a very quaint place. I was in Australia last year, in Canberra. Now there's a planned city and it is the most cold and sterile city I've ever seen. I don't like it.

John Bellinger, President
First Hawaiian Bank

The rapid population growth of Honolulu on limited island land has resulted in continuous changes in land use, at times causing destructive alteration in the landscape, as well as traumatic displacement of people, and in some areas, eradication of traditional rural land uses. Modern developments have sometimes been imposed rather harshly upon the island.

The ancient Hawaiian mullet ponds at Kuapa near Koko Crater were dredged by industrialist Henry Kaiser into the Hawaii Kai complex of marinas and townhouses that continue to expand in all directions. Fifteen years ago there were only fish, *kiawe* trees, and pig farms in Maunalua Valley.

When Kaiser first moved into Maunalua and Kalama, the pig farmers and newly arrived counter-culture people joined in an effort to preserve the small farms and rural lifestyle they enjoyed at low rents on old Bishop Estate leaseholds. The farmers lost, but only after staging a sit-in in front of the bulldozers. Police dragged them away as they pleaded for the right to live on the land that Hawaiian Princess Bernice Pauahi Bishop inherited from their ancestors, land that Bishop Estate trustees had now leased to Kaiser.

I had previously struggled with Kaiser myself as land use commissioner, and in the process we grew to know each other well. Kaiser first started in business as a studio photographer, and he often took time from his busy schedule to proudly show me his early photographs when I called at his office. I tried to convince him that a little mix of people and occupations in the vast development at Hawaii Kai would be very desirable. I also tried my best to keep his houses off the dramatic ridges around Kuapa Pond, but to no avail. He was a very stubborn man.

When I tried to convince my fellow commissioners to deny urban zoning for the narrow ridges and for Oahu's south shore beyond the Blowhole, Kaiser personally drove himself downtown to the Land Use Commission office and, with his associates waiting hesitantly in the hallway, loudly expressed his extreme displeasure at a public zoning body that would deny him the right to do anything he wanted with his land. Kaiser said he would sue me, and he threatened to abandon the entire multimillion-dollar Hawaii Kai project unless he immediately received permission to subdivide Kalama Valley and build on every ridge. The "progress" and growth-oriented commission members quickly retreated, and I was unable to muster sufficient votes to prevent Kaiser from receiving almost everything he demanded. He never consulted with the small farmers and Hawaiian families living deep inside Kalama Valley. The zoning change was decided by Kaiser.

As so often happens in Hawaii, the struggle between Kaiser and myself fostered a lasting friendship. I was the only photographer to photograph his home on Koko Head, where he lived until his death, when Hawaii Kai was still in early stages of construction. We would ride off together in his pink jeep to watch his pink bulldozers and pink landmovers rearrange Maunalua land. Even his dredge and tugboats were pink. His "Five Companies" built Boulder Dam on the Colorado River and a Liberty ship a day during World War II. He was one of the many immigrants to Hawaii who substantially changed the shape of things.

There was a stir of political reaction to Kaiser's confrontation with the farmers, causing legislators to debate a bill recognizing the existence of semisubsistence farming in a rural environment. Senator Nadao Yoshinaga called for a study of population stabilization in a racially and economically mixed community, which would recognize the prior rights of people living on the land. He wanted consideration of individually styled communities appropriate to counter-culture lifestyles of people who want to live on the land in their own way in hand-built structures exempt from conventional building codes. The bill was defeated by a legislative majority that would have none of this rural lifestyle nonsense.

The erection of personal "country-style" homes without regard to expensive zoning restrictions and building codes has been difficult to halt on Oahu, where isolated valleys and wooded land along the shore support many

---

We got to restrict the population and tourists to certain numbers. You can't let them grow hog wild. If we imposed ourselves on San Francisco or Los Angeles and over-populated their space they'd call a halt to it. So, I think the Governor has got a good idea. We've got to watch it. So far so good. Certainly the islands haven't suffered from these tourists, but when it gets out of hand you gotta prepare for it . . . They have these conventions all the time. We shouldn't go out and solicit these conventions. Let 'em get down on their knees to come to Hawaii. Let them start begging a little bit. Then we can be a bit choosy.

Vernon "Red" McQueen
Sports writer

hidden shacks that building inspectors have never seen. Some who do have permits constructed innovative dwellings and plain single-walled cottages on unpaved roads in remote areas where water is still collected off the roof to make the inside plumbing work. The need for concrete sidewalks is hardly necessary for bare feet.

The building department ordered a beach shack in Wai'anae torn down because no building permit had been obtained and it claimed the structure was not safe. The inspector said, "They have to follow the same kind of construction as conventional building construction. By that I mean they have to use nails. They can't hold it together with ropes." The Hawaiian grass shack is apparently no longer acceptable at City Hall.

Hawaiian families living on small semisubsistance farms in Waikane-Waiahole valleys are still struggling to prevent their valleys from being converted into expensive rural subdivisions. They like low rents and don't object to unpaved roads. When adjacent Kahana Valley was purchasd for a state park and eviction notices posted to allow "proper development" of the park for public use, families in the valley successfully halted their ouster. Lydia Dela Cerra, speaking for the park families, said, "This valley has housed our ancestors for many, many years. Isn't it a privilege that we, the offspring of Hawaiian ancestry, should be given rights to remain in the valley which once held the *mana* of the natives here, which is

slowly dispersing into thin air?"

"We love our land," said her neighbor in the next valley. "We also love our ancestors, and we cannot and will not see them ripped out of the land by bulldozers. They kill a little bit of us every time they take our land."

The Hawaiians have now gone to Congress to get back the land they claim is rightfully theirs. They ask for "compensation for losses resulting from the overthrow of the Hawaiian Kingdom." They want one billion dollars, plus title to all federal lands in Hawaii that become surplus to government needs. A congressional commission has been appointed to study methods of possible compensation to native Hawaiians for their lost lands. Their attorney adds that the claim is just as valid as the settlement recently received by Alaskan Indians and Eskimos.

The Hui Malama 'Aina Ko'olau, a Hawaiian community organization, says they do not pretend to stop development, but with their race nearing extinction and so few pure-blooded Hawaiians remaining, they do ask to participate in the decisions that shape their future and their land. "We demand that it be development that builds on the life of the people," says Hui Malama, "that preserves our values and that nourishes the children of all the native people of Hawaii. We cannot any more allow development that destroys the things that make Hawaii what it is." ∎

In crime statistics the local population is broken down into its respective components. Caucasians are, as always, lumped into one category without distinction as to ethnic background . . . It's high time that people here realize that ethnic identity is not limited to "minority groups" like Korean, Samoan, Chinese, and that Irish, Germans, Italians, French et. al. have backgrounds as diverse and valuable as any other group . . . To be honest, I find this whole ethnic breakdown business to be utterly valueless and grossly distracting from the fact that we are all fellow human beings, but if it is to be done to one group, why not for all? . . . Who's kidding whom? Are we to continue with the divisive nonsense or are we finally going to wake up to the fact that we're all just people? Ethnic identity is fine when it includes all, but all too often it obscures our common identity and is used to fuel the fire of racism.

Gregory Shepherd, Kailua
English teacher

This community is the kind of place where I can really affirm the doctrine of creation.

Bishop Edmond Browning
Episcopal Diocese, Honolulu

A tropical fruit stand at Kahalu'u invites buyers in shoes or bare feet.

The Aloha Spirit Is Not A Myth

In January, Japanese *tofu* makers take alternating two-week vacations so there will always be *tofu* on supermarket shelves. Of course, not everyone does this; the Kewalo pickle factory took just one week's vacation last year, and it was long enough for fresh bottled pickles to disappear. I drove into a service station in Kane'ohe town, giving the usual request, "Fill 'er up," only to hear the candidly honest Hawaiian attendant tell me, "I'm all out of super. I forgot to order." I'll always remember my visit to a hotel gift shop, where I inquired why my paper-cover book, *Kauai*, was not in stock. The pretty clerk told me my book was a lot of trouble, because it was always selling out and she had to reorder!

Honolulu is that place where the world goes by outside while we "do our own 'ting," as it is said in local pidgin, and ignore what is considered normal elsewhere. Our relaxed and kindly attitude has successfully resisted brutalization despite plantation *lunas*, politicians, and war. We are nice to each other and kindly to strangers. With all our troubles (and we do have troubles) the people of Hawaii have remained alive and vibrant. The "aloha spirit" is not a myth.

Spanish galleons carrying plundered gold from Manila to Acapulco sailed within less than a hundred miles from the islands. If our consistant, year-round trade winds had changed ever so slightly, we would be speaking Spanish today. Now there is serious discussion in political chambers on how to maintain our traditional ethnic balance of Oriental, Polynesian, and *haole* to prevent Honolulu from becoming mostly *haole* like all the other states. We don't want to lose what we have, but we're not quite sure how to keep it.

One of the problems involved in maintaining cultural integrity is knowing what you have, but in many specific areas we don't know what it is. I wouldn't know how to inventory ethnic assets, and I know it would be impossible — and unwise — to determine what the best racial combination is. Our life modes and way with people can easily be exported — our philosophy and people relationships taken home as souvenirs — and we should encourage spreading the message far and wide. It is perhaps the most valuable commodity anyone can possess, and it is free. The visitor can look at our scenery, but must not touch. They can take away everything else, because we have lots of good living.

For those concerned about Hawaii's growth rate, this book is a disaster — now everyone will want to live here! It is truly a dilemma. When people telephone me in Honolulu, I generally tell them it is raining and has been for the past week. (Actually, to a certain extent this is true, because it rains almost every night in the mountains back of Manoa. Upper Manoa Valley averages about 90 inches a year — this is more than monsoon weather in central India.) Perhaps this might discourage a few. But I know it doesn't rain all the time. I can only write a book about a very wonderful place and hope the philosophy behind it all is exportable — a lifestyle that visitors can emulate and take back home. Perhaps we can be copied in every detail in other places.

We are reminded by every decision that scars the earth or our people that we must live on earth's terms. If we want a beautiful island — a livable island forever, with a remunerative economy in future years — we must make it so by rational and thoughtful decisions based on nature's restrictive terms — not ours. Even planning for so-called "controlled growth" is meaningless if there is no actual limit. The carrying capacity of the island is determined by our needs for open space, clean air, agriculture, and places to live, eat, and enjoy, and these needs must be the determinant of the island's optimum population. Over the short term we can grow fat and rich if we wish to duplicate Las Vegas; but in the process we will destroy our way of living and our island in the sun.

Please understand the need to tread gently upon our island. We cannot build a hotel on every beach or a condominium apartment on every hillside. There is only room for so many people at a time, and when we are full, some will have to wait their turn. If we allow entry to all visitors who are able to afford a ticket, our unique island treasure may be lost — to everyone. Please understand if sometimes the people of Honolulu occasionally must advise, "No more reservations are available — the island is full." ∎

Honolulu is the example I hope someday all America will follow . . . it's the Aloha spirit we have — no other place has it.

Charles Clark, Superintendent
State Department of Education

King Kamehameha draped in plumeria flower *leis* on his birthday celebration. The original statue was lost at sea on its way to Honolulu from its Italian sculptor. This is the second.

Kualoa on Kaneʻohe Bay.

Dedicated to my Honolulu children:

Tad Miki
Jay Koki
Miyo Nancy
Chiye Rana

HERALDRY

HERALDRY

HENRY BEDINGFELD, ROUGE CROIX PURSUIVANT
PETER GWYNN-JONES, LANCASTER HERALD
FOREWORD BY THE DUKE OF NORFOLK, EARL MARSHAL

BISON GROUP

First published in 1993 by
Bison Books Ltd
Kimbolton House
117A Fulham Road
London SW3 6RL

ISBN 0-86124-994-1

Printed in Hong Kong

PAGE 1:
The Royal Arms, 1603-88.

PAGE 2:
TOP: *The Royal Arms, 1340-c.1400.*

MIDDLE: *The Royal Arms, 1707-14.*

BOTTOM: *The Royal Arms, 1714-1801.*

CONTENTS

Foreword   7

1   Origins   *Henry Bedingfeld*   8

2   The Heralds   *Henry Bedingfeld*   22

3   The Science of Heraldry   *Henry Bedingfeld*   40

4   The Art of Heraldry   *Peter Gwynn-Jones*   50

5   Heraldic Monsters   *Peter Gwynn-Jones*   78

6   Fauna and Flora   *Peter Gwynn-Jones*   96

7   Royal Heraldry   *Henry Bedingfeld*   112

8   International Heraldry   *Peter Gwynn-Jones*   136

Glossary   154

Index   158

Acknowledgments   160

For Further Reading   160

TOP: *The Royal Arms, 1801-16.*

BOTTOM: *The Royal Arms, c.1400-1603, and one of the crests used by Edward IV.*

OPPOSITE PAGE: *The arms of the Duke of Norfolk, surrounded by the Garter and ensigned by a duke's coronet.*

FOREWORD

by the Duke of Norfolk KG, GCVO, CB, CBE, MC
Earl Marshal of England

You will discover when you read this book that heraldry is a very old subject but, I am delighted to say, evergreen. From the period of the tournaments to the present day it has gradually evolved to fulfil the needs of the changing times, and today it is arguably more popular than ever before. Apart from the national Heraldry Society based in London, there are a number of provincial heraldry societies across Britain which cater for a proper study of the subject.

The two authors, Rouge Croix Pursuivant and Lancaster Herald, are full-time practising heralds at the College of Arms and are well versed in their chosen profession and the intricacies of heraldry. They have, I believe, given a fresh approach to this intriguing and colourful subject, and have taken many illustrations from the official records of the College of Arms which have not hitherto been published.

Norfolk.

1
ORIGINS

Henry Bedingfeld

Throughout Europe shields of arms are used to identify countries, counties, towns, cities and families and, partly as a result of past European colonial expansion, almost the whole world uses armorial symbolism, especially if national flags are included. The flag of the United States of America, said to have been based on the arms of George Washington, is even to be found on the moon, set in place by the first astronauts to land there.

The origins of armorial symbolism are diverse: there was no single 'great inventor' of heraldry. The original meaning of the word includes all the activities of heralds whether it be design of armorial insignia, genealogical research, ceremonial duties or, in the past, ambassadorial duties. Today the word has become synonymous with the study of armorial bearings and, because of this, it is used here in this context. If we have to pinpoint a time and place for the beginnings of heraldry it is almost certainly in Plantagenet Anjou and Maine in France in the mid-twelfth century, but the evidence for this is incomplete. The idea of painting a shield with simple, coloured designs fulfilled both the practical need of identifying one's opponent either in battle or during a tournament, and appealed to the individual's love of display. The twelfth-century Renaissance may have exercised a certain amount of cultural influence on the highest echelons of society, who may also have been drawn by Arthurian tales of courtly romance in which knights battled not merely to kill or capture an opponent, but in order to fulfil some sort of chivalric ideal. Above all, a brave and skilful knight would not wish to remain anonymous, and prominent insignia, either carried as a banner, or on his surcoat or shield, ensured that the world could recognise him.

The feudal system and the growth of large noble households may have encouraged magnates to display banners and flags bearing their own devices simply for the purpose of identification. On the battlefield, members of a lord's retinue needed to be able to identify their leader; in an illiterate age a magnate required a seal to authenticate his orders, and his mark had to be clearly recognisable. It became convenient for a nobleman's son to adopt his father's mark, and by the end of the twelfth century it is clear that armorial bearings had become hereditary. Heraldry started with the great magnates, whose vast landed

BELOW: *Bodiam Castle, Sussex.*

OPPOSITE, ABOVE: *The battle of Crécy, from Froissart's* Chronicle, *fifteenth century.*

possessions set them apart from ordinary knighthood; it gradually spread down the social ladder, so that by the fifteenth century, esquires and gentlemen adopted arms too. It undoubtedly spread throughout Western Europe from the mid-twelfth century as knights travelled to tournaments or to war.

Heralds, whose job was to proclaim the venues of tournaments, emerged as the first recorders of heraldry. They had to announce the lists of combatants by name and so needed to be able to recognise the insignia of the individuals. Heralds became expert in advising knights on the appropriate insignia to adopt and, from being mere recorders, grew to be controllers and, eventually, creators of armorial bearings.

Heraldry has been defined by Sir Anthony Wagner, Clarenceux King of Arms as, 'the systematic use of hereditary devices centred on the shield'. 'Systematic', because the science and art of heraldry developed a descriptive language and system of rules; 'hereditary devices', because certain designs passed from one generation of a family to another, usually from father to son; and 'centred on a shield', because the shield, with its simple, flat shape, was the best part of a knight's accoutrement upon which to paint devices. It provided a practical protection of the person as well as an ideological defence of family, territory, honour and virtue.

Today there are virtually no surviving medieval pennants, flags, or surcoats, and shields were destroyed in tournaments or on the battlefield. The only evidence of early heraldry is recorded in manuscripts such as rolls of arms, illuminated manuscripts,

BELOW: *The arms and crest of von Hassendorf, 1483, a modern painting.*

RIGHT: *A modern library painting of the armorial bearings of the Bowyers Company.*

The Armorial Bearings of
THE BOWYERS COMPANY

College of Arms
London

Rouge Croix Pursuivant

BELOW LEFT: *Seal of Roger de Quincy Earl of Winchester, c.1235.*

BELOW RIGHT: *Joanna Stuteville, c.1266. A rare seal showing a lady riding sidesaddle.*

ations of the first owner's descendants. They provide the earliest practical evidence of heraldic designs and devices, most of which were simple geometric shapes.

The first seal of Waleran, Count of Meulan and Earl of Worcester, has been dated between 1136 and 1138 and shows the shield and horse trapper (a horse blanket reaching almost to the ground to protect the horse from blows) as checky; the counterseal (reverse side) shows the same checky pattern on shield, horse trapper and lance pennon. Waleran's maternal uncle, Ralph, Count of Vermandois, had a seal showing a checky lance flag, and in a second seal, on a charter of 1146, he bears the chequers on both flag and shield. The checky shield has claims to be the oldest in heraldry, but this example is particularly interesting as Waleran has clearly inherited it from his mother's family. The Counts of Vermandois continued to bear the checky shield, and later the descendants of his mother's second marriage, the Warenne Earls of Surrey, bore the same shield, as did another branch of the Warennes, the Earls of Warwick, who added an ermine chevron as a further distinguishing feature.

The de Clare family bore the simple shield of chevrons. The seal of Gilbert de Clare, Earl of Pembroke, has been dated at about 1141, but is only known from a later drawing, and that of his nephew Gilbert de Clare, Earl of Hertford, has been dated at about 1146.

chronicles and, to a certain extent, romances and poems, or on the seals used by kings and magnates to authenticate their charters and orders.

Heraldic seals seem to have appeared first in France, England and Germany in the second quarter of the twelfth century, and it is clear that they were used by several gener-

13

ABOVE: *The tomb plate of Geoffrey Plantagenet, Count of Anjou and Maine, d.1151.*

common arms among feudal tenants in East Anglia in particular, notably the Fitzwalter, Pecche, Baynard, and Walpole families.

Another shield of this period is that almost certainly borne by Geoffrey de Mandeville, Earl of Essex (died 1144), which is quarterly gold and red. Variations of this shield were borne by a group of families, all connected to Geoffrey de Mandeville and his wife, including Say, Beauchamp of Bedford, Clavering, Vere, Lacy and others.

Elsewhere in Europe the existence of heraldry at this time is shown in the seals of Count Amadeus III of Savoy (died 1148); Henry the Lion, Duke of Saxony (died 1195); Raymond Berengar of Provence in 1150; Welf VI, Marquis of Tuscany and Prince of Sardinia in 1152; and of Raymond Berengar IV of Aragon in 1157.

Mention must be made here of the arms of Geoffrey Plantagenet, Count of Anjou and Maine (father of King Henry II of England). A Cluniac monk, Jean of Marmoutier Abbey in the Loire valley in France wrote a history of Anjou in about 1170-80, in which he describes Geoffrey's ceremony of knighthood in 1128 at Rouen. It took place a week before his marriage to Matilda, daughter of Henry I, King of England. In the ceremony, the king hung a shield bearing six golden lions about Geoffrey's neck. This passage has frequently been taken as the first written record of a shield of arms and thus the first mention of heraldry. Unfortunately Jean of Marmoutier is thought to be unreliable (Dr Elizabeth Hallam, editor of *The Plantaganet Chronicles*, describes Jean's tales as 'lively and often apocryphal'). Certainly Jean must have seen Geoffrey's enamel tomb plate at Le Mans Cathedral (he died in 1151), and it is quite possible that the chronicler, writing 20-30 years later, could have embellished his tale by adding the heraldic detail to the ceremony. However, if the written description of the first armorial shield cannot be believed, at least the tomb plate still exists in Le Mans Museum and is the first *coloured* example of heraldry that survives today. That it is heraldry is demonstrated by the fact that Geoffrey's bastard grandson, William de Longespée, Earl of Salisbury, bore the same shield, which today can be seen on his tomb in Salisbury Cathedral.

Rolls of arms are another important source of evidence for the origins, and particularly the development, of heraldry. The *Chronicles* of Matthew Paris, a Benedictine monk in the Abbey of St Albans, are illustrated with

The shield shows six chevrons, but is better known in its later form with just three chevrons. It is the first surviving example of a fairly common design and instigated a whole series of arms, notably by changing the central chevron to a fess. A fess between two chevrons, in a variety of colour combinations and with certain additions, became

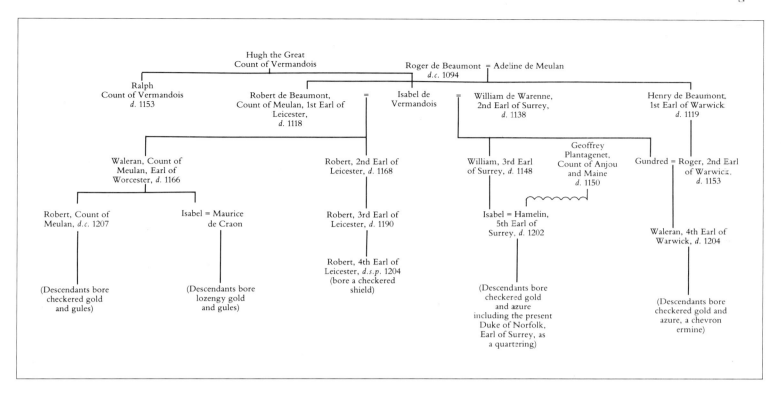

the shields of arms of figures mentioned in his text. Paris worked at St Albans between 1217 and his death in 1259, writing a variety of texts, one of which was a summary of events in England between 1200 and 1250. The

heraldic record is secondary to the historic content of his work, but is nevertheless crucial to a study of early English heraldry. A day's journey from London, St Albans was visited by many of the eminent, including the

ABOVE: *Pedigree showing descent of checky arms.*

BELOW: *Flower's Ordinary c.1520, showing Warenne and other checky banners and shields.*

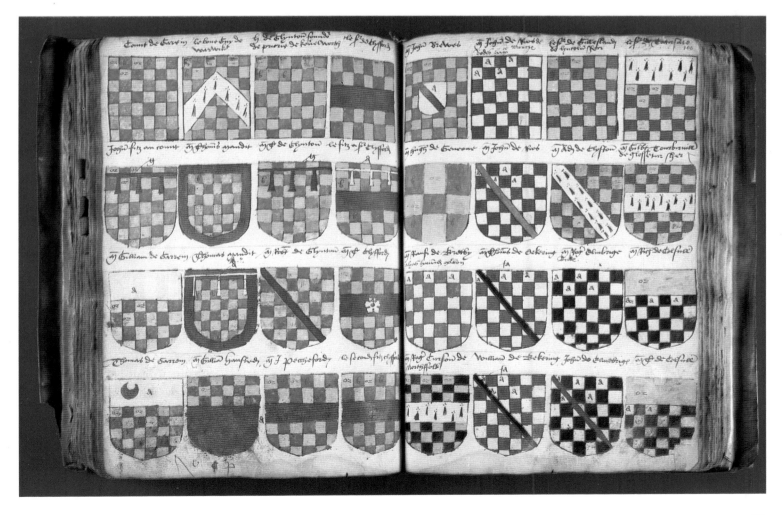

record of their arms. Sir Anthony Wagner commented that 'the Matthew Paris shields are the work of a clerk, a keen and accurate observer, but one who looks at heraldry from the outside'. Other contemporary rolls of arms, such as Glover's and Walford's Rolls, are probably the work of heralds or even knights professionally involved with the subject.

The Bigot Roll, known from a seventeenth-century copy of the original, was composed after the campaign of Charles, Count of Anjou, in Hainault in 1254 against John, Count of Avesnes. It lists nearly 300 participants and gives their arms in blazon, the technical language used to describe arms. Glover's Roll (named after Robert Glover, Somerset Herald, 1570-88, who possessed a copy of the now lost medieval original) has been dated at 1255 or slightly earlier. It lists 55 names and the blazons of their arms, but unlike the Bigot Roll it is not a record of a discernible event, and it is not clear how the compiler decided on his choice of entrants. Starting with the king and his eldest son, it records the arms of earls, barons and knights from almost every English county. Walford's Roll, *c.*1275, exists as a nineteenth-century copy edited by W S Walford, and lists some 180 names and blazons. Like Glover's Roll, it seems to be a personal collection of the

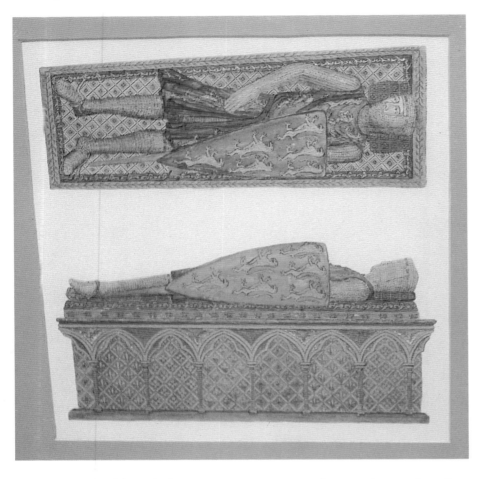

ABOVE: *A painting of the tomb of Will am de Longespée, Earl of Salisbury, an illegitimate grandson of Geoffrey of Anjou, at Salisbury Cathedral.*

king, Henry III. Matthew Paris was therefore able to gain a wide-ranging knowledge of events and people, including, of course, a

RIGHT: Holles Ordinary, *mid-seventeenth century. Arms derived from the Clare arms.*

FACING PAGE: *Matthew Paris shields, c.1244.*

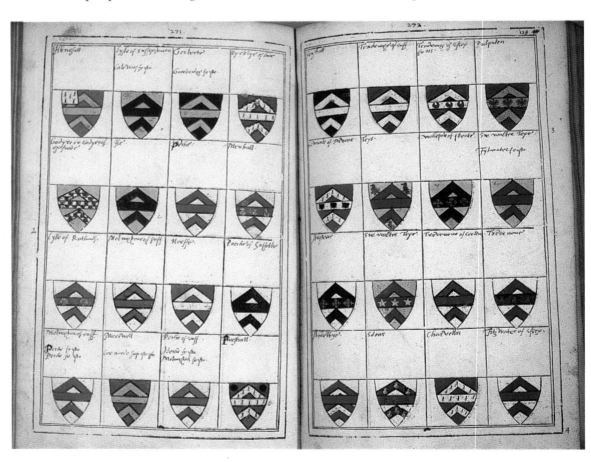

RIGHT: Holles Ordinary;
various lozengy coats.

FACING PAGE: *A miniature from
the Westminster Psalter c.1250.
It shows the typical equipment of
a knight at the time.*

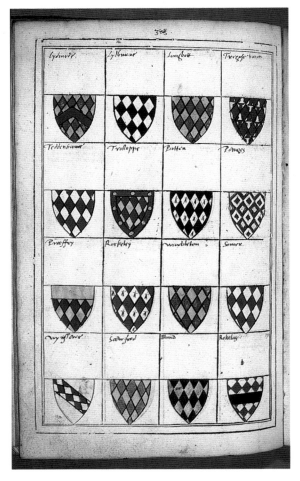

BELOW: Holles Ordinary;
various quartered coats.

compiler, though as it also includes a number of foreign arms, it is likely that he was fairly well travelled. All the arms of these early rolls are described in Anglo-Norman blazon, the forerunner of a later-perfected system. The earliest roll commemorates a particular event, the Hainault campaign, and until 1500 it seems to have been fairly common for a herald to compile a roll after a military campaign, siege or tournament, recording the arms of the combatants.

Romances and poems are also important as heraldic records, but have a different relevance to that provided by seals and rolls of arms. The romances are primarily literary models of chivalry, drawn from a world of fiction and fantasy where men and events are larger than life. They were written from the end of the twelfth century – a century before the first rolls of arms were compiled – and provide the first literary references to heralds, banners, and shields of arms. Shield devices were mentioned as being used as a means of recognition on the field of combat, although descriptions of them are inevitably poetical, rather than by blazon. As Maurice Keen noted in *Chivalry*, the romances project an ideal world, 'the romantic authors habitually

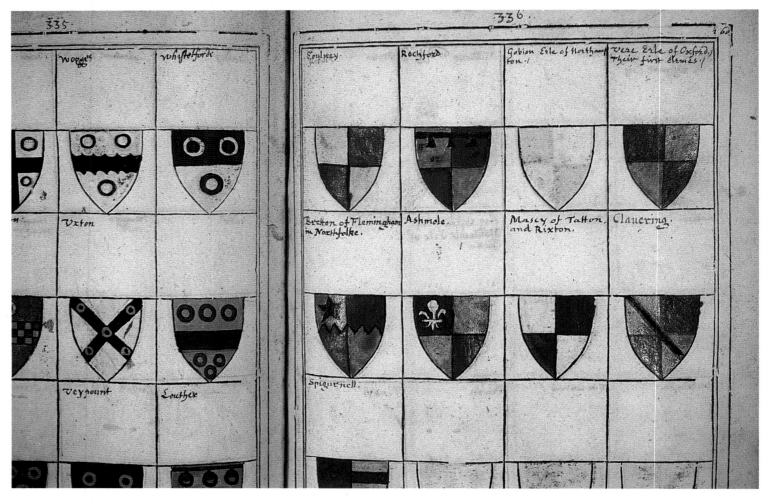

associating together the classic virtues of good knighthood: *prouesse, loyauté, largesse, courtoisie,* and *franchise* (the free and frank bearing that is visible testimony to the combination of good birth with virtue)'. The romances were undoubtedly popular with contemporaries, but how much effect courtly ideals had on the behaviour of the average knight in the thick of battle or in the tournament mêlée is questionable. The harsh realities of life may have negated the civilising influence of chivalric principles.

Heraldry was an essential part of the chivalric ideal, the symbolic element of it in fact. Chivalry is a difficult concept to understand because it means different things to different people at different times. In essence it is an ideal by which a man achieved knighthood and by which he was supposed to live in honour and virtue. There are a number of surviving treatises on chivalry which provide an insight into the precise meaning of the concept. Their popularity lasted for centuries, and they were still being read in the fifteenth and sixteenth centuries. The *Ordene de Chevalerie*, written by an anonymous northern French poet before 1250, describes

the ritual by which a man was created a knight, and explains the meaning of each part of the ceremony. The candidate underwent a ceremonial bathing to remove the stain of sin, supposedly emerging as clean as an infant from the baptismal font. This particular formality is still recalled in the modern order of chivalry, the Order of the Bath.

In the late thirteenth century the Majorcan writer, Ramon Lull, described the origins of chivalry, the duties of a knight and the qualities required of an esquire before he could attain knighthood, in the *Libre del ordre de Cavaylería*.

Geoffrey de Charny, himself a renowned warrior who was killed defending the French royal standard at the Battle of Poitiers in 1356, wrote three works, the *Livre*, the *Livre de Chevalerie*, and *Questions*, in which he discusses the joust, the tournament and war, and describes the different degrees of honour attached to each activity. Success in the joust is praiseworthy, but success in the tournament is better, and in war still more so. Gaining honour in war at home is accorded less prestige than battle honours acquired on a foreign battlefield.

BELOW: *Knights jousting c.1480, from the Military Roll of Arms.*

uilipendentes. inestimabili gaudio perfusi — moliebatur cū filuf suif uuuentibz duobz uide

Each of these authors shows a practical and humane understanding of what chivalry meant, and while the *Ordene* is entirely secular, Lull's and Charny's works have additional underlying Christian themes. There is a common thread running through all three works: that all candidates for knighthood must be of good birth, good lineage, and must have sufficient wealth to sustain their rank. Geoffrey de Charny extends these criteria to include men-at-arms as well as knights. From the time of early heraldry it was necessary to be well born to be a knight. This social distinction had a practical foundation, as any potential knight had to be wealthy enough to provide himself with at least one horse, as well as the other accoutrements of knighthood. The expense of knighthood thus helped to restrict the use of armorial bearings to those of the knightly class or above.

Heraldry, then, was an invention of the noble and knightly classes and evolved partly from the practical needs of combat, and partly from a desire to display. A combination of circumstances and ideas – feudalism, the chivalric ideal, the love of abstract decoration, and the desire for recognition in combat – fused together to produce conditions ideal for the development and flowering of heraldry. As Maurice Keen has commented, 'heraldry offered a means whereby both the class pride and the ideals of knighthood could be symbolically expressed, and the heralds, as experts in its history, literature and rituals became a kind of secular priesthood of chivalry'.

LEFT: *Seal of Margaret de Quincy, Countess of Winchester, c.1207-18.*

2
THE
HERALDS

Henry Bedingfeld

The first mention of a herald in literature seems to be in the romantic poem known as *Le Chevalier de la Charette*, written by Chrétien de Troyes between 1164 and 1174. At a joust the herald sees a shield which he does not recognise hanging outside a poor lodging. He enters barefoot, wearing only a shirt (he had pawned his other clothes for a drink at a tavern), in order to discover whose arms he has seen, and he finds Lancelot within. As Sir Anthony Wagner has written: 'It is unlucky that the first recorded act of the first recorded herald should be his failure to recognise a shield of arms!' But to be fair to our wayward herald, Lancelot was taking part in the joust in disguise, having been released from captivity on parole, and it is therefore not surprising that he was not recognised. Two things become apparent from this story. Heralds were known and written about as being involved in jousting in the third quarter of the twelfth century, and were evidently expected to be able to recognise arms only a short time after heraldry first came into being and before it became fully established as hereditary.

The tournament and joust, in fact, created the herald. It was he who had to proclaim the event, he who had to announce and acclaim the knight as he took to the field in combat, and he who had to be able to explain to the onlookers who was who. Chrétien de Troyes, in the *Chevalier au Lion*, calls them 'Li hera qui des vaillanz crie le ban?' In *Le Chevalier de la Charette* Chrétien de Troyes also points out the combatants to the Queen and her ladies: 'Do you see that knight yonder with a golden band across his red shield? That is Governau de Roberdic. And do you see that other one, who has an eagle and a dragon painted side by side on his shield? That is the son of the King of Aragon, who has come to this land in search of glory and renown. And do you see that other one beside him, who thrusts and jousts so well, bearing a shield with a leopard painted on a green ground on one part, and on the other azure blue? That is Ignaures the well-beloved, a lover himself and jovial. And he who bears the shield with the pheasants portrayed beak to beak is Coguillanz de Mautirec.' This is a vivid picture, at an early date, of the herald's skill of personal identification at a tournament.

Not only did the herald acclaim the knight entering the lists, but knowing a man's history gave him enough power to mar his reputation. He has been called the journalist of that age and perhaps because of this certain provincial newspapers include the word 'herald' in their names. Certainly present-day heralds are aware that they may be mistaken as a London representative of these journals.

For the first hundred years or so of heraldic history the French romantic poems seem to be the only sources that provide any mention of heralds and their activities, almost all of which were connected to the tournament. While they may not relate factual history, they do at least portray the conditions of the time. It is not until the latter part of the thirteenth century that we have the beginnings of documentary evidence mentioning heralds, rarely by name, but by title, and often in the company of minstrels or confused with them. The *Statutum Armorum* of 1292, containing new laws for the conduct of tournaments, forbade any king of heralds or min-

strels from carrying hidden weapons or swords unless pointless, and ordered that kings of heralds should wear their surcoats of arms only. For making minstrelsy before Edward III at Christmas, a 1338 wardrobe document records a payment of wages to 'Master Conrod, King of the Heralds of Germany' and *ten other minstrels* of divers great lords of Germany. In 1348 payment was made to 'Magistro Andreae Roy Norreys' (Master Andrew Norroy King of Arms), Lybekin the piper, Hanekin, his son and *six other minstrels* of the king.

It is thought that heralds were originally minstrels who somehow managed to specialise in the tournament. Minstrels would undoubtedly have been present at tournaments as well as at the courts of magnates, and would have been familiar with who bore which shield of arms. There seems to have been a certain amount of rivalry between the two groups. There are a number of romantic poems which contain detailed heraldic references and which may have been written by heralds. However, judging by the number of disparaging comments about heralds, they are more likely to have been penned by a jealous minstrel: 'Heralds are boorish and deceitful and no one is greedier than a herald in pursuit of his perquisite of broken armour'. Heralds were entitled to collect broken armour when it had fallen from a

ABOVE: *The Earl of Warwick jousting at Calais, 1414. The Earl's herald stands holding two saddles, while on the left the joust is watched by an English royal herald sitting between two French royal heralds.*

LEFT: *William Dethick, Garter King of Arms, depicted in the initial letter 'T' in a grant of arms to Charles Hewet of Dublin in 1597.*

CHESTER
HERALD

LANCASTER
HERALD

RICHMOND
HERALD

SOMERSET
HERALD

WINDSOR
HERALD

YORK
HERALD

BLUEMANTLE
PURSUIVANT

PORTCULLIS
PURSUIVANT

ROUGE CROIX
PURSUIVANT

ROUGE DRAGON PURSUIVANT

Badges of Officers of Arms

knight, and probably resold it later in the tournament. There is a complaint that 'every knight has to maintain three or four heralds and cannot get rid of them' and another that 'there is no profession more convenient for an idle, greedy man, nor any in which one may talk so much and do so little'. It is not difficult to draw the conclusion that heralds, by specialising in tournament work, were in greater demand than minstrels and therefore financially more successful.

The heraldic fraternity was divided early on into three grades: Kings of Arms, heralds, and pursuivants. Kings of Arms controlled a given province and heralds acted under them, with pursuivants as followers learning their profession. In France and Germany in the Middle Ages there were hundreds of heralds but in England, it seems, not nearly so many. The king and the great magnates in England each had their own heralds and pursuivants, and so, too, did the rich knight. each herald

OPPOSITE PAGE: *The badges of office of the present English Heralds and Pursuivants in Ordinary.*

FAR LEFT: *The arms of Peter Gwynn-Jones, Lancaster Herald.*

LEFT: *The arms of Henry Bedingfeld, Rouge Croix Pursuivant.*

and pursuivant having a title of office. A study of the *College of Arms Monograph of the London Survey Committee, 1963* yields all the known names and titles of the English heralds. Apart from the obvious titles of territories conquered or acquired, such as Anjou,

LEFT: *Henry Bedingfeld wearing a tabard of the Royal Arms.*

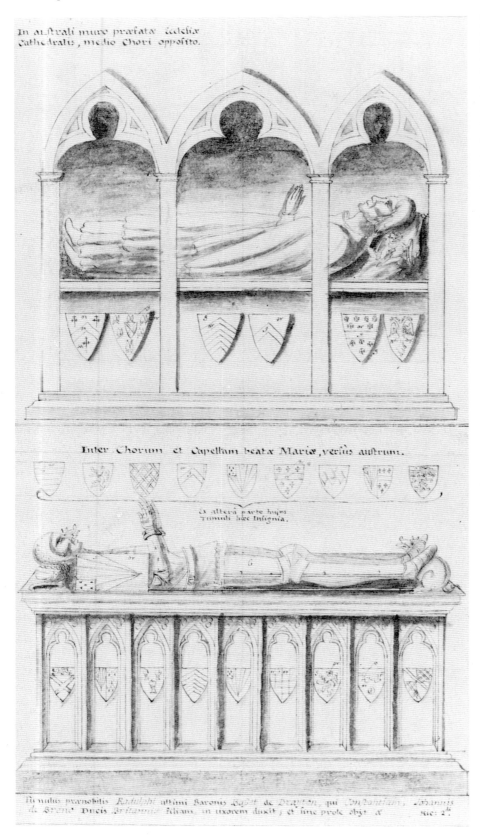

In australi muro praefata ecclesiæ
cathedralis, medio Chori opposito.

Inter Chorum et Capellam beatæ Mariæ, versùs austrum.

Ex altera parte hujus
Tumuli hæc Insignia.

Tumulus prænobilis Radulphi ultimi Baronis Basset de Drayton, qui Constantiam, Johannis d. Brene Ducis Britanniæ filiam, in uxorem duxit; et sine prole obijt. sic 2^di

ABOVE: *Drawings of two
monuments in Lichfield Cathedral
made at the Visitation of
Staffordshire by William
Dugdale, Norroy King of Arms
in 1663/64. The lower one shows
the effigy of Ralph, Lord Basset
of Drayton, d.1390.*

Aquitaine or Guyenne, Ireland and Agincourt, Kings of Arms' and heralds' titles derived from lordships and castles like Lancaster (dating from 1347, both king and herald), Derby (1384), Nottingham (1399), Northumberland (1472), and Montorgueil (1494).

The titles of pursuivants are much more fanciful. These are taken from mottoes,

badges and supporters, and include Bon Espoir (1419), Rouge Croix (1418/19), Il faut Faire (1443/44), Secret or Segret (1425), Bontemps (1434), Bonaventure (1445), Bon Rapport (1448), Tyger (1477) and Blanc Sanglier (c.1483, from the badge of Richard III). Lancaster Herald derives his name from the Earls and Dukes of Lancaster and his badge of office is the red rose of Lancaster royally crowned. The present incumbent is the forty-fifth to hold this office.

Rouge Croix Pursuivant was first created by Henry V and is named from the red cross of St George, badge of the Order of the Garter and sometime national flag of England. His badge of office is a red cross, and the present Rouge Croix is the eighty-second to hold this office.

Tyger Pursuivant, a title taken from the man-tyger supporters of Lord Hastings, from 1471 the Lieutenant-General of Calais, is known only from a letter from Edmund Bedingfeld, dated at Calais 17 August 1477, to Sir John Paston in Norfolk. Having conveyed local 'tydyngs' to Paston, and reported that King Louis XI of France is besieging St Omer, he goes on to say that 'the said French King within these three days railed greatly of my lord to Tyger Pursuivant, openly before 200 of his folks; wherefore it is thought here that he would feign a quarrel to set upon this town if he might get advantage'. Louis XI was using Tyger Pursuivant as a messenger, knowing that he would tell his master, Lord Hastings what he had heard.

Il faut Faire derives his name from Sir John Fastolf's motto. Secret or Segret, by name Laurence de Fugiers, was another of Fastolf's pursuivants and he and Roger Legh, Gloucester Herald (later to be Clarenceux King of Arms), suffered a most unfortunate incident in 1432 when they were robbed on the road between Rouen and Dieppe and barely escaped with their lives.

Before 1415 the chief of the English royal heralds held varying heraldic titles, but in that year Henry V created William Bruges Garter King of Arms, named after the Order of the Garter. Shortly after his creation he was present at the Battle of Agincourt with other English heralds, as was Montjoie, the French King of Arms. In 1406/07 the French royal heralds acquired the use of the Chapel of Saint Antoine le Petit in Paris and, endowed with a set of ordinances, had thus acquired corporate status. It was not until Richard III's charter of 1484 that the English royal heralds gained similar status, being

BELOW: *The Garter feast in St George's Hall, Windsor Castle, 1672. The Hall was built by Edward III in 1363 and was completely altered in 1682. This engraving by Wenceslas Hollar shows the heralds standing in line before Charles II.*

given a residence known as Coldharbour on the northern bank of the Thames in the City of London. This corporation is now known as the College of Arms. After the Battle of Bosworth in the following year, Henry VII removed Coldharbour from the heralds, who were obliged to conduct their business from the Court or their residences in London. This unhappy state of affairs was resolved in 1555 when Queen Mary gave them by charter a house in the City of London called Derby House. This was burnt down in the Great Fire of 1666, though the records were saved. A new College of Arms was built on this site and, with a lucky escape in World War II, it remains the home of the heralds today.

Tournaments must have been the chief occupation of the heralds until Tudor times, but from it they developed a further skill in ceremonial matters, whether for ceremonies of knighthood or coronation. They also acted as messengers between their masters and others. Certainly Tyger Pursuivant's diplomatic language must have been tested to the limit when he was railed at by the French king. Senior heralds were employed on special missions by the king (or queen), for example when taking the Order of the Garter to a foreign sovereign, and in their diplomatic capacity they had the equivalent of diplomatic immunity.

From the twelfth century the heralds' function evolved: from being observers and heraldic advisers at tournaments they became recorders, then controllers, then creators of arms. As the king's Court officials they came under the control of the High Constable and Earl Marshal and were in attendance upon their court, the Court of Chivalry, which regulated the use of arms. The growing number of armigerous individuals and complicated family descent involving arms meant that many cases were brought before it, one of the most celebrated being that of Scrope *v* Grosvenor, which lasted from 1385 to 1390. An argument over who had the right to bear *Azure a Bend Or* was finally decided in Scrope's favour by Richard II after a long case in which John of Gaunt and Geoffrey Chaucer were among the witnesses. The court still exists today as the Earl Marshal's Court, and the last case brought before it was in 1954.

Until the late thirteenth century, it seems that individuals could assume arms as they wished. Gradually, arms came to be regarded as property which could be inherited, and by

the mid-fourteenth century it is clear that they were regarded as marks of privilege, dignity or nobility, grantable by royal authority through Letters Patent. The first known grant by Letters Patent was in 1338 by the Holy Roman Emperor Louis IV; the first known English grant, by Edward III, has not actually survived, but is referred to in a grant by Richard II. In 1393 he granted arms to Otes de Maundell, mentioning that this was a fresh grant to replace the one made to his father, Peter, at least 20 years earlier. The earliest surviving Letters Patent again dates from Richard II's reign and shows how arms had come to be regarded as a mark of distinction. In 1389, Richard granted arms to Johan de Kingeston so that he could 'faire certeins faitz et pointz d'armes' against a French knight in the tournament lists. He was raised to the rank of gentleman, the lowest rank of nobility, and then to esquire, but it is clear that without the right to bear arms, he was unable to respond to the challenge laid down by the French knight in tournament.

BELOW: *The heralds in the Garter procession at Windsor Castle.*

Richard II had a keen interest in heraldry, and made several grants during his reign, but generally grants of arms by English kings are rare. Unlike their European counterparts, they delegated the power to grant arms by Letters Patent to the Kings of Arms. Henry V appointed William Bruges Garter King of Arms in 1415, and the first of his grants that survives is to the Company of Drapers in London on 10 March 1438/39. The assumption of arms was obviously an area in which Henry wished to exercise control, because in 1417 he issued a writ to the sheriffs of Hampshire, Wiltshire, Sussex and Dorset, which referred to the assumption of 'Cotearmures' by men on recent military expeditions. He empowered them to stop this practice unless men had ancestral rights to arms, or had received an authoritative grant. Those that had borne arms with the king at Agincourt were, however, exempt, and could continue to use any arms they had assumed. This seems to lend credence to the words Shakespeare gave the king in his play *Henry V*:

*For he today that sheds his blood with me
Shall be my brother; be he ne'er so vile
This day shall gentle his condition.*

Another form of heraldic control, which started later but ran parallel to the Court of Chivalry, only to cease at the end of the seventeenth century, was the system of Heralds' Visitations. These developed from the production of rolls of arms and were heraldic surveys made from the mid-fifteenth century by the provincial Kings of Arms, ie Clarenceux, whose province is England south of the river Trent; Norroy, north of the Trent; and March, whose province was Wales and the west of England. March disappeared in Henry VII's reign and his province was divided between Clarenceux and Norroy. On appointment each King of Arms took an oath at his creation which required him to know and record the arms of noble gentlemen within his province. The earliest of these visitations was made by Roger Legh, Clarenceux (1435-60), the same man who was robbed in 1432 with Segret Pursuivant. In 1498-99 Henry VII issued a 'placard' or licence to John Writhe, Garter, and Roger Machado, Clarenceux, to visit the arms of gentlemen and to reform them if necessary, according to their oath at their creations.

In 1530 Henry VIII issued a Commission by Letter Patent under the Great Seal to Thomas Benolt, Clarenceux, to visit his province and 'to reform all false armory and arms devised without authority' and to 'deface and take away' all unlawful arms. Thus began a series of county visitations made by the provincial Kings of Arms or their deputies which lasted until the revolution of 1688, recording the lawful arms of the gentry visited, together with their pedigrees; those arms not acceptable had to be disclaimed. The series of visitations are a most important source of armorial and genealogical knowledge, unique in Europe, and they show that the royal heralds with direct royal authority had complete control over armorial matters during this period.

An unexpected controversy arose as a result of the 1530 Visitation Commission. Clarenceux and Norroy Kings of Arms both had clearly-defined provinces over which to exercise their jurisdiction, but Garter King of Arms, the senior heraldic officer, did not. With jurisdiction over Knights of the Garter and peers of the realm, Garter could, theoretically, grant arms to suitably qualified individuals in any area of the country. When he

did this, he encroached on the territorial powers of the junior Kings of Arms and acrimonious disputes often resulted. It was not until 1680 that the Earl Marshal, who is responsible to the Crown for the College of Arms, was able to resolve the problem. He ordered in 1673 that all grants of arms were to be recorded at the College of Arms and, in 1680, that they were to be made jointly by Garter and Clarenceux in the south, and by Garter and Norroy in the north. A clause was also added to the Kings of Arms' patents of creation whereby they could only make grants with the Earl Marshal's consent by Warrant, and these orders apply to this day.

Since 1673 the College of Arms has kept a continuous series of grant volumes, which has now reached volume 158. Well over half these grants have been made in this century

ABOVE: *Rouge Croix Pursuivant reading the Letters Patent granting armorial bearings to Hampshire County Council. They were presented to the Lord Lieutenant of the county, Lt Col Sir James Scott, Bt, seated left. In the background is 'King Arthur's' Round Table, made in the late thirteenth century in the reign of Edward I.*

alone, and this is a clear indication that there is a strong and increasing demand for arms.

Heralds are visible to the public twice a year in full Court uniforms and tabards at the State Opening of Parliament and at the Garter Service in Windsor. They spend most of their time, however, engaged in heraldic and genealogical research. Regarded as learned officers of the Crown, they conduct themselves accordingly, but over the years there have been a few rogues entrusted with the job. Several have died of drink or insolvent in a debtors' gaol. William Radclyffe, Rouge Croix, however, did something far worse. In order to establish a claim to the estate of the Earls of Derwentwater, he entered a false pedigree in the College records, having forged a marriage entry in a parish register to act as proof. He was tried at York Assizes in 1820 and was sentenced to three months' imprisonment which he served still as Rouge Croix, not resigning his office until 1823. He died five years later. Others, such as Sir John Vanbrugh, seemed to have used their position as a sinecure. A celebrated architect and dramatist, Vanbrugh was not at all notable as Clarenceux King of Arms (1704-25). It was said of him that he knew nothing about heraldry and genealogy, and cared even less; in fact he ridiculed both and neglected his official duties.

Fortunately, many others have brought learning and considerable application to the

LEFT: *Her Majesty The Queen with her heralds at the time of the quincentenary of the foundation of the College of Arms, 1984.*

BELOW: *John Charles Brooke, Somerset Herald, 1778-94. Portrait painted on glass.*

job. William Camden, Clarenceux King of Arms (1597-1623) was a writer and antiquarian of note, as well as an extremely active herald who visited by deputy 20 counties in his southern province between 1612 and 1623. Probably the most famous member of the College was Sir William Dugdale, Garter King of Arms (1677-86). He accompanied Charles I to Oxford during the Civil War and at Charles II's restoration he was appointed Norroy King of Arms. He carried out Visitations to all ten of the counties in his province, usually with his clerk. A great benefactor to the College, he presented copies of his own works, some important transcripts, and arranged the gifts of many books and manuscripts by others. His clerk, Gregory King, was enormously talented; described as Dug-

dale's 'little clerk', he was not able to mount a horse from the ground for several years. He started working for Dugdale when he was 14 and, apart from his clerical duties, was also something of an artist. He was, by turn, a distinguished herald and genealogist, an engraver and cartographer, a draughtsman, one of the fathers of population studies, and a town planner. He laid out parts of Soho in London; Soho Square was originally named after him as King Square and the present-day Greek Street was originally Grig Street after his Christian name Gregory. He was Lancaster Herald from 1690 until 1712.

John Anstis, Garter (1719-44), was one of the most learned men of the College. It was mainly at his instigation that the Order of the Bath was instituted in 1725 by King George I.

He left a large manuscript collection to the College, and his most important published work is *The Register of the Order of the Garter.*

Elias Ashmole, Windsor Herald from 1660–75, gave Oxford University in 1672 a large collection of material he had acquired on the death of the naturalist John Tradescant, and he is best known as the founder of the Ashmolean Museum at Oxford. He had great ability as a herald and boundless energy, and wrote *The Institution of the Order of the Garter.* Sir Isaac Heard (Garter King of Arms from 1784 to 1822), fostered the Anglo-American connection. His first wife was a Bostonian and he visited America several times, corresponding with George Washington during his presidency. He is credited with being one of the first heralds to take an active interest in American genealogy, an interest continued by later heralds.

ABOVE: *Rouge Croix with the Lord Lieutenant of Hampshire, Lt Col Sir James Scott, Bt, with Mr F Emery-Wallis (left) and Councillor D A Keep, chairman of Hampshire County Council (right) in July 1992.*

LEFT: *The Letters Patent granting armorial bearings to Pickering Kenyon, solicitors. The decorated borders are composed of red and green filing tapes, and a symbol for each partner is included as a play on his name.*

· DE · MIEVLX · EN · MIEVLX ·

Robt Cooke alias Clarencieulx
Roy d'armes

3
THE SCIENCE OF HERALDRY

Henry Bedingfeld

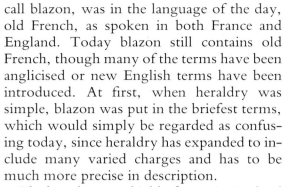

From the earliest heraldic times, or at least from the thirteenth century when the earliest rolls of arms were written, a language has been employed to describe shields of arms, crests, badges and supporters. Originally this language, which we call blazon, was in the language of the day, old French, as spoken in both France and England. Today blazon still contains old French, though many of the terms have been anglicised or new English terms have been introduced. At first, when heraldry was simple, blazon was put in the briefest terms, which would simply be regarded as confusing today, since heraldry has expanded to include many varied charges and has to be much more precise in description.

The best-known shield of arms in England is the Royal Arms, which can be described in everyday speech as a red shield with three golden lions one above the other with their heads facing the viewer. This is both rather longwinded and somewhat inelegant. The earliest roll of arms, Glover's Roll of *c*.1255, has the first known blazon of the Royal Arms as follows: *Le Roy d'Angleterre port l'escu de gules oue trois Lupards d'Or* ('The King of England carries a red shield with three gold lions'). This was clearly sufficient at the time, and everybody would have known these arms well, but this blazon does not quite describe the arms precisely. Compare the earlier description with the latter blazon and the following modern blazon: *Gules three lions passant guardant in pale Or*. In early heraldry a lion passant guardant was called a leopard, or 'Lupard'; the term 'in pale' denotes that one lion should be placed above the other. The colours, '*Gules*' for red and '*Or*' for gold, are the same today as they were in the thirteenth century. (Heraldic convention has it that the claws and tongues of these lions are blue, though this is not blazoned.)

Fundamental to an understanding of heraldry is the fact that the left side of the shield is known as the *dexter* (the Latin word for right) and the right side of the shield is known as the *sinister* (the Latin for left). This is not a deliberate plot by heralds to confuse, but it describes the shield from the point of view of the *bearer* – the man carrying the shield.

The first step in blazoning a shield is to describe the background colour. This can be red (*Gules*), blue (*Azure*), black (*Sable*), green (*Vert*) or purple (*Purpure*) – these are called the tinctures. The other colours, gold (*Or*) and white (*Argent*) are called the metals. The background can also be patterned to show a fur, the principal ones being *Ermine* (black tails on white), *Vair* (a pattern of blue and white), and *Potent* (a crutch-like interlocking pattern). The background colour, called the field, can be a single metal, tincture, or fur; it can also be divided or parted. If the field

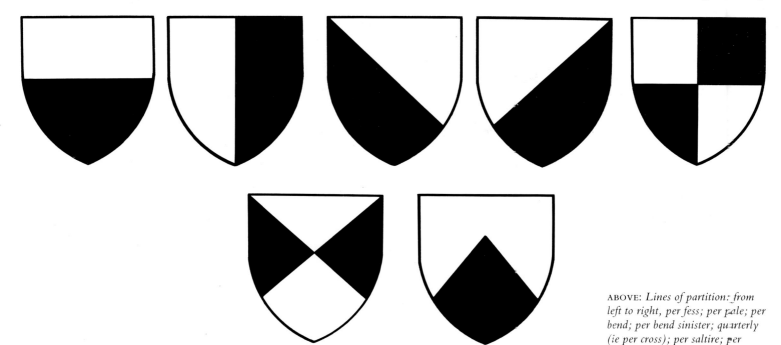

is parted vertically it is *party per pale*; if horizontally it is *per fess*, if diagonally it is *per bend* or *per bend sinister*. It can also be *per chevron*, *per saltire* or *quarterly*. These partition lines can be multiplied so that many *per chevrons* on the shield becomes *chevronny*, *per saltire* multiplied becomes *lozengy*, and *quarterly* becomes *checky*. A multiplied *per pale* becomes *paly* and a multiplied *per bend* becomes *bendy*; they can be mixed so that *paly* combined with *bendy* becomes *pale bendy*. The straight lines of partition can also be decorated.

The second step in blazoning is to describe the principal shape or *charge* upon the shield. These geometrical shapes are usually referred to as the *Ordinaries* and are: *pale, fess, chevron,*

chief, bend, bend sinister, pile, pale, saltire and *cross*. The width of these charges can vary, depending on whether they are plain or whether they have a device upon them. As a general rule, the *pale, fess* and *chief* are about one-third of the height or width of the shield, and the others are in the same proportion. They should be wider if they have charges upon them, and more narrow if they are between other charges. The edges of each can be straight, *engrailed* (indented in a series of curves which point outwards in a concave pattern) or *invected* (indented with a series of curves pointing inward). The most simple Ordinaries have diminutives: *pale* becomes *pallets*; *fess* becomes *bars* or *barry*; bend

43

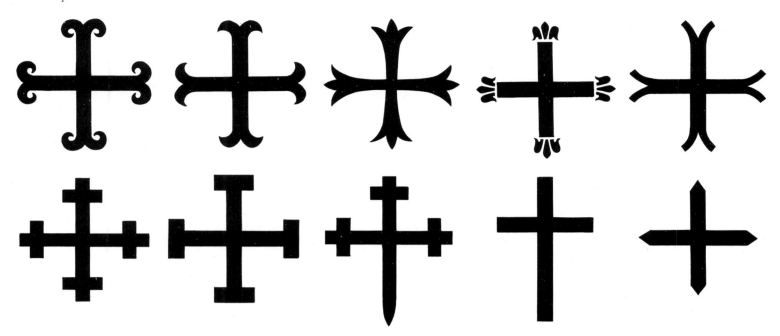

ABOVE *Differing forms of cross: from left to right, recercely; moline patonce; fleuretty; fourché; crosslet; patent; crosslet fitchy; passion cross; pointed.*

BELOW: *Various charges: from left to right, an eagle displayed; a lion rampant; a lion passant; a gryphon segreant; a boar sejant; a pheon; a pomegranate; a mullet; a maunch; a lymphad; a portcullis.*

becomes *bendlets*; and *chevron, chevronels*. There is no diminutive for *chief, pile* or *saltire*, and the cross has many variations.

If there is no Ordinary on the shield, the principal *charge* or charges are described next. A shield can have a single charge or figure, or a combination, and they are usually animals, mythical beasts, or inanimate shapes. The postures of animate charges must be described with terms such as *rampant* (a beast or monster standing on one hind leg), *passant* (walking past), *displayed* (a bird such as an eagle, with outstretched wings), *sejant* (seated erect).

In colouring charges, heralds observe a strict rule: tincture is not to be placed upon tincture, nor metal upon metal. Thus a red field with a black fess is not possible, nor a white field with a gold pale, for the simple reason that from a distance they would not be noticed.

The third step is to describe any secondary charges resting on the surface of the field. Thus the arms of de Montmorency are *Or a Cross Gules between four Eagles displayed Azure*, and those of the College of Arms are *Argent a Cross Gules between four Doves the dexter wing of each expanded and inverted Azure*.

The fourth step is to describe secondary charges placed upon the Ordinary, or main charge. Thus the arms of the City of York are, *Argent on a Cross Gules five Lions passant guardant Or* (recorded without tinctures at the Visitation of 1584). For a combination of the third and fourth steps, the arms of the University of Cambridge are *Gules on a Cross*

Ermine between four Lions passant guardant Or a Bible lying fessways of the field clasped and garnished of the third the clasps in base (granted in 1573 and recorded at the Heralds' Visitation of 1575).

The fifth step is to describe important charges on the field which do not occupy a central position, such as a *chief, canton* or *bordure*. Therefore the arms of the Paston family are blazoned *Argent six Fleurs-de-lis 3, 2 and 1 Azure and a Chief indented Or*, those of Noel, (Earls of Gainsborough), *Or fretty Gules and a Canton Ermine*, and those of Montague (Earls of Sandwich), *Argent three Fusils conjoined in fess Gules within a Bordure Sable*.

The sixth step is to describe charges placed upon the chief, canton or bordure. Examples are *Azure a Fret Argent and on a Chief Or three Crescents Sable* (Hood) and *Quarterly 1st and 4th Azure three Fleurs-de-lis Or 2nd and 3rd Gules three Lions passant guardant in pale Or upon a Bordure Azure Fleurs-de-lis alternating with Martlets Or* (Henry Tudor as Earl of Richmond (Henry VII)).

It should be added that the field or Ordinaries can be *semy*, that is, strewn with charges as in the medieval French Royal Arms: *Azure semy-de-lis Or*, which shows many fleurs-de-lis strewn equally over the field. Another form of scattering is when droplets of liquid are displayed on the field, Ordinary or charge. Each of these droplets, or *gouttes*, has its own name. Droplets of water become *goutty d'eau* (white) and others are *goutty de sang* (red), *goutty des larmes* (blue), *goutty de poix* (black), *goutty d'huile* (green), and *goutty d'or* (gold).

Roundels (circles) also have their own picturesque descriptions. Gold roundels are *bezants* (when strewn they become *bezanty*), white roundels are *plates* (*platy* when strewn); a red roundel is a *torteau*, (*torteaux* when strewn); blue roundels are *hurts*; green roundels, *pomeis*; black roundels are *pellets* (*pellety* when strewn); and purple roundels are *golpes*. If the roundel is *barry wavy Argent and Azure* (representing water) then it is called a *fountain*.

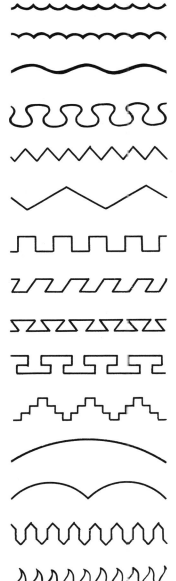

ABOVE: *Decorated lines of partition: from top to bottom, engrailed; invected; wavy; nebuly; indented; dancetty; embattled; raguly; dovetailed; potenty; embattled grady; arched; double arched; urdy; rayonny.*

The Most Noble Lord Horatio Nelson, Viscount and Baron

LEFT: *The armorial bearings of Viscount and Viscountess Nelson.*

Finally, marks of cadency are blazoned to denote the bearer as eldest, second, or third son etc; eldest sons bear labels, second sons, crescents, third sons, mullets, and so on.

When arms are shown with helmet, mantling, crest, supporters and motto, the whole combination is called the 'achievement of arms'. Next in importance to the shield of arms is the crest, which is three-dimensional and sits on top of the helmet. The full achievement is sometimes incorrectly referred to as the crest. From the helmet flows mantling on each side; this is depicted as a cut and shaped cape, thought originally to have shaded the knight from the heat of the sun or protected the neck from blows; it is coloured with a tincture on the outside and is lined with a metal. The mantling is held in place on top of the helmet with a crest wreath, depicted as twisted material coloured with an alternating metal and tincture (usually the first metal and the first tincture of the

blazon), or a crest coronet. From either of these arises the crest.

The helmet denotes the rank of the bearer: a steel tilting helm for esquires and gentlemen; steel with raised visor for baronets and knights; and steel with gold bars to the visor for all peers. The sovereign's helmet is wholly gold. Esquires' and gentlemen's helmets face the dexter; Baronets' and knights' and peers' face the dexter or can be *affronty* (facing the viewer). Supporters are an extra mark of honour and can only be borne by peers, Knights of the Garter and Thistle, and Knights Grand Cross of the orders of chivalry; only those of hereditary peers are inheritable. If the bearer is a Companion or Commander of one of the orders of chivalry, or more senior, or a Knight of the Garter or Thistle, then he can place the appropriate circlet of the order around his shield of arms and in addition show, suspended on ribbons below the shield, his orders and decorations. The motto can be in virtually any language though English, Latin and French are the most common. Mottoes are not part of a grant of arms but are adopted by the bearer and can be changed at any time.

So far we have discussed armorial bearings as borne by men, but women are subject to slightly different rules. Maiden ladies bear their paternal arms on a lozenge, a diamond shape that can have a decorated edge with a knotted bow at the top, known as a true lovers' knot. Married ladies bear their arms on a shield alongside those of their husbands; husband on the dexter, wife on the sinister. Widows continue to bear their marital coat, but on a lozenge rather than a shield, and divorcées revert to their paternal arms on a lozenge. Ladies do not bear crests because they do not wear helmets and are not combatant. However, it has recently been decided that women may take an 'active defence' role in the British armed services and, if commissioned, may in the future aspire to a grant of arms with crest, helm and mantling. History will have to relate as to whether the Kings of Arms will accede to this aspiration.

The marshalling of arms is a term used to describe the joining together of two or more coats of arms. Marshalling began with the compounding of arms, that is to say, taking part of one coat and adding to it part of another. John de Dreux, Duke of Brittany and Earl of Richmond, for example, was a grandson of Henry III and he placed the lions of England on a bordure around his own checky

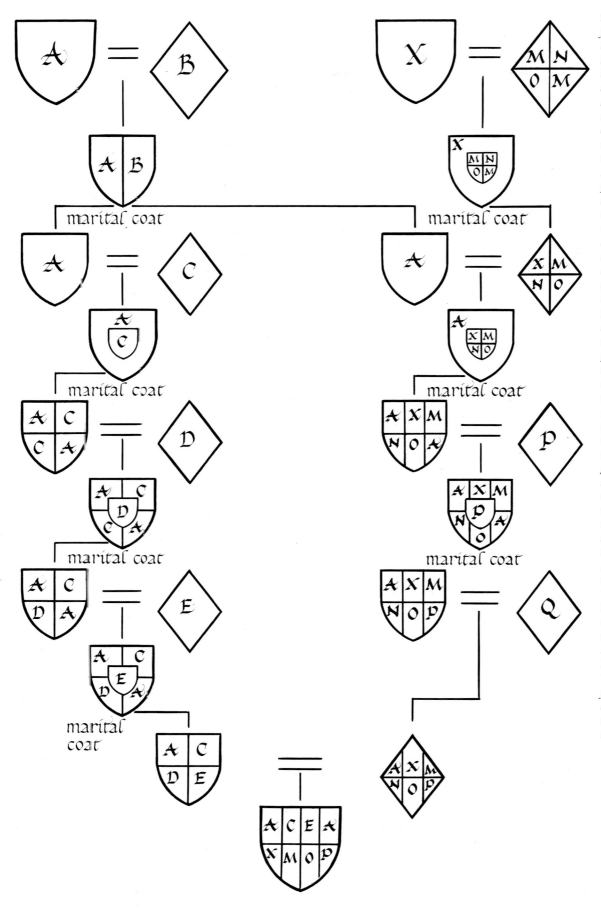

LEFT: *The system by which families may bear quarterings is based upon marriages to heraldic heiresses. A marries B who has brothers and is consequently not an heiress. A and B's marital coat shows the arms as impaled, but this arrangement ceases upon B's death. A and B have two sons; the first marries heiress C, and the marital coat shows the arms of A with an inescutcheon of pretence showing the arms of C, as A is said to be pretending to represent the family of C after C's father has died. After C's death their son can quarter the arms of C; the paternal arms A are placed in the first and fourth quarters, with C in second and third. This son then marries heiress D and the marital coat shows the quartered coat of AC with D on an inescutcheon of pretence. When D dies their son can then add the arms of D to his other quarterings so that his shield is quartered (1)A, (2)C, (3)D, (4)A. This system continues, and quarterings can be added whenever the family A marries other heiresses. The second generation of family A shows a second son (top right). He has married a Miss X, an heiress, who is already entitled to quarter the arms M, N and O. Their son, after X has died, can therefore quarter with his arms of A all those quarterings which his mother brought to the family. This process continues until one branch of A marries the heiress of the other branch of A, the son of this union being able to quarter A, C, D, E, A, X, M, N, O, P. Although the word 'quartering' would indicate only four divisions, in heraldry all the arms placed on one shield are termed as such, regardless of number.*

coat with a canton of Brittany overall. The arms of the de Bohun, Earls of Hereford, are said to have been compounded by adding the lions rampant of William de Longespée, Earl of Salisbury, to the attributed arms of two bends of Milo, Earl of Hereford. The arms of Prince John of Eltham: *England with a bordure of France*, is another example.

RIGHT: *The standard of Sir William Paston of Paston, Norfolk, 1532.*

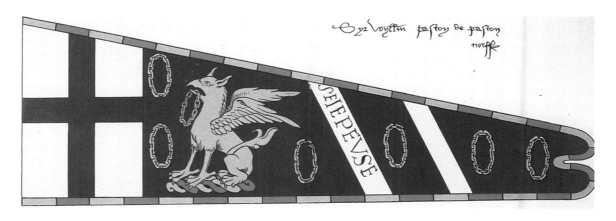

BELOW: *Standards of the Joscelyne family, part of a herald's funeral certificate, 1652-81.*

Later, in the reign of Edward I, one sees the introduction of the practice of dimidiation, that is impaling (putting side by side) two coats on one shield, with each shield having first been cut in half vertically. This produced rather odd results. Edmund, Earl of Cornwall, dimidiated his shield of a lion rampant within a bordure of bezants (gold roundels) with the three chevrons of de Clare; being dimidiated the results show the lion cut vertically in half and the chevrons also, the latter appearing as three bendlets. Better known are the arms of the Cinque Ports, which consist of the arms of England dimidiating *Azure three ships hulls fesswise in pale Argent*, the result of which shows the front half of the lions joined to the back half of the ships' hulls. Another famous coat is that of Great Yarmouth in Norfolk, which shows the front halves of three lions joined to the rear halves of three herrings.

Dimidiation was clearly unsatisfactory, and in time it gave way to simple impalement. In personal heraldry, the husband's arms are placed in entirety on the left-hand side of the shield and the wife's arms in entirety on the right. Similarly, in arms of office, the arms of the corporation or institution are placed on the dexter and the arms of the head of that body are placed on the sinister, but only during his term of office. This applies to bishops, Kings of Arms, masters of livery companies, and chairmen of both civic and corporate bodies.

The marshalling of arms by quartering first occurred in England when Eleanor of Castile and Leon married Edward I. Her arms can be seen at Westminster, as the castle for Castile quartering the lion of Leon. Edward III's Great Seal of 1340 shows the ancient arms of France (*Azure semy de lis Or*) in the first and fourth quartering, with England in the second and third. King Edward's mother was Isabelle of France, the sister of kings Louis X, Philip V and Charles IV of France, who all died without male issue; and through his mother, Edward claimed the throne of France, reinforcing his claim heraldically by quartering the French arms. In about 1400 the French kings reduced the number of fleurs-de-lis on their arms to three, and the kings of England followed suit. British monarchs quartered the French Royal Arms until 1801, after the French mon-

archy had ceased to exist. Quartering indicates four divisions on a shield, but in fact the number of possible divisions is almost infinite. Families are entitled to quarterings if they have a descent in the male line from any forebear married to an heraldic heiress, that is, a woman entitled to arms who has no brothers (or deceased brothers without male issue). Marshalling by quartering is also possible when a 'name and arms' clause appears in a will. These were relatively frequent in the eighteenth and nineteenth centuries, and require beneficiaries to ask for a variation of the Laws of Arms, which state that arms descend down the legitimate male line. The beneficiary under the will (if unrelated) would need special permission from the sovereign (a Royal Licence) to put this clause into effect. This means that he could inherit property if he changes his name and arms to those of his benefactor, or adds the new name and arms to his.

Thomas powle
ond of the sixt part
of the Wynmylles

Rychard hewlett
of Sydnam in com
Kent

Antony butler
of Rolles in
com Lyncolne

Jane Collyns
wyffe to Edward
west

Stonyng

Robert Morley
de com north

John paterson
de London

Thomas wood
Brodene de
Barkshier

John Clyffe of forgrave
de com Kent

Olyver
Dawkesbury

William
Inffer

Myrygland
west

4
THE ART
OF HERALDRY

Peter Gwynn-Jones

LEFT: *Grants of William Hervey,
Clarenceux King of Arms, made
in 1559. These include arms for a
woman, Jane Collyns, the wife of
Edward West (top right).*

It is often assumed that most medieval armorial bearings have specific meaning. As many were no more than bands of contrasting colours or tinctures, much has been written to attribute qualities to each of these tinctures, and to arrange them in order of importance. This practice in England can be traced back to John de Bado Aureo who wrote his heraldic treatise, *Tractatus de Armis*, in the last years of the fourteenth century. De Bado Aureo and later writers distribute virtues to the tinctures in a variety of different ways. Gold, for example, shifts from being the tincture exclusively used by royalty to that associated with obedience. Faith was another attribute of gold and in this form it must have overlapped with blue as the tincture of loyalty. Blue varied as a tincture of war or of peace and friendship. There is nothing to suggest that medieval heraldry incorporated these ideas or that they have in any way affected post-medieval heralds in their task of creating and designing new armorial bearings. As Joseph Edmondson wrote in his *Complete Body of Heraldry*, in 1780, 'but as to such ridiculous fancies, the mere mention of them is fully sufficient'.

The numerous medieval arms featuring bands or stripes were greatly influenced by the twelfth-century Renaissance which awakened a love of decoration in the knightly classes. In addition, the structure of the shield was ideal for those who wished to decorate it in contrasting tinctures.

Any attempt to analyse early heraldry and the physical nature of the shield must take into account the Bayeux Tapestry, which depicts the Norman invasion of England in 1066. It shows knights armed with shields adorned with wavy geometrical designs and indeterminate dragon-like creatures. Twenty years later, in her eye-witness account of the First Crusade, the Byzantine princess Anna Comnena noted that the shields of Western European knights were plain with polished metal bosses and plates. Clearly, it is difficult to reconcile these two sources of evidence as it seems unlikely that the style and nature of shields would have altered so dramatically within 20 years. The Bayeux Tapestry designs almost certainly did not contribute to the heraldic designs which emerged approximately a century later. The centrifugal wavy patterns emanating from the centre of many shields on the Tapestry was not a formation found in early heraldry, which also had no place for dragon-like figures. Recently doubts have been cast on details found in

BELOW: *The Bayeux Tapestry – although not considered heraldic, the geometric configurations of the shields of knights have never been satisfactorily explained.*

LEFT: *Simple geometric forms of bars, bends and crosses in early medieval heraldry, seen in the College of Arms' Mowbray's Roll, painted c.1365-70.*

53

William Lorde Knowles, Baron of Grayes, Viscount Wallingford, Treasorer of his Maiesties Housholde, Maister of his Maties Court of Wardes and Lyueryes, Knight of the moste Noble order of the Garter, and one of his Maiesties moste honorable priuey Councell Anno . 1 6 1 6 .

the Tapestry, pointing out that some of the eating habits and items of dress depicted did not exist in Western Europe in 1066. There is a growing school of thought that later custodians of the Tapestry effected doodles and infillings; but until its threads are subjected to scientific examination, these doubts will remain unanswered. Given the possibility of later infillings, these shield decorations should be treated with a measure of suspicion.

Anna Comnena's account of plain shields with polished bosses and plates agrees with the general supposition that early twelfth-century shields were made of wood and covered on both sides with leather to which extra defences of metal were added. Exuberance of spirit and love of colour manifest in the twelfth-century Renaissance would allow for these bands of metal to be painted in contrasting tinctures. Similarly, studs and bosses, when painted in different colours would give rise to distinctive forms, which may have been the origin of many roundels or circles, the escarbuncle (a boss-like formation with decorated spokes) and some forms of heraldic cross which can be seen as a simpler form of the escarbuncle. Later theories often attribute the cross to the presence of the original user of the arms on a crusade. However, a shield strengthened with one vertical metal band and one horizontal one would provide a cross formation, and a decoratively-treated stud or boss could account for the variety of smaller crosses as individual heraldic charges.

The incidence of simple charges in early heraldry is manifested by the crescent. An analysis of *Smith's Ordinary*, a collation of medieval armorial bearings made in the sixteenth century, demonstrates the importance of the crescent. Out of the 9000 shields of arms depicted, 168 are listed under crescents – nearly one in 50 shields therefore bore this charge. It seems doubtful whether the medieval knights were inspired to adopt an Islamic device, as their later descendants have so often claimed, overlooking the fact that their ancestor often never partook in a crusade. Cognate heraldry may have played a part, that is to say the adoption of the crescent from the existing arms of a family connected by blood or feudal tenure. However, the frequency of the crescent suggests that its use had a more practical origin. The addition of a simple sliver of metal to a shield would serve to deflect an antagonist's weaponry; practicality in the twelfth century may have meant that the crescent was no more that a glancing device used to drive off a sword or an arrow at an oblique angle and a vital part of self-preservation in warfare.

The evidence that pieces of metal were used as deflecting devices on shields is given further credence by the mullet, shaped like a

ABOVE: *Crescents may have originated with pieces of metal hammered onto the shield to deflect weapons, as seen in the College of Arms'* Jenyn's Ordinary; *painted c.1380.*

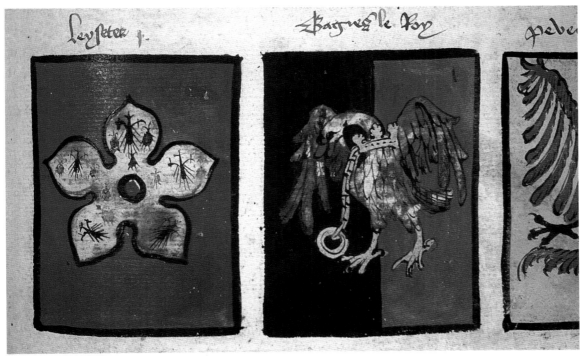

LEFT: *The swan badge of Bohun, inherited by Henry V through his mother, Mary Bohun, adjacent to the Leicester cinquefoil; painted c.1480.*

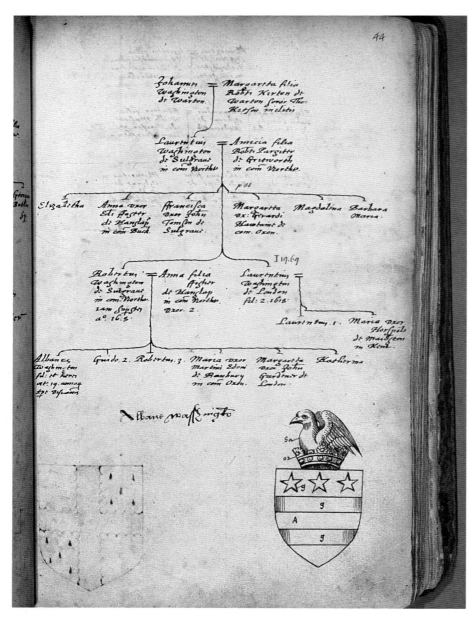

the principle of never placing colour (*Sable, Azure, Gules* or *Vert*) on colour, nor metal (*Argent* or Gold/*Or*) on metal. The limited use of green in early shields of arms is thus explained: it simply did not show up against the natural colours of the countryside.

In addition to permitting the structure of the shield to dictate the nature of much early heraldry, the medieval knight drew heavily upon fauna, exercising a subjective desire to be associated with the masculine and warlike characteristics of certain animal species. Many also wished to demonstrate a blood or feudal link with other families and the resultant grouping of families bearing similar arms is known as cognate heraldry.

The research of Sir Anthony Wagner, Clarenceux King of Arms, has admirably demonstrated the importance of the swan in cognate heraldry and in so doing has demonstrated that pre-heraldic legends may have provided the inspiration for certain heraldic charges. One eleventh-century legend tells of an unknown knight who disembarked from a river boat towed by a white swan in order to protect the widowed Duchess of Bouillon and her daughter Beatrice. His subsequent marriage to Beatrice imposed on her an oath never to question him as to his birth. A daughter, Ida, was born to the couple before Beatrice ultimately asked the fatal question. The Swan Knight departed as he came, never to be heard of again. Ida subsequently married Eustace, Count of Boulogne, and many of their descendants adopted the swan as their heraldic charge. Other versions relate that the Swan Knight rescued and married the widowed Duchess of Brabant, from whom sprang the ducal line of Cleves and other noble families, who also adopted the swan as a heraldic device.

The heraldry of the Washington family also exemplifies the cognate and the choice of a charge based on allegiance to another family. It is known that in 1182 one William de Hertburn purchased the manor of Wessyngton in County Durham, from which he and his descendants subsequently derived their surname, Washington. There is a plausible suggestion that the original William was the son of Patrick of Dunbar, the second son of Earl Gospatric of Dunbar. Certainly his thirteenth-century Washington descendants featured on their shield a lion similar to that of the Dunbar family. In 1278 Robert de Washington held the manor of Routhworth from the Barony of Kendal. The Barons of Kendal bore arms, *Argent two bars Gules*; and

ABOVE: *The Washington pedigree and armorial bearings entered at the Heralds' Visitation of Northamptonshire, 1615. The arms may have inspired the American flag.*

five-pointed star and frequently pierced in the centre. The term 'mullet' means 'little mill' or 'wheel', referring to the spur rowel. As a small, sharp piece of metal, it may have been hammered onto the shield for protective purposes and subsequently painted in contrasting tinctures to the background of the shield. *Smith's Ordinary* lists 280 shields charged with mullets. If mullets were used in this way, it is possible that charges such as annulets or rings, and billets or rectangles, may also have originated with pieces of metal employed as shield deflectors. Smith lists 93 and 73 shields for these charges respectively.

The practical nature of much early heraldry dictated by the structure of the shield can, to some extent, be seen in the choice of tinctures. Although these were seldom, if ever, chosen for symbolic reasons, a desire for recognition on the field of battle or tournament, and a love of bright colour gave rise to

FACING PAGE: *Martlets in the arms of Valence: tomb of Aylmer de Valence, Earl of Pembroke (died 1323) at Westminster Abbey.*

Robert de Washington and his descendants exchanged their lion for the well-known arms, *Argent two bars Gules in chief three mullets also Gules*. It is thought that these arms may have inspired the armorial bearings of the United States adopted by Congress in 1782, and the stars and stripes of the American flag.

A constantly recurring charge in medieval heraldry is the cinquefoil. This combines the cognate with the pun. Puns have always provided inspiration for the choice of charges from the inception of heraldry down to the present day. Some cinquefoils are now believed to have originated with the pimpernel flower adopted as a punning charge by Robert FitzPernell, Earl of Leicester. The earldom and the pimpernel flower, stylised into the cinquefoil, subsequently passed to Simon de Montfort, Earl of Leicester, in the thirteenth century. In the baronial wars which split England during the reign of Henry III, it seems likely that many of de Montfort's supporters incorporated the cinquefoil in their arms to demonstrate their allegiance.

This combination of punning and cognate heraldry can be discerned with many charges. It explains much of the popularity of the martlet (ie the swift, swallow or martin). Although the speed of the martlet probably had an attraction in its own right, other families such as Valence, Earls of Pembroke, and Arundel adopted it as a punning device. *Volans* means flying, and *hirondelle* is the French for swallow. Both these families were linked to other families who thereby chose the martlet to feature in their arms.

The pun explains the use of many inanimate charges which might otherwise have had limited or no appeal. Many inanimate charges fall into this category. Leaky is said to have borne water bougets or goatskin containers; Seffington bore scythes and Shakerley and Shuttleworth bore shuttles. Spades were adopted by the families of Standelf, Gardner and Swettenham: a *delf* is that which is delved or dug, and vigorous digging usually produces sweat. Inanimate charges such as bugle horns and horseshoes are also frequent in medieval heraldry. Horseshoes were borne by the families of Ferrers, Ferounes and Shoyswell; horns by the families of Horne, Horner, Forrester, and hence Foster and Forster.

Over the centuries a number of romantic tales have emerged to account for charges appearing in some medieval armorial achievements. Most of these tales are apocry-

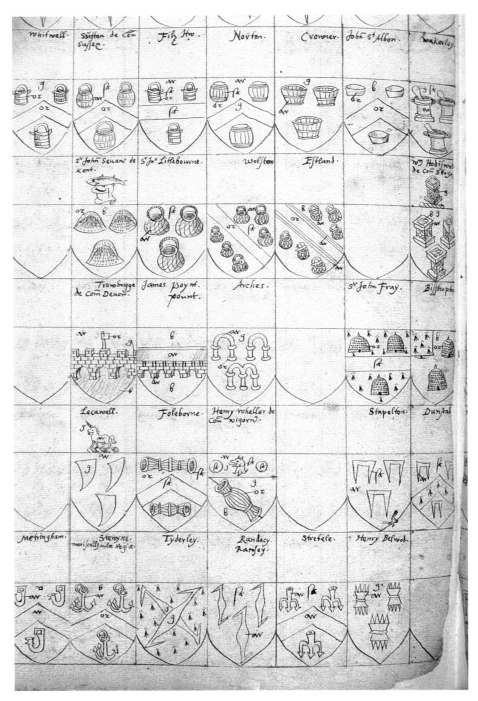

However, in dismissing fanciful tales, the sceptic must be wary, for a few medieval heraldic charges may owe their origin to unusual events. The heart in the arms of Douglas is one such example. In 1330 Sir James Douglas undertook to convey the heart of Robert Bruce to the Holy Sepulchre at Jerusalem in accordance with the latter's dying wish. Sir James was killed on the journey, and both his body and the heart of Bruce were brought back to Scotland, where the heart was incorporated into the arms of the Douglas family. Another legend which may be based on fact concerns the FitzGerald monkey. A tale is told of Thomas FitzMoric, the thirteenth-century ancestor of the FitzGerald Earls of Desmond. On the news of his father's death, 'Suddainly the nurses running forth cryeing and lamenting the childe was left all alone, when a monkey that was kept in the house tooke him out of the cradle, carried him to the topp of the castle, there unwrapped him out of swaddling clothes, licked and lapped the childe and folded ye child up in cloathes againe and . . . brought him downe againe in safety, and left the sayed child where first he found him, and finding the nurse settled by the cradle gave her a sound boxe on the eares, as it is thought thereby warneing and admonishing her to looke better hereafter to her charge'. The crest of the Earls of Desmond, however, is a boar, but another branch of the family, the Earls of Kildare, bear a monkey. This suggests that it may have been John FitzThomas FitzGerald, 1st Earl of Kildare, **an** exact contemporary of Thomas FitzMoric, who was

ABOVE: *A page from the sixteenth-century Smith's Ordinary showing inanimate objects in medieval arms; many were used as a punning allusion to the surname.*

RIGHT: *Although many families of Forester, Forster and Foster used stags or hunting horns as a punning allusion, one medieval family of Forster was more direct and used a forester himself, equipped with bow, arrows and horn.*

phal and do not stand the test of critical enquiry. Traditionally, the Prince of Wales' badge of feathers was adopted by Edward, the Black Prince, from the crest of the blind King John of Bohemia who was slain at the battle of Crécy. This story ignores two facts: the crest of King John consisted of two eagles' wings scattered with linden leaves, and the ostrich feathers are known to have been used by some of the Black Prince's brothers. It is now recognised that the feathers were introduced into English regal heraldry by Philippa of Hainault, the mother of the Black Prince, and the feathers are likely to be a punning allusion to Ostrevans, a county held by her family.

FAR LEFT: *An ostrich feather and the motto* HIC DIEN [Ich Dien] *shown as a badge of Edward III and now accepted as being derived from his wife Philippa of Hainault. Painted in the studio of Sir Thomas Wriothesley, Garter King of Arms, early sixteenth century.*

LEFT: *The heart of Robert Bruce in the arms of Sir James Douglas, Earl of Douglas and Avondale, c.1461. The crest is a dog-like salamander breathing fire (see chapter on heraldic monsters).*

carried off by the monkey. Here the legend recites that the infant was rescued by the castle monkey during a fire.

Moreiddig Warwyn was a twelfth-century Welsh chieftain who ruled over a territory roughly covered by Breconshire and North Carmarthenshire. Warwyn means 'fair neck' and may refer to a birthmark. Medieval superstition attributed this to an adder which frightened his mother while she was resting in a garden during her pregnancy. The mark of the snake was laid upon the neck of the child, his place of birth was named Lle-Dychrynllyd, the place of horror; and his descendants thereafter bore a boy's head with a snake entwined about the neck.

Towards the end of the Middle Ages several developments become apparent which were to influence the nature of future heraldry. Design began to break through the

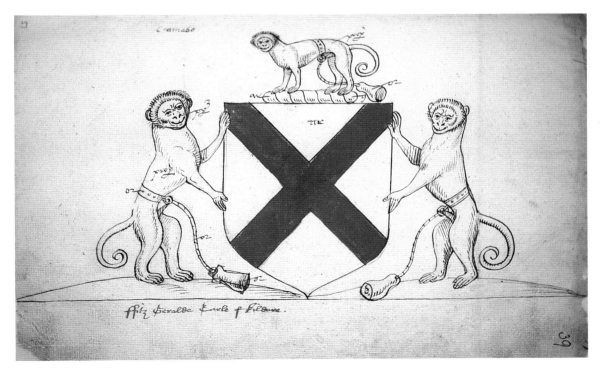

LEFT: *The FitzGerald monkey, supporters and crest of Gerald FitzGerald, Earl of Kildare, drawn c.1601.*

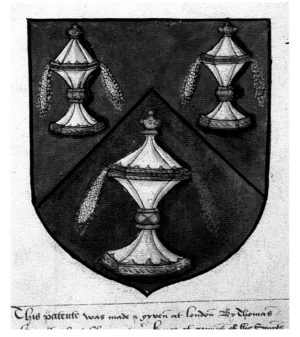

medieval reluctance to place one charge upon another. Invariably a fess or a chevron had been placed between three devices of similar nature. Gradually these devices were placed on the fess or chevron, making it possible to set three other charges in the blank areas of the shield. This new arrangement was to be exploited by the early Tudor heralds to provide a style of heraldic design far removed from anything known to their medieval predecessors.

A second development stems from the granting of arms to corporate bodies such as the mercantile companies of London, begin-

ning with the Drapers Company in 1438. These grants incorporated charges which reflected the craft or trade of the grantee and thus introduced a number of inanimate objects unknown to early heraldry. Charges long used as puns now acquired a new meaning as occupational heraldry. The arms of the Clothworkers Company granted in 1530, for example, featured the teasel, havettes and the ram. These charges recall the ancient crafts of fulling and shearing. New cloth was trampled in water for cleansing and thickening in a process known as fulling. Thereafter the fuller scoured the cloth with teasels or thistle

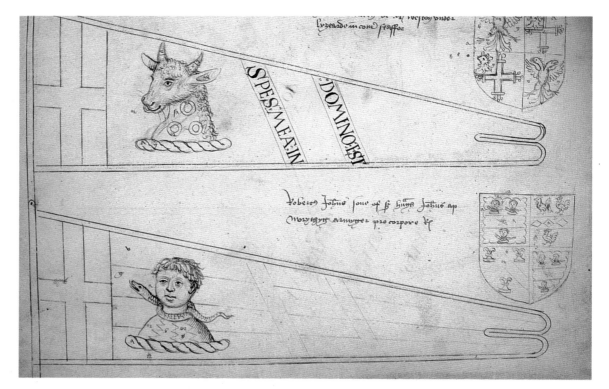

LEFT: *In later medieval heraldry devices appear charged on the Ordinaries. Examples from the Fenwick Roll, painted during the reign of Henry VI, include escallops on a bend, a lion on a chief, estoiles on a saltire, and lozenges on a bend.*

heads to remove loose particles and raise a nap before it was passed to the shearman, who stretched the material over a padded bench with the aid of a havette, a form of double hook. The crest of a ram is a clear allusion to the source of the raw material, but may also imply the shearman's stretching frame which in France was known as a *rame*. The choice of charges reflecting the grantee's career or occupation was increasingly to influence the nature of heraldry.

With the incorporation of the royal heralds in 1484, and the subsequent growth of Tudor bureaucracy, a better system of record-keeping came into existence. It therefore becomes gradually easier to ascertain the original grantee or bearer of the arms, to know more about him and the reasons why particular charges were chosen. At the same time the granting King of Arms can be identified and his particular preferences in design can be discerned.

In 1484 John Writhe was Garter King of Arms, a position which he held from 1478 to 1504. New grants of armorial bearings made by John Writhe and his fellow Kings of Arms during the two-year reign of Richard III numbered five, namely Whiting, Rede, Gough, Horton and the Company of the Wax Chandlers. Of the personal grants, only Rede included a crest, that of a duck, possibly a shoveller, *bendy Or* and *Argent*; his arms may be blazoned as *Gules on a bend wavy Argent three ducks Sable beaked and legged Gules*. The ducks, being birds frequenting reeds, are clearly a straightforward pun, showing that the pun as an inspiration of design was still in use. Of the remaining

ABOVE: *Typical grants of armorial bearings made by Sir Thomas Wriothesley, Garter King of Arms, 1505-34. Crests are made pale, bendy or checky and hold, or are placed between sprigs of foliage, and arms are heavily charged with different devices.*

RIGHT: *Blue and murrey, the livery colours of the house of York in the arms granted to Isabella Myberry, illegitimate daughter of Edward IV (right); the same marshalled with those of her husband John Awdeley (left).*

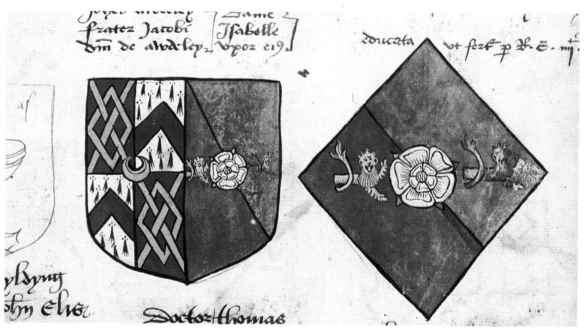

personal grants, Horton is notable for including a *fess compony countercompony between
three crossbows*. The reason behind the crossbows may be elusive; but the compony or
chequered fess was granted with the chequers
in blue and murrey, the livery colours of the
house of York. This inclusion of royal livery
colours is a feature of several fifteenth-
century grants and extends also to the blue
and white of the house of Lancaster. Cognate
heraldry, like punning heraldry, had survived the Middle Ages.

The apparent paucity of grants of armorial
bearings that can be attributed to John Writhe
and his colleagues at the end of the fifteenth
century is misleading. It was a period enormously rich in heraldic creation, but the
records of the College of Arms giving details
of specific grants are sparse. Badges and supporters proliferate, yet documentary Letters
Patent issued by the Kings of Arms granting
them seem non-existent. The power to grant
and confirm all armorial bearings had been
vested in the Kings of Arms since the early
fifteenth century, when this could have been
interpreted as applying only to the shield of
arms. Badges and supporters were therefore
not considered to come under royal jurisdiction, and Letters Patent would have been
unnecessary. Another reason for the lack of
documentary evidence may have been that it
was only the upper echelons of armigerous
society who assumed badges and supporters:
people whose gentility was never in doubt,
and who required no authority to prove their
social status. The style of heraldic designs in
this period, however, suggests a common
designing source, and it seems unlikely that
many people would have assumed arms
without recourse to the heralds. The monster
supporters of the late fifteenth century, such
as the pantheon, bagwyn and enfield, appear
to come from the imagination of one man or
group of men, presumably the heralds. The
Kings of Arms were therefore probably far
more active in granting arms than the surviving documents would imply, only issuing
Letters Patent to those whose right to bear
arms might be challenged. Discussion and informal sketches rather than formal documentation may also have been sufficient to produce arms. This may explain the absence of
any documentation for the grant of the College of Arms itself; none would query the
right of the Kings of Arms to grant armorial
bearings to their own corporation.

Writhe's son, Thomas Wriothesley, succeeded his father as Garter King of Arms in

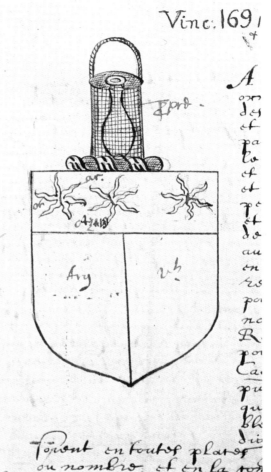

LEFT: Ung orynall dedens son
case en leurs propres coleurs, *a
urinal in its basket, granted as a
crest by John Writhe, Garter
King of Arms, to Louis Caerlion,
1493.*

BELOW: *Typical of puns used by
Sir Thomas Wriothesley, Garter
King of Arms, is the rabbit
within a warren, the crest in the
grant of armorial bearings made to
Ralph Warren of London,
c.1528, who subsequently became
Lord Mayor in 1536.*

1505, an office he held until 1534. Wriothesley and his contemporary Thomas Benolt, Clarenceux King of Arms, 1511–34, were responsible for a period of heraldry unique in its creativity and distinctiveness. Approximately 500 Wriothesley/Benolt arms have been identified. With the exception of those made to women and clergymen, all include a crest, which was a major break with medieval practice. Until the early sixteenth century, crests were borne by the limited few of tournament rank, whose attributes in the fifteenth century also included supporters. Wriothesley and Benolt now allowed crests to be granted with all arms, while restricting the use of supporters; and this practice has continued to the present day. A typical Wriothesley/Benolt crest was subject to an exaggerated form of the art and science of heraldry previously found in the shield. Crests of animals were therefore divided by a paly, barry, quarterly or bendy formation charged with additional devices, and were frequently provided with a sprig of foliage to hold in beak or claw. The shield itself drew heavily upon the late fifteenth-century practice of charging Ordinaries with a further device; typical arms of the Wriothesley period contained two or three charges in combination with an Ordinary such as a chevron or fess, in stark contrast to medieval heraldry where only one such charge would have been used. The result is arguably cluttered and lacking in control; but it is nonetheless exciting and allowed English heraldry to break away from its medieval restrictions, providing for future freedom of design.

The reasoning behind Wriothesley's choice of charges is too often obscure. Cognate heraldry accounts for the frequent use of blue and murrey, the livery colours of the house of York, which had been adopted by the Tudors in addition to their more familiar colours of green and white. Similarly, association with the Crown doubtless accounts for the many Wriothesley grants incorporating the greyhound which was, *par excellence*, the royal beast of the Tudors. (Henry VII used two greyhounds as his supporters.) Occupational heraldry, as found in the arms of fifteenth-century mercantile companies, is not immediately obvious. In 1493 John Writhe had granted Louis Caerlion, Doctor of Medicine, the crest of a urinal in a basket. During the Wriothesley period such an obvious allusion to the grantee's occupation seems to have been confined to simple charges, for example, bezants or gold roundels for a goldsmith.

In contrast, the heraldry of Wriothesley and Benolt is liberally sprinkled with puns; Edmund Haselwood's crest is typical: *a squirrel sejant Azure collared and charged with three roundels in pale Or and grasping a branch of hazel Vert fructed Or*. Ralph Warren was granted the crest of: *a mount Vert environed of a palisade Or thereon a rabbit statant Sable eared and footed Or about the neck a collar compony Argent and Gules cottised Or*. The crest of Richard Chopping was: *an oak tree Vert fructed Or the trunk bendy wavy of four Argent and Gules thereon a green woodpecker proper*. (The woodpecker is, of course, the ornithological chopper.) The crest of John Chrystmas sports a cubit arm grasping a branch of holly, as do the crests of William Hollys and William Grene. John Pasmere was granted the crest of: *a demi sea hare Azure scaled Argent the ears and forefeet Gold*. 'Puss' is a term still used by beaglers for the hare and *mare* is Latin for sea.

The mid-sixteenth century witnessed a return to simplicity in design for which Thomas Hawley, Clarenceux King of Arms from 1536 to 1557, would appear to be largely responsible. Hawley favoured engrailed crosses or chevrons, placing these between animals or animals' heads. His grants demon-

LEFT: *A page of crests granted by Sir Thomas Wriothezley, in which three arms hold bunches of holly as a pun on the surnames of Chrystmas, Hollys and Grene.*

strate that the personal whims and tastes of individual heralds have played a major part in heraldic design and the choice of charges. At times these seem to have dominated, to the near exclusion of any wishes or preferences of the grantee.

There was also a large increase in the number of grants of arms, and recent evidence suggests it may have been by as much as ten-fold. It is now known that Hawley's successor, William Hervey, Clarenceux King of Arms from 1557 to 1567, was responsible for approximately 80 grants a year. Many of these relate to the growing number of Court officials and members of the professional and mercantile classes. A typical page of Hervey grants in the official records of the College of Arms contains 23 entries, with grants to the Queen's physician, a skinner of London, a sergeant at law, an alderman of London, a doctor of the arches, a knight, a Londoner, a gentleman of unspecified location or occupation, a gentleman of Devon, a Londoner, a water bailey of London, another Londoner, a gentleman of Warwickshire, a gentleman of Norfolk, another of unspecified residence, another of Cornwall, two master cooks to the Queen's Majesty, the Lord Mayor of London, the latter's wife, a gentleman of Kingston in Surrey, and two goldsmiths of London.

By 1584, the centenary of the College of Arms, the simplification of heraldic design first seen under Hawley as a reaction to the Wriothesley period had intensified, and was being applied to a growing number of new grantees. The heraldry of 1584 was largely the responsibility of the industrious Robert Cooke, Clarenceux King of Arms.

William Segar, Garter King of Arms from 1604 to 1633, wrote of Cooke that he 'confirmed and gave Armes and Crests without number to base and unworthy persons for his private gaine onely, without the knowledge

LEFT: *Sea hare crest of Joan Pasmere, granted c.1520. 'Puss' is a term used for a hare, and mare is Latin for sea.*

of the Erle Marshall'. 1584 was certainly a year of activity in Cooke's office. *Hare's Ordinary* lists 25 Cooke grants specifically for that year. Of other undated grants from this same source, between 14 and 21 are likely to have fallen within the same period, which suggests that Cooke was approaching something in the region of a new grant each week. However, this is misleading. It is now known that Cooke's predecessor, William Hervey, granted approximately 80 new grants a year. There is every reason to suppose that Cooke accelerated this rate. The troublemaker Ralph Brooke, York Herald, accused Cooke of making nearly 500 grants over 30 years, a figure long accepted as reflecting the late Tudor situation. An analysis, however, considerably exceeds this figure. Furthermore, there are late Tudor armorials in the College which would seem to relate exclusively to contemporary grants. Taking these factors into account, it seems that Brooke's statement is missing a nought – the figure intended was 5000 and not 500. For genealogists, this sheds new light on the Heralds' Visitations, which are not so much a record of old arms-bearing families, but of new Tudor grantees; current research is showing that in mid- to late Tudor Visitations, it is usually the man who heads the pedigree who was the original recipient of the armorial bearings. Cooke may therefore

have granted as many as 150 new armorial bearings in 1584 alone.

Cooke's style is in stark contrast to the complexity of Wriothesley/Benolt heraldry. He made full use of the Ordinaries, generally leaving these plain. When he departed from this, it was usually to adopt the engrailed line, although other varied lines were avoided. Twelve examples of engrailing occur in 100 consecutive grants made around 1584. The Ordinaries were then combined with an additional charge, repeated three times when fess or chevron were used, or five when placed between or on a cross or saltire. In only seven out of these same 100 grants is a further additional charge to be found. These charges were essentially traditional: lions, lions' heads, faces and gambs, boars' heads, mullets and escallops abound in Cooke's heraldry. The result is neat and well-composed, but arguably it remains somewhat dull. Gone is the exuberance of early Tudor heraldry which, for all its lack of balance and control in design, possessed excitement and a sense of innovation.

As with Cooke's arms, so his crests relied heavily on traditional charges. In 25 consecutive Cooke crests granted in 1584 there feature two human arms, two lions, two eagles, a phoenix, a dove, a fox, a talbot, a bull, a swan, a gryphon, an ermine, an ounce, a tyger, an ostrich and a fleur-de-lis.

These crests are then differenced in a simple way; issuing from, or gorged with, a coronet being a much favoured expedient. The more exotic creatures found a hundred years before, such as the pantheon, bagwyn and enfield, were generally eschewed, and the heraldry of 1584 provided nothing new to take their place. It may be thought that this conservatism was to Cooke's own taste, but perhaps it reflected a wider and popular sentiment that new heraldry should be traditional. This view was to become increasingly apparent during the next hundred years.

By 1684 the conservatism of heraldry was such that its survival seemed in question. Linked with the increasingly unpopular Heralds' Visitations, soon to be terminated with the final Visitation of London in 1687, heraldry appeared ill-suited to adapt to the changing times. On the one hand there was a failure to innovate which might otherwise have provided an outlet for creative heraldic design. On the other hand there was the apparent inability, perhaps excusable under the existing circumstances, to check the growing number of 'new men', the product of increasing economic and social changes, from quietly appropriating or self-assuming armorial bearings to which they had no entitlement. This situation was to reach its nadir in the first decade of the eighteenth century, but a measure of its seriousness was already apparent at the bicentenary of the College of Arms in 1684. The number of grants made in

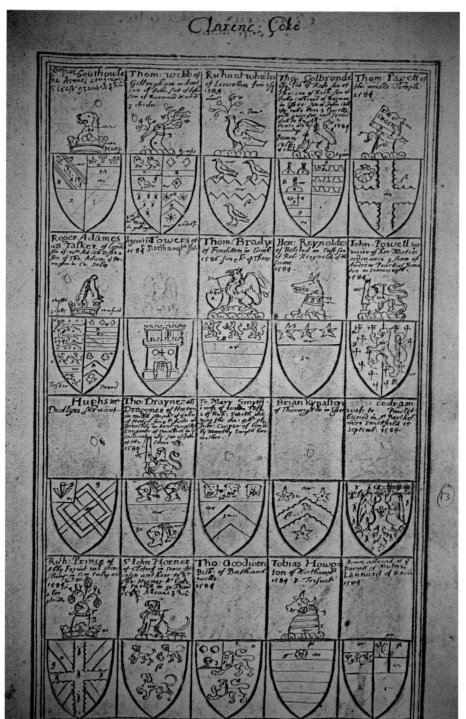

that year was only eight. Of these eight, one was to a corporate body, the Corporation of Clergymen's Sons, a charity established for the relief of the widows and children of clergymen. A gloomy grant made at a gloomy time in the history of heraldry, it was blazoned as *lozengy Argent and Sable on a chief Purpure a cross paty Or between two books opened Argent the leaves cover and clasps Gold*; and for the crest: *the Efigies of Charitie standing on a wreath of the colours of the field habited in a loose Garment Sable, her face, breast, hands and feet proper, her hair dishevelled Or, accompanied with three naked boys, vis one on her dexter side*

ABOVE: *Grants of Robert Cooke, Clarenceux King of Arms, made in 1584 and contained in* Hare's Ordinary.

LEFT: *The armorial bearings of the Corporation of Clergymen's Sons, granted 1684.*

RIGHT: *The armorial bearings granted in 1784 to the brothers Charles and William Smith suggest that good composition and design were not always of importance in late eighteenth-century heraldry.*

BELOW: *The armorial bearings of John Zephaniah Holwell, Governor of Bengal, and survivor of the Black Hole of Calcutta, granted in 1762.*

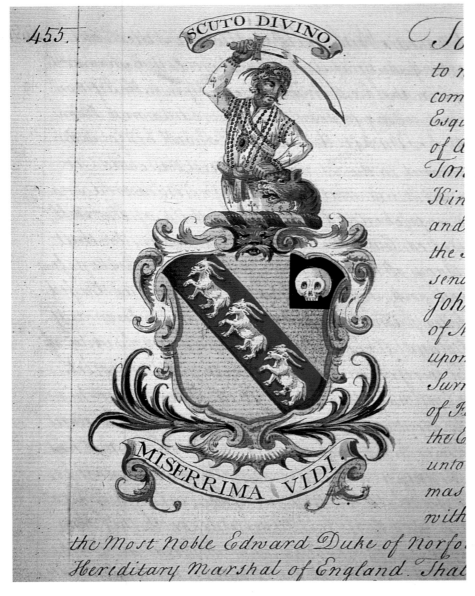

and the other in her arms all proper and crined Gold. If the depressing nature of this design is anything of a guide, it is perhaps as well that heraldry found no major outlet in new corporate grants at this time. Such was not to happen for many years to come.

Of the remaining seven grants made in 1684, one was to John Dugdale, Windsor Herald, being arms for his wife, Elizabeth, the daughter and heir of Thomas Pigeon: *Azure a chevron between three pigeons' heads erased Argent.* Presumably a grant to a herald is a good indication of the taste prevailing at the time. That taste would not appear to have changed from the days of Robert Cooke. Six grants remained for other individuals: a Doctor of Physick from Norwich, the Recorder of the City of London, one of the chaplains-in-ordinary to the king, an ex-High Sheriff of Hertfordshire, an alderman and sometime mayor of Cambridge, and a would-be gentleman from St Albans. The design of these 1684 grants is notable in that it differs little from that of the Cooke era. Only the pegasus crest of the Doctor of Physick provides a little interest among otherwise plain-lined Ordinaries, lions, eagles, roses and other familiar and conservative charges. Much has been written praising the qualities of late seventeenth- and early eighteenth-century heralds. Dugdale and Anstis are famous names, and none doubts their ability as scholars, administrators and genealogists, but as heralds creating new heraldry their record is nothing less than abysmal.

By 1784 the position had improved, with 40 new grants being made. Of these, many were based on earlier armorial bearings which had hitherto been used by the grantee without proper authority. Some families were at least being made aware that appropriating the arms of another family of the same surname with whom there was no known connection was not a proper way to behave, and were proceeding to have grants of armorial bearings in their own right.

Other grants of 1784 exemplify a groping for new ideas. Typical of this is the grant to Charles Smith, an officer in the Royal Artillery, and to his brother William Smith, a captain in the East India Company. The arms manifest the use of dissimilar charges scattered with Ordinaries and Sub-Ordinaries with little sense of design. The charges are obvious, relating as they do to the careers of the two grantees with a different crest for each brother. However, it can be argued that this choice of the obvious in late eighteenth-century heraldry was too often made at the expense of the aesthetic.

The importance attached to the meaning of charges during this period, at the apparent expense of design and good composition, is demonstrated by a number of grants which recite a specific event in the grantee's life which subsequently inspired the choice of a particular device. In 1762 a grant of armorial bearings was made to John Zephaniah Holwell, sometime Governor of Bengal. His armorial bearings are blazoned as: *Or on a bend Gules three goats passant Argent attired and unguled of the field on a canton sinister Sable a human skull proper*, with this motto MISERRIMA VIDI; *and for the crest a demi-man representing Surajud Dowla, Subah of Bengal in his complete dress, the left hand resting on the head of a tiger inspired with fury the right hand grasping a scimitar in attitude of striking the blade broken all proper and over it this motto* SCUTO DIVINO. The Letters Patent to John Zephaniah Holwell then recites at some length the events leading up to 'the dreadful Confinement and Suffocation in the Black Hole Prison in Fort William at Calcutta in the East Indies in the nights preceding the 20th day of June one thousand seven hundred and fifty six', during which 'One Hundred and Forty Six being crammed into a Dungeon at Eight o'clock in the Evening from whence the said John Zephaniah Holwell and Twenty Two more only survived at Six in the Morning . . .'

In the same grant book is that made in 1758 to John Garmston of the City of Lincoln, whose gruesome crest is blazoned as *a shark's head regardant and couped Argent swallowing a negro man proper* with the motto OPERA DEI MIRIFICA. Regrettably the recital does not tell the tale which must lie behind this choice of crest, and one is left to wonder whether the unfortunate victim survived his ordeal.

The tiger in the crest granted to Robert Adams in 1732 was not so lucky. The recital of the Letters Patent states that Adams, when Governor of the Coast of Malabar in 1729, was 'attacked by a tiger who seized him by the left Arm the marks whereof are Still to be seen, but through Providence he had the good fortune to destroy that furious Beast by ripping open his Belly with a Lance that his Guts fell out and immediately died on the spot . . .'

John Hockin, Vicar of Oakhampton and Rector of Lydford in Devonshire, received a grant of armorial bearings in 1764, which recited that 'in Time of War with France, at the Beginning of Queen Anne's reign a large

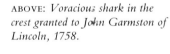

ABOVE: *Voracious shark in the crest granted to John Garmston of Lincoln, 1758.*

LEFT: *The tiger killed by Robert Adams, Governor of the Coast of Malabar, was granted in his arms and crest, 1732.*

69

RIGHT: *The arms granted to John Hockin in 1764 commemorate his father's single-handed repulsion of a French raiding party.*

HOCIN DEUS RUPES LOCO

pretend to use them without lawful Auth
John Hockin, Clerk, Master of Arts.

French privateer cruising in the Bristol Channel, came to Anchor off an Estate called Godrevey then in the possession of John Hockin his Grandfather before mentioned who was one of the principal Inhabitants of the Parish, and it being conjectured that the Privateer's Intent was to send in her Boat to plunder the House which stood alone, and carry off the Cattle from the Estate, The said John Hockin and his Family were alarmed and collected their Friends and Neighbours to keep Watch that Night on the Cliff or Beach. At Daybreak they all dispersed, thinking the Danger over but just as Thomas Hockin, His father aforesaid, a young Man was getting into Bed, another person whose Fears had led him out more than once to take a View, came in a great hurry and told him that a Boat full of Men was making for the Shore as fast as they could row, on which the said Thomas Hockin slipped on his Clothes and catching up a Gun and a Pole to feign the appearance of another ran out and down a steep hill to the Sea in sight of the Boat from whence he was fired at several Times, and then got behind a Rock which served him as a Breastwork and from thence with his one Gun only fired on the Boat with so much vigour and Effect as to prevent the Crews Landing, and at last make them turn about and row back again to their Ship as fast as they could . . .' The Arms of Hockin commemorate this event by depicting the English lion with gun and scattered French fleurs-de-lis in the sea.

Another marine episode is celebrated in the grant of 1828 to Thomas Stott of the City of Quebec, sometime Paymaster of the 29th Regiment of Foot, and in 1828 Paymaster of the 4th Royal Veteran Battalion. His Letters Patent recite that 'in the night of 10th November 1816, being on board the Harpooner Transport on his Voyage from Canada to England, the Ship struck on a Rock off the Island of Newfoundland where the Memorialist and two hundred and six other Persons only out of a Crew of three hundred and eight four Souls were most providentially saved by means of a Rope conveyed by an English Bull Dog which swam to an uninhabited part of the Island previously reached by some Sailors from the wreck . . .' The crest granted for Stott was blazoned as *issuant out of waves of the sea a demi bull dog proper around his neck and reflexed over the back a Log line Or holding between the paws a Wreath of Oak fructed also proper.*

It is perhaps regrettable that the practice of reciting events which dictated the choice of charges was discontinued, leaving the observer of heraldic design to guess as to the reasoning behind the choice. However, this loss was more than compensated by the refreshing developments in heraldic design which had occurred by 1884. The number of new grantees had more than doubled and numbered 82 in 1884. Of these, three were impersonal: the Borough of Harrogate, the Borough of Ramsgate, and the newly-constituted Diocese of Southwell. Although only a small number, it marked the beginning of a resurgence in corporate heraldry.

Of personal grants, supporters for new peers numbered only three and included those to Lord Tennyson: *two leopards guardant Gules ducally crowned and semi of fleurs de lis Gold.* There was also the grant of supporters by Royal Licence to a baronet, Sir Henry William Dashwood: *two male gryphons Argent gorged with a collar flory counter flory.* This exemplifies something of the new spirit in heraldry with the reintroduction of a fifteenth-century

creature so untypical of the conservative heraldry of the intervening centuries. The grants of 1884 included one to a single woman, Sophy Felicite de Rodes. Grants to women have never been numerous, but they have been consistent and may today be poised to take a greater percentage of the total.

71

RIGHT: *The arms of Pring, granted 1884, use the varied line (ie the dovetailed pale) and place this between four annulets, an arrangement characteristic of the period.*

PETIT ALTA

BELOW: *One of the first badges to be granted after their revival in 1906 was the crowned catamountain's face of Sir Alfred Scott-Gatty, Garter King of Arms.*

The number of grantees from overseas in 1884 had risen, which reflects the imperial expansion of the age. There were six, among them being Sir John Hall, the Prime Minister of New Zealand, the Rajah Oodai Pertab Sing of Bhinga, and James Matthew Taylor, vice-consul in Corfu. Grants to the administrative and professional classes also increased. Those in the Commission of the Peace in 1884 accounted for 16 grantees, suggesting that a concerted effort was being made to approach Justices of the Peace to ensure that they became properly armigerous. The Church, the Law, the Army and medicine account for four, three, three and two respectively. There is also an officer of Arms, Arthur Staunton Larken, Richmond Herald.

No attempt was made in 1884 to introduce new charges. Even the unusual, such as the snail, cameleopard and the Dashwood male gryphons were reintroductions rather than creatures making their first appearance in heraldry. The lion accounts for 15 crests, the human arm for ten, the stag six and the eagle five, showing that long-used charges were still preferred.

Nonetheless, in contrast to 1784, the heraldry of 1884 is refreshing. It manifests a new and frequently successful approach to design. There is a spirited treatment and rearrangement of charges, particularly in arms. The segmented heraldry, that is to say the placing of different and frequently discordant charges above and below fess or chevron, is largely absent. Good design suggested that two identical charges above a chevron should be repeated by a third identical charge beneath. Varied lines are used to cover the more unusual forms, such as flory, counterflory, dovetailed, and rayonny. Ordinaries are frequently cotised; crosses are parted and fretted, made formy or botonny; and there is a liberal use of gouttes, ermine spots and party divisions.

By 1884 it is also clear that the traditional arrangements were beginning to break down. No longer was it necessary to place three charges on a bend, fess or chevron. Two greyhounds are courant on a bend and five horseshoes are charged on a chevron. A fess is set between two talbots' heads, and there is a cross couped charged with four bombs all between two anchors; the heraldry of earlier centuries would have used three talbots' heads, two above the fess and one below, and five bombs with four anchors.

The heraldry of 1884 is simple, neat and interesting, with a unity in its design and none

LEFT: *The arms of Culham of New Zealand bring together a crowned hammer (a culling implement) and a boar's head (a further allusion to ham), to create a badge-like device. This is then used as a single charge to be repeated three times in the shield, demonstrating the influence of badge formations in the arms of twentieth-century heraldry.*

of the segmented clutter with which this period is so often wrongly credited. Two names stand out as designers, and any history of heraldry must give them due credit. They are Alfred Scott-Gatty, Rouge Dragon Pursuivant, and Henry Farnham Burke, Rouge Croix Pursuivant. Both of them were destined to become Garter King of Arms.

In 1984, the quincentennial year of the College of Arms, the number of grantees had risen to 191. Of these, 28 were impersonal, demonstrating an upsurge in corporate heraldry. Twelve came from overseas, including a grant to the University of Hong Kong. Local authorities accounted for 11 of these 28 grants. The remainder were diverse: the Australian Shipping Commission, the Chartered Institute of Building, the Roman Catholic Diocese of Toronto and the Engineering Council.

Grants from overseas may have constituted a high percentage of corporate grants, but personal grants from overseas were surprisingly low, only 23 out of a total of 191. Ten were honorary grants to Americans, an enigmatic source which may develop in the future, seven were Canadian and there were three each from Australia and New Zealand. The small number of personal grants from Australia in 1984 is in contrast to greater numbers in previous years. The five grants to Australian corporate bodies in 1984 do, however, show that heraldry is thriving in that country.

The year 1906 saw the revival of the badge; and its use and development is characteristic of twentieth-century heraldry. There were no known grants of badges between the sixteenth century and 1906, but in 1984 there were 73. In the Middle Ages badges were borne by followers and retainers of armigerous individuals. Today they are used by bodies or people associated with a corporate body, or by members of the grantee's family, such as non-armigerous sons-in-law, and grandchildren in the female line, who are not entitled to bear and use the arms and crest.

The reappearance of the badge has been a major factor influencing design in arms where styles have become increasingly diverse and ingenious. As the badge is freestanding and not enclosed within the restricted area of a shield, it has encouraged the combining of charges to provide a single new device which has then been introduced into the arms. Typical examples of this are fleurs-de-lis with the petals terminating in animals' heads, or with the outer petals extending into wings; a harp terminating in a stag's head; martlets flying through coronets; pickaxes enfiling mullets; and a variety of charges encircled by annulets, frequently treated with a compound outer edge, such as embattled or potenty. The medieval leopard's face, *jessant de lis*, now has many successors, following its tradition of combining separate charges to form a single device. The badge may also be influencing the positioning of charges. As badges are often circular or symmetrical in design, this has encouraged a realignment of charges in arms so that they no longer all point upwards or face to the dexter. Heraldry

BELOW: *The armorial bearings of the All England Lawn Tennis and Croquet Club (Wimbledon); sport and the arts are major factors in twentieth-century heraldry, with grants of arms made to corporate bodies and leisure allusions contained in the arms of individuals.*

is now rich in examples of animals respecting (facing) each other, and flora and inanimate objects with stalks or apexes pointing inwards or outwards. With this has come a further move away from the traditional two-one arrangement of upright charges. The positioning of the Sclater bees and the Tesco cloves provide examples (see illustrations in the chapter on fauna and flora).

A less rigid attitude to heraldic design during the twentieth century has manifest itself in several ways, particularly with the wider use of unusual Ordinaries and Sub-Ordinaries; the flaunch, for example, is now much favoured. Curiously this is not true of the varied lines, where only embattled and wavy have held their own. Similarly gouttes and ermine spots are much less apparent. There is no doubt that this freedom of design in modern heraldry has allowed for the continuous rearrangement of traditional charges, rather than a search for new ones. The principal exception to this is found with the use of flora and fauna from around the world, although many such charges are rapidly becoming, or have become, traditional. The maple leaf and the wattle are obvious examples of this, as are the lyrebird and the Australian magpie. All were absent in 1884, but are familiar charges in current heraldry.

Novel inanimate charges in the 1980s were rare. There was some oriental weaponry, a cream-skimmer, a pair of swivels and the prow of a Viking ship in 1982–83, and the following year produced a ko (a Maori digging stick) and a koruru (a Maori carved head), a tuning cone, and a reed hook. There were also signs that chemical symbols had begun to establish themselves in heraldry, with the appearance of the DNA chain, the benzene ring and conventional representations of a neutron and an atom. There is no doubt that the benzene ring in particular will become increasingly popular as a simple and distinctive heraldic charge.

The choice of charges in the second half of the twentieth century frequently reflects the occupation and career of the grantee or his ancestors. The pun is still apparent, and cognate heraldry is widely used in the sense of taking charges from the arms of a county or school with which the grantee has been associated. A new and important source of design inspiration is provided by the leisure pursuits of the grantee, which have provided scope for subtle use of the Ordinaries and Sub-Ordinaries. Pily arms can suggest a backgammon board; and when piles Argent are

The Armorial Bearings of the
ROYAL PHILHARMONIC ORCHESTRA

College of Arms
London

Bluemantle Pursuivant of Arms

voided and engrailed on a blue field, they suggest coral and are suitable for those with snorkelling interests in tropical waters. Similarly, mountaineering, camping and sailing need not be represented by realistic crampons, tents or sailing boats. A lozengy or checky field can be effective. If each lozenge is divided per fess Argent and Azure, a series of snow-capped mountain peaks against the sky is suggested. Similarly, if the Azure is rendered Vert, the effect of tents in the countryside is obtained. Chequers divided per bend Argent and Azure provide white sails on a blue sea. Those interested in the theatre have recently made use of papillonny, a rare field used during the Middle Ages which is reputed to be derived from scales of a butterfly's wing. Papillonny can suggest the seats in an auditorium. It has recently spread

ABOVE: *The armorial bearings of the Royal Philharmonic Orchestra incorporate violin bridges in arms and badge, an example of a new inanimate charge in heraldry.*

ABOVE: *The use of simple field divisions can suggest leisure pursuits, for example, sailing (top left), camping (top right), mountaineering (bottom left) and photography, with a vairy potenty field providing a series of black camera formations (bottom right).*

RIGHT: *The armorial bearings of Mead, granted 1975, show that simple yet distinctive heraldry can still be obtained in the twentieth century. The arms combine the pun of green and yellow fields for meads or meadows, with an allusion to the grantee's ancestry, which had connections with America. The two flaunches suggest the continents of North America and Europe.*

FACING PAGE: *Papillonny field in the arms of Holborn Law Tutors suggesting seats in an auditorium; the nuts are the fruit of the hazel, the ancient tree of wisdom.*

from leisure heraldry into educational heraldry, where it can also represent seats, as in the arms of the Holborn Law Tutors, and into occupational heraldry where it implies roof tiles.

The means by which heralds arrive at a suitable design has probably altered very little since the fifteenth or sixteenth century. It therefore serves to describe the process as it operates today. An approach is made by the would-be grantee to the College of Arms, the Court of Lord Lyon (in Scotland), or the requisite authority under whose jurisdiction he or she comes. At the College of Arms such approaches are either made to a herald known to the grantee or to the College in general. If the latter is the case, then the grantee becomes the responsibility of the herald-in-waiting (ie on duty) at the time. The first job of a herald is to ensure that the grantee is eligible for a grant of arms to be made by the Kings of Arms, who are empowered to grant only to 'eminent' men and women. In practice, anyone who holds a civil or military commission, a university degree or professional qualification, or who has achieved a measure of distinction in a field beneficial to society as a

whole is eligible to bear arms. Similarly, grants of armorial bearings are made to corporate bodies such as local authorities, places of education, professional bodies and leading commercial companies. The herald, acting as agent to the Kings of Arms, will then draft the relevant petition or memorial, addressed to the Earl Marshal. If the latter approves the application, he issues his Warrant to the Kings of Arms to grant such armorial bearings as they deem suitable.

The herald and grantee draw up an acceptable design together. For the herald's part, he must ensure that the design is distinctive in its own right; and that being different from anything already on the register, it constitutes in the full sense a new coat of arms. It is also his job to uphold the principles of good heraldry, and to be the guardian of good heraldic taste. Within this limitation, however, it is right and proper that the grantee should be allowed whatever charges he wishes. In practice, few grantees come forward with firm proposals for a design, and leave the herald to use his own ideas and methods to produce suitable arms. Individual allusions and charges are perhaps less important than the ultimate visual effect of the design; they are simply a means to achieve a distinctive and pleasing result. The process has provided rich and varied results in the past and should ensure that heraldry has an exciting future.

POTESTAS·EX·VOLUNTATE

Lancaster

POTESTAS·EX·VOLUNTATE

Ex.ᵈ

C·S
Y+R
Pᵗ ˡⁿᵍ

TO ALL and SINGULAR to whom these Presents shall come, Sir Alexander Colin Cole, Knight Commander of the Royal Victorian Order, upon whom has been conferred the Territorial Decoration; Garter Principal King of Arms, Sir Anthony Richard Wagner, Knight Commander of the Most Honourable Order of the Bath, Knight Commander of the Royal Victorian Order; Clarenceux King of Arms, and John Philip Brooke Brooke Little, Esquire; Commander of the Royal Victorian Order; Norroy and Ulster King of Arms Send Greeting! Whereas Valerie Aggett Feme Sole, Bachelor of Laws of the University of Durham, Solicitor of the Supreme Court of England & Wales, Principal of Holborn Law Tutors Limited hath represented unto The Most Noble Miles Francis Stapleton

le Roy Edward

5
HERALDIC
MONSTERS

Peter Gwynn-Jones

LEFT: *Dragon supporter to the attributed arms of King Cadwalader, painted in the early sixteenth century.*

Popular belief has a tendency to credit heraldry with the invention of gryphon, unicorn, cockatrice and other fabulous monsters. Such a belief, though flattering to past heralds, is far from the truth. Any understanding of heraldic monsters must take into account the medieval bestiary, that curious compilation based on the work of Physiologus who, at some unknown date between the second and fifth centuries AD, wrote his book of beasts. This book later grew with the factual and fanciful additions of many writers, until it finally evolved into a kind of zoological scrapbook, proving one of the most popular and avidly read works of the Middle Ages. No attempt was made to differentiate between fact and fancy, the medieval mind happily accepting that the gryphon or unicorn were as real as the familiar animals of the domestic farmyard.

Although the occasional monster of the bestiary found its way into early heraldry, it was not until the fifteenth century that heraldry turned its attention in earnest to this source, and began that steady recruitment of the fabulous which was to reach a climax during the Tudor period. The zoologist, meanwhile, turned to science and, following the sixteenth-century Swiss naturalist Conrad Gesner, began collecting specimens at first hand and noting the finds of the new explorers and discoverers of the wider world. The process of discarding the monster in favour of real, though less exotic, creatures had begun and, but for its preservation by the heralds, it might have been destined for complete obscurity.

The gryphon was probably the first of these bestiary monsters to find its way into heraldry. As early as 1167 it features on the seal of Richard de Redvers, Earl of Essex. Bestiary accounts state that the gryphon had the size and strength of over 100 eagles and the ability to seize and carry off an ox in each foot. It was guardian of mines of gold, hidden in the high mountains where it built its nest which was lined with the precious metal. There are accounts of a feud between gryphons and a race of horseborne Scythians who attempted to steal this gold. Bitter antipathy arose between gryphons and horses, which suggests that the charging of a gryphon on a shield of arms may have been a deliberate attempt by the medieval knight to instil fear into the horses of his opponents. Goblets in the shape of gryphons' claws or eggs were highly prized in the courts of medieval Europe, and were usually made from antelope horns and ostrich eggs. The gryphons' gold can be traced back to Aristeas, a Greek of the seventh century BC. This remarkable traveller reached the mountains of central Asia and returned to report of a people who stole gold from fearsome creatures which he called gryphons. There is much here to suggest that the creature was the bearded vulture or lammergeyer, a huge bird with a wingspan of nearly ten feet, which nests in inaccessible cliffs in the Asiatic mountains. In spite of sceptical zoologists, the lammergeyer is still held to be able to seize and carry off sheep. The gold of the region is real enough and is still mined today.

Aristeas seems to have confused these gryphons with gryphons already known to him in his domestic Greek culture. The Greek gryphons, upon which Aristeas grafted the lammergeyer, and the latter's association

BELOW: *Gryphon supporter to the arms of Cardinal Wolsey.*

with gold, appear from seals to have had a Middle Eastern origin. They are probably nothing more than a composite creature, the symbolic combination of the eagle, the king of the birds, with the lion, the king of the beasts. If not an eagle, the bird may have been the gryphon vulture, sacred to the Egyptian god Osiris and other deities. Its characteristic ruff may account for the gryphon's stylised ears, which certainly predate the Aristean merger. It is these ears which distinguish the head of the gryphon in heraldry from the otherwise identical head of an eagle.

The dragon was another early arrival in heraldry and continues to enjoy widespread popularity, frequently appearing in grants of new armorial bearings to Welshmen. It is also popular with grantees associated with the City of London, two dragons featuring as supporters in the city's armorial bearings. Like the gryphon, the dragon has remained largely unaltered by heraldry, except perhaps for the extra pair of legs which it acquired in the fifteenth century, for which the heralds seem largely responsible. Earlier dragons have two legs, and are known as wyverns, and the four-legged simply as dragons.

The dragon is thought to have been brought to Britain by the Romans who used it as the badge of the Roman cohort. They were inspired by the Dacian tribesmen from north of the Danube, who used long wind-sock banners, in the mouths of which they placed lighted tapers or torches. These banners were called *dracones* and would seem to be responsible for the wings of the dragon of heraldry, and also for its fire-breathing qualities. These characteristics were merged with the earlier dragon of the classical bestiaries, which is described as the largest of the snakes and one that lassoes its prey in a knot with its tail and suffocates it; this is a very passable description of a python. In Britain, the Romano-Britons retained the dragon in their iconography. The Welsh word *draig* or dragon is also used for 'leader' and the attributed arms of Uther Pendragon (the reputed father of King Arthur) are *Or two dragons addorsed Vert crowned Gules*.

The heraldic dragon of the West is not to be confused with oriental dragons. These wingless and bewhiskered monsters are closely associated with water, and their origin may owe something to the crocodile. Such dragons are relative latecomers to heraldry, and are chiefly associated with the armorial bearings granted to persons associated with the Far East.

Like the python, the cobra also played its part in the creation of a fearsome heraldic monster: the cockatrice or basilisk. Although the basilisk is now depicted in heraldry with an additional dragon's head at the end of its tail, the cockatrice and basilisk have a common origin. It was never the size of a dragon; the bestiaries give it a length as small as six inches. It was regarded as the king of the snakes, the name basilisk being derived from *basileus*, the Greek for 'king'. Its venom was so deadly that even birds flying over it could be overwhelmed and would drop dead from the sky. Nonetheless, the cockatrice or basilisk could be conquered by weasels. This emphatic statement in the bestiaries clearly refers to the mongoose; and the cobra fits, its head being responsible for the cockscomb

ABOVE: *Wyvern crest of Sir William Fitzwaryn, created Knight of the Garter c.1360.*

ABOVE: *Cockatrice in the arms and crest granted to John Langley, 1632.*

as blasphemous. The fabulous and miraculous horn of the creature was considered the most valuable of all charms against poison and sickness. So prized was it, that the horn belonging to Queen Elizabeth I was valued at £100,000. This and other such horns can now be identified as the spiral horn of the narwhal, a species of small whale found in northern seas and sporting a tusk of fine ivory that can develop to the length of seven or eight feet.

There are two generally-held theories on the origin of the unicorn: firstly, it is thought that the animal might be the Arabian oryx (a species of antelope); the second theory favours the single-horned Indian rhino. Neither of these takes into account the medieval legend of the unicorn, which held that the only way to catch the creature was to send a virgin, preferably nude, into the forest. The unicorn would then come and lay its head trustingly in her lap and follow her faithfully wherever she went. This legend, together with the horn – an obvious phallic symbol – have strong pagan and sexual undertones. Again, oryx and rhino do not explain the old nursery rhyme, 'The lion and the unicorn were fighting for the crown; the lion beat the unicorn all around the town'. This enmity between lion and unicorn is one of the oldest concepts found in mythology. Frequently the unicorn was chased across the sky by the lion and was slain by it. It is known that the lion was a solar symbol, and the sun in turn was sacred to the ancient gods of the Indo-European peoples. By inference the unicorn was a lunar symbol; this is borne out by its frequent appearance on ancient seals and coins in conjunction with a crescent moon. The moon was sacred to the goddesses of the Indo-Europeans, who were governed by matriarchal systems until they were replaced by male-dominated societies several thousand years before Christ. The unicorn's goddesses thus linger on in the medieval virgin legend and the unicorn itself has taken refuge in heraldry. The legend enabled Christ to be associated with the unicorn, the virgin being identified with the Virgin Mary.

and wattles. Once the head had been associated with a cock, this element was fancified until the creature was believed to be half-cock and half-snake, and reptilian wings were therefore introduced. A later addition can be traced to the English so-called naturalist, Alexander Neckham, who in about 1180 stated that the cockatrice was hatched from the egg of an aged cock incubated by a toad; other versions give the incubator as a snake. Intriguingly, so great was the fear instilled by the cockatrice that in the fifteenth century a cock was put on trial in Basle on the charge of having been found laying an egg. It is not known how the trial went except that the cock was found guilty in spite of having his own defence counsel. It is to be wondered how the cock and his counsel communicated.

Although popular in the heraldry of recent centuries, the unicorn was rare in the Middle Ages. As bestiary writers likened Christ to the unicorn, its use in heraldry was regarded

The unicorn may have originated as a calendar creature, one that is composed of parts of several animals each sacred to a particular season of the year, with the horn as a fertility symbol, the symbol of life. Unreliable though he is, it may be significant that Ctesias, writing in about 400 BC, states that the unicorn's horn was white, red and black, the colours of womanhood: white for the virgin, red for the sexually-active woman and black for the aged hag. On the other hand, the unicorn may after all have a natural origin. It is known that the white bull was also sacred to many of the ancient goddesses. It is just possible that one or more tribes learnt to graft the horn buds of a young calf into the centre of its forehead. This is physically possible and results in a single massive horn.

Gryphon, dragon, cockatrice and unicorn were familiar monsters of the bestiaries and as such have remained largely unchanged by their use in heraldry. Less familiar creatures underwent a process of heraldic evolution. The use of three-dimensional crests from the fourteenth century and appearance of supporters in the fifteenth century brought a need for new heraldic source material. Supporters in particular required beasts with claws and feet to support arms – geometrical or inanimate objects were no good for this. So the heralds turned in earnest to the bestiaries as well as to the natural world around them. During the sixteenth century heralds became bolder and more imaginative; and, by the end of the Tudor period, remarkable changes had taken place. The results can therefore be regarded as heraldic monsters in their own right. One of the new arrivals, dating from the beginning of the fifteenth century, is the yale. Bestiary accounts provided it with the remarkable ability of being able to swivel its horns at will, laying one back in battle, keeping it in reserve in case the forward attacking horn was damaged. Apparently it also enjoyed wallowing in water. Although some tend to favour the wildebeest as the origin of the yale, medieval mapmakers consistently depict it as an animal of the East. Its physical characteristics point to the water buffalo, which attacks with sudden swipes of the horn, and this possibly accounts for the swivelling characteristics.

Although comparatively slight, the evolution of the yale in heraldry can be discerned in the treatment of the animal's horns in the fifteenth century. It first appears as a supporter to the arms of John, Duke of Bedford, who intended it to be a punning allusion to his earldom of Kendal, or Kend-eale. The Bedford yale had straight horns and a long tail. It subsequently passed with the earldom to Sir John Beaufort, Duke of Somerset; and two yales were used by the latter's daughter and heir Margaret, Countess of Richmond, the mother of Henry VII. The Beaufort yale is slightly different, with convoluted horns and a short tail.

More noticeable changes are apparent with the heraldic antelope. This originated with the antelope of the bestiary, which was essen-

ABOVE: *Unicorn supporters of Robert Monckton Arundel, Viscount Galway, who died in 1810.*

LEFT: *Yale supporter to the arms of John Beaufort, Duke of Somerset and Earl of Kendal, c.1440.*

RIGHT: *Heraldic antelope, the dexter supporter to the arms of Henry VI. It is not clear whether he used supporters, or whether these were attributed to him shortly after his death; painted in the early sixteenth century.*

tially a gentle creature and can be identified with the black buck, an animal which was then widely distributed in the Middle East before it retreated to its present limited range in India. Heraldry evolved the black buck into a monster of ferocious countenance, with tufts of hair, a tusked nose and serrated horns. The serrated horns may be an exaggerated and stylised rendering of the spirals found in the natural animal.

The heraldic tyger was a particularly popular charge at the beginning of the sixteenth century. It too originated with the bestiary where it was placed correctly between lion and leopard. The bestiary writers stated that the tyger was exceedingly fierce and swift and that the only way to escape it was to throw down mirrors or looking-glasses. The tyger was then distracted by its own image, believing itself to be one of its cubs. Curiously, the bestiaries do not mention the tyger's stripes; but these were Persian tigers which were rather less pronounced in their striping than their Bengal counterparts. So the tyger came into heraldry as a cat-like creature, albeit unstriped. Developments at this stage enhanced its ferocity by making its face wolf-like, adding serrated ears and a horn or tusk to the end of its nose. The heraldic tyger in its fully-evolved form is essentially a creation of heraldry, and bears little resemblance to the tiger of nature or to the tyger of the bestiaries. The former has since been introduced into heraldry in its own right.

An extreme case of heraldic evolution is the male gryphon, which should not be confused with the gryphon described previously; the male gryphon has a spiky, wingless body. A clue to the origin of the male gryphon is in a supporter to the arms of St Leger, painted in 1530, showing a creature with a hairy mane, two horns, and sparks of fire emanating from various points of its anatomy. Eventually the hairy mane was depicted in feathery form and the horns discarded. The only

RIGHT: *Male gryphon, the sinister supporter to the arms of Sayntleger (St Leger), confirmed in 1531. This transitional creature retains the horns and hairy mane of its bison origins.*

maned and horned creature in the bestiaries is the bonacon. Interestingly, the bestiaries report that the bonacon defended itself by means of a fiery emission from its backside, which was capable of setting fire to every-thing contained in several acres behind it. It seems that the heralds found descriptions which were not precise in stating from which part of the anatomy the fire came, and there-fore placed fiery emissions at random.

RIGHT: *Male gryphon supporters granted in 1834 to Sir Henry William Dashwood, baronet. A special Royal Licence was required to allow supporters to be borne by a baronet. In this evolved state the male gryphon has lost its horns and hairy mane. The latter is now normally replaced by feathers, as with the more familiar winged gryphon which features in the Dashwood crest.*

Such an emission from the mouth may subsequently have been mistaken for a beak.

With the bonacon, identification with a natural animal is possible. Some bestiaries state that its horns curled back on themselves so that if you bumped into it 'you did yourself no harm'. It was reddish in colour, with a woolly mane. All this points directly to the European bison, *Bison bonasus*, which was adapted and evolved in heraldic use to the male gryphon found in heraldry today.

At the high point of bestial heraldic evolution, the early Tudor period, there is some indication that monsters reverted to their original bestiary form, suggesting that earlier changes were not always deliberate, but were instead misinterpretations. The salamander evolved into a fire-breathing dog-like monster with a lion's tail before reverting to its bestiary origin as an amphibian (see the illustration of the arms of Douglas in the chapter on the art of heraldry). Salamanders of any form were held to be so cold that they sought the hottest flames as their haunts, where they survived unscathed. This fabulous characteristic has rendered it a popular heraldic charge for fire-fighting organisations. There is

no good reason to associate the natural salamander with fire. However, the bestiary account received lingering credence from no less than Benvenuto Cellini, the Renaissance artist and silversmith, who recalled that in 1505 his father 'saw in the midst of the hottest flames a little animal like a lizard which was sporting about in midst of the most scorching blaze'.

The panther provides further indication that heraldic evolution was somewhat haphazard. The supporter to the arms of Queen Jane Seymour shows a creature with a striped skin of multicolours. Doubtless this was based on a bestiary which referred to the colours, but omitted to describe how they were arranged. That a mistake had been made would seem to have been accepted by later members of the Seymour family, who reverted to the more familiar spotted creature. However, the panther was subjected to another change. Sir William Segar, Garter King of Arms, wrote of the panther at the beginning of the seventeenth century, 'this beast . . . is admired of all other beasts for the beauty of his skyn being spotted of variable colours; and beloved and followed of them for the sweetness of his breath that streameth forth of his nostrils and ears like smoke, wch our paynters mistaking, corruptly do make fire'. In this form it is known as the 'panther incensed', and it is significant that 'incensed' can mean either enraged or sweetly smelling. The kindly-disposed panther of the bestiary was thus transformed by heraldic painters into a monster characterised by fire, flames and ferocity. The original panther, or pard, is likely to have been a cheetah, for the leopard was held to be the bastard offspring of lion (ie leo) and pard. The natural leopard is more akin to the lion in shape, but is spotted like the cheetah, thus inheriting characteristics from both of its supposed parents.

Birds as well as mammals were the subject of heraldic evolution, a good example during the Tudor period being the heathcock or moorcock. A study of contemporary renderings of the bird show clearly how it originated with the blackcock, which was then abundant in southern England and the Midland counties. The first stage in the evolution was to exaggerate the wattles of the blackcock, which are prominent in the mating season, into something resembling those of the domestic farmyard cock. This was soon followed by the elongation of the tail feathers. At first the elongation retained the distinctive lyre-like formation of the natural bird, but in a later stage the tail feathers were

LEFT: *Salamander crest and badge of Baron Sterling of Plaistow.*

LEFT: *Panther supporter to the arms of Jane Seymour, third wife of Henry VIII, painted c.1536.*

RIGHT: *Panther 'incensed' crest of Japan Tobacco (UK) Limited.*

GRATIA · PLACENDI

The Armorial Ensigns of

J.T. (U.K.) LIMITED

College of Arms
London

Lancaster Herald

straightened and swept upwards in two sharp points. In this way heraldry created its own monstrous bird; only the retention of the black plumage provides a tenuous link with its natural origin. In time, this may also be discarded.

In addition to drawing on the bestiaries, Tudor heralds introduced new monsters of their own imagination. Into this group fall a number of composite monsters such as the bagwyn, a roebuck with a wolf's tail, and the more complicated enfield with the head of a fox, the chest of a greyhound, the talons of an eagle, the body of a lion and the hind legs and tail of a wolf. One such creature is the alphyn, which is similar to the heraldic tyger. Combining the body of an existing heraldic monster (the tyger) with the forelegs of an eagle, it also possesses an unexplained knot in its tail; it has recently enjoyed a revival of popularity.

Perhaps more successful was a monster that did not combine parts of existing creatures, but sprang from outright imagination: the pantheon. Held to be an inhabitant of the skies, it is hence usually depicted

ABOVE: *The heathcock or moorcock evolved from the blackcock.*

BELOW: *The alphyn crest of Roberts.*

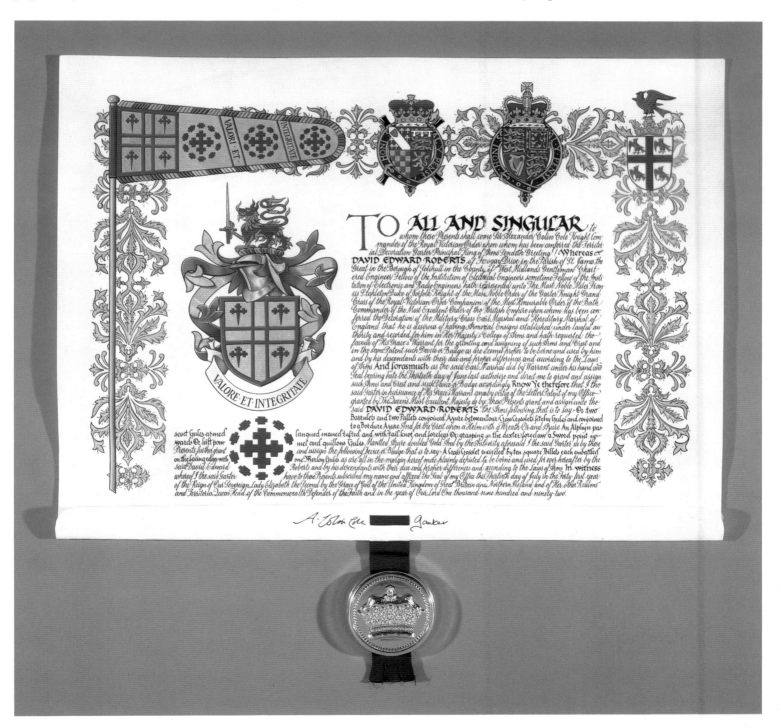

FACING PAGE: *A Chinese phoenix derived from the argus pheasant, and blazoned as a* fynye in ys ꝼper collers *(ie a phoenix proper). The crest of the Company of Painter Stainers with three Chinese phoenix heads in the arms, granted in 1486.*

RIGHT: *Pantheon supporters of Charles Powlett, Duke of Bolton, who died in 1699.*

BELOW: *A sea monster, generally believed to be a sea calf, granted c.1520 to George Witwang of Northumberland.*

in purple or black and liberally sprinkled with stars. It is increasing in popularity as a charge or heraldic device suitable for this age of space travel and developing technology.

Closely allied to the composite monster are the monsters of sea and air. They were not strictly a Tudor invention, since there lurked a medieval belief that everything on land had its counterpart in the sea, and extreme belief sometimes extended this to the air. Tudor heralds made good use of these ideas and placed wings, scales, fins and fishtails on a variety of land animals. This practice has been revived in recent years, and many such marine and airborne monsters occur in modern grants of arms.

Renaissance heraldry showed a surprising reluctance to adopt the new discoveries made by contemporary travellers and explorers as charges, and this attitude continued well into the nineteenth century. One exception to this was the Chinese phoenix, which was adopted by two city livery companies in the fifteenth century. This is a clear indication of the City of London's immediate interest in foreign trade and shows a growing awareness of the importance of the Orient.

RIGHT: *Classical phoenixes based on the eagle; supporters to the arms of West Midland County Council.*

RIGHT: *The Werewolf crest of Kaylewaye, one of the few new monsters to enter heraldry in the late sixteenth century.*

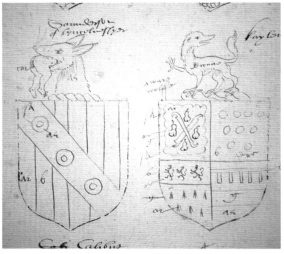

The argus pheasant native to China had evolved in Chinese culture into the *feng huang*, which was confused by travellers from the West with the legendary European phoenix. Further alterations by English heraldry turned it into an exotic fowl, now known as the Chinese phoenix. The more familiar European phoenix was, in fact, derived from a real eagle with painted wings, which was burnt with spices in a nest of palm branches by the ancient Egyptians. This took place at Heliopolis every 160 years as a sacrifice to the sun and to celebrate the leap year. This practice had been recorded in garbled form in the bestiary, and had given rise to the belief in a fabulous bird separated from its aquiline origin.

The apparent failure to make use of the zoological findings of explorers and adventurers marked the beginning of a new and conservative age in heraldry. From the late Tudor period for some 250 years, heraldry was essentially retrospective, preferring to rearrange the old rather than adopt the new. Virtually the only novelty was in the use of human beings or bits of human beings. Heralds seemed mesmerised by the human arm as crest material, giving it every sort of object to grasp. For supporters there are endless military and naval figures, as well as

LEFT: *A missed opportunity: a drawing of an explorer's first impression of an opossum with a bulging pouch from South America (1516). Sixteenth-century heraldry failed to utilise such discoveries, which might otherwise have evolved further into the monstrous.*

natives of conquered territories, a clear reflection of Britain's preoccupation with the developing empire.

LEFT: *Winged lynx supporters to the arms of the College of Ophthalmologists.*

But heraldry did not remain static, and the nineteenth century saw a reawakened interest in monsters. The medieval bestiaries again provided a useful source. The lynx of the bestiary, credited with remarkable eyesight and capable of seeing through solid objects, has become increasingly popular. The addition of wings symbolises the speedy dissemination of its visual services, and introduces a new monster to heraldry. Another recent addition, also endowed with useful qualities, is the caladrius. Bestiary writers reported that

Zoology then features on ten other shields, a meagre number in comparison. Of these, one is charged with a bear, one with a crow or raven, three with luces or pike, three with eagles and one with a crane. Since the thirteenth century the lion's popularity has fluctuated, but its place as the pre-eminent zoological charge has never been challenged; from 1952 to 1972 it featured in nearly 20 per cent of all supporters granted. Its use has now surpassed that of the human being, which was in wider use during the last century.

The lion apart, any study of early heraldry will reveal only a sprinkling of animal species. Inevitably these reflected the nature of the bearers of coat armour. The medieval barons and knights were crude, rough men, preoccupied with war and self-advancement. When not pitting their strength against each other, it was directed towards the baiting and chasing of animal life. This unsophisticated and martial masculinity is reflected in the heraldry of the age, where stag, bull, bear, wolf and boar represent the pursued, and the horse, greyhound, talbot (the original hunting hound) and birds of prey represent the pursuers. Speed was signified by the martlet which loosely covered the swift, swallow and species of martin. These characteristics became so deeply engrained in the system that even today there are many who would

regard the foxhound as more heraldic than the poodle or Pekinese, and the stag beetle to be preferred to the more effeminate butterfly. It is debatable whether it is right to maintain this attitude.

The pun was exceptional in breaking through this barrier and accounts, for example, for species of fish borne on the shields of families such as Tench, Breame and Herring. Again, the Lucys bore luces or pike, the Roches bore roach, the Ellises bore eels and the family of Gournay bore a gournard.

It was not until the fifteenth century that heraldry turned its attention in earnest to the animal world and began recruiting the non-indigenous, a process stimulated by the new practice of adorning the helmet with a crest and the subsequent use of supporters. Once again, the medieval bestiary was a rich source of inspiration. Two popular additions entering heraldry in this way were the elephant and the ostrich, the former often bearing a castle on its back as a derivative of the Indian howdah, and the latter holding in its beak a key, horseshoe or other metal object as an exaggerated reference to its liking for roughage to assist the gizzard. More frequently, heraldry turned to the indigenous, adding to the small number of those mammals and birds found in the heraldry of earlier centuries, and embracing such humble species as

the hedgehog, rabbit, and squirrel. No attempt was made to study animal life at first hand, and curious medieval accounts of nature passed unverified into heraldic use. Baby adders burst to life from their mother's belly, cranes held rocks in their raised claws to prevent them falling asleep, and hedgehogs caught falling grapes on their spines to carry away to their young.

The use of zoology in heraldry had reached and passed a climax well before 1600. The Tudor heralds never showed any real inclination to move beyond the bestiary or the native European species. In the meantime zoological knowledge had increased immensely as explorers pushed back the frontiers of the

known world. Heraldry was left behind, and it was not until the nineteenth century that any attempt was made to catch up. Of the 182 grants of crests made by the Kings of Arms between 1674 and 1700, only seven feature non-indigenous animals: three cranes, two peacocks, one camel and one vulture.

In any generalisation there are bound to be exceptions, and sixteenth-century heraldic ornithology provides three interesting examples. At the beginning of Henry VIII's reign, Sir Thomas Wriothesley, Garter King of Arms and Thomas Benolt, Clarenceux King of Arms, granted a tragopan as a crest to Robert Lord, alias Laward, of London. Improbable though the bird may seem, it is not, as previously thought, a product of Tudor imagination. It is a species of pheasant which displays with horn-like wattles, which are clearly depicted in the Laward grant.

In the mid-sixteenth century the turkey made its appearance in a grant by Thomas Hawley, Clarenceux King of Arms, to Robert Cooke. The turkey's name is, of course, misleading. The turkey is a native of North America, and its introduction to Europe in the sixteenth century as a domestic fowl brought it to the attention of the heralds who used it to provide a suitable pun on the grantee's surname.

Towards the end of the sixteenth century Robert Cooke, Clarenceux King of Arms (not to be confused with the turkey grantee) introduced the bird of paradise as a crest for John Browne of Spexall in Suffolk. First knowledge of the species, now known as the great bird of paradise, was obtained by Western explorers, who found skins which had been stripped from the body, leaving behind the legs. Cooks's grant is therefore accurate in its depiction of a legless bird.

RIGHT: *Tragopan crest of Laward, alias Lord, of London, early sixteenth century.*

the mammal. Once the current preference of depicting the mammal in its natural colours ceases to be an important factor in the system, and it becomes more acceptable to colour it in heraldic tinctures, then perhaps it will match the present popularity of the bird. There is no sound heraldic reason why an armadillo, for example, should be preferred in natural pinkish brown. A green armadillo plated in gold, the crest of Oliver, stands in the good heraldic tradition of the Middle Ages, when mammals were invariably rendered in primary colours.

The new interest in mammal and bird may soon be extended to fish and insect. The dolphin, long regarded as the king of fishes, and the marine equivalent of the lion on land and the eagle in the air, was the only 'fish' regularly used in heraldry, the use of others being generally restricted to the pun. However, game fishing has recently encouraged the use of the salmon, trout and other more exotic species. Even the fishing fly is now found as a heraldic charge. The recent appearance of such as sunfish, flying fish, parrotfish and angelfish reflect interests in sailing and snorkelling in tropical climes.

A small number of insects, arachnids and crustaceans featured during the Renaissance and Tudor periods. The grasshopper, or greshop, of Gresham, and the stag beetle of Hartwell are two punning examples. The bee is also popular as a symbol of industry, and more recently the octagonal cell formation of the honeycomb has been introduced as a field for the shield. Twentieth-century heraldry has increased the range of invertebrates. The slater (a long-antennaed relative of the wood louse) is a punning crest for Sclater, and a water boatman displayed gold is the crest for Hammond, alluding to the rowing interests of that grantee. Combining the pun and career is the elephant hawkmoth of Lord Delfont. This insect provides not only a pun on his title, but moths are associated with bright lights at night and are hence appropriate for a notable impresario.

Less popular as heraldic charges are reptiles and amphibians, except for a number of snakes which feature in various knotted formations in late Tudor grants subsequently. Snakes have remained frequent as a component part in the Rod of Aesculapius, the classical god of medicine, and in the caduceus

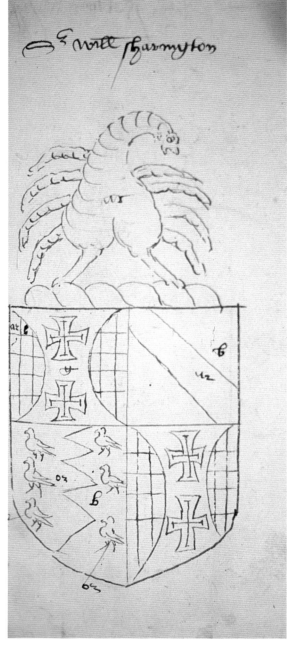

ABOVE LEFT: *Stag beetle crest granted in the early sixteenth century to William Hartwell.*

ABOVE RIGHT: *A curious interpretation of a scorpion, the crest of Sir William Sharington (Sherrington), c.1547.*

RIGHT: *Bees and a slater in the arms and crest of Sclater.*

or wand of Mercury, a charge suitable for those connected with the media of communication. The chameleon is a recent arrival, and its ability to change colour offers considerable scope for grantees involved with the theatre. There are several species of chameleon which, with their various horns and facial embellishments, make for excellent and distinctive crests.

For the amphibians, the frog remains a rarity; but a notable exception is a sixteenth-century crest which shows a leaping frog as a delightful pun for the family of Dryland. The increasing interest in wildlife conservation and ecology may now help the heraldic position of frog and toad. The East Hampshire District Council, for example, was recently granted the natterjack toad, thus helping to cement the link between twentieth-century heraldry and wildlife conservation.

The mollusc has a long heraldic history. As a pun for families such as Shelley, its use is obvious. More difficult to ascertain is to what extent its common use in heraldry derives from its adoption as a pilgrim's badge. Whelks provide a pun for names such as Wilkinson. Cowrie shells, hitherto used as a currency in tropical regions of the world, have featured in the arms of bankers; and there is much scope in mollusc charges for persons concerned with the building industry, or insurance, with its emphasis on protection.

Two types of animal fur have been widely used since the inception of heraldry in the twelfth century, reflecting the sartorial fashion of the time. Ermine is a white fur covered with black spots representing the tail tips of the natural animal. Vair is composed of the grey-blue back skins of a type of squirrel, stitched alternately with its white belly skins. Originally both ermine and vair were probably stitched over shields, but paint was soon substituted, allowing their forms to be represented in different colours. A misunderstanding of the French word 'vair' led to translators confusing this with the word *verre* meaning glass, and so Cinderella was given

LEFT: *The natterjack toad crest of East Hampshire District Council; beechnuts feature in the arms.*

BELOW: *Examples of vair in the Holles Ordinary.*

slippers of an impossible material instead of fashionable squirrel skin.

Heraldic botany has invariably come a poor second to zoology. The rose and fleur-de-lis, the garb or sheaf of corn, (particularly associated with the earldom of Chester) and the simple devices of cinquefoil, quatrefoil and trefoil, these alone made any real impact on medieval heraldry. Trees, fruit and leaves appeared rarely as charges, usually as punning allusions to surnames. Other forms of flora were negligible or non-existent. Tudor heraldry made some attempt to rectify this, but in general its botanical charges played a secondary role. More often than not they featured as a simple sprig held in the feet or mouth of a zoological charge to render this more distinctive from existing devices featuring the same animal, or as a pun.

The rose is particular, and is the botanical counterpart to the zoological lion. The plucking of red and white roses in the Temple gardens by John Beaufort, Duke of Somer-

set, and Richard Plantagenet, Duke of York, is the traditional origin of their adoption as the badges of the rival houses of Lancaster and York. The truth is different. Eleanor of Provence introduced a golden rose into English heraldry which was subsequently adopted, as a badge, by her eldest son Edward I. Her second son, Edmund Crouchback, Earl of Lancaster, changed his rose to red in order to distinguish himself from his brother. Thereafter, this red rose adhered to the title of Lancaster. Meanwhile, the white rose had anciently been a Mortimer badge, and features in arms from the area of the Welsh Marches, the Mortimer stronghold. For example, the town of Ludlow in Shropshire bore *Azure a lion couchant between three roses Argent*. It was through his Mortimer descent that Richard Plantagenet, Duke of York, laid claim to the English throne and thus linked the white rose to the Yorkist cause. Some cinquefoils and even quatrefoils may have a rose origin, being simplified and

BELOW: *Sprigs, twigs and flowers feature as secondary charges in the crests of many Tudor grants.*

stylised versions of that flower. Others may reflect an ancient loyalty to Simon de Montfort in the baronial wars of the thirteenth century.

The fleur-de-lis is one of the more controversial charges in heraldry. Although it is found in the arms of seemingly unconnected families throughout Europe, it is most familiar in the Royal Arms of France. As such, it was appropriated by Edward III and remained a feature in British regal heraldry until discarded in 1801. French legend asserts that Clovis, King of the Franks, received the fleur-de-lis as a divine gift in return for his conversion to Christianity in 496. It is possible that Clovis, trapped between an army of heathen Goths and the river Rhine may have noticed the water iris growing far out into the river. Recognising the possibility of fording at that point, he managed to lead his army to safety and subsequently adopted the iris, in the form of the fleur-de-lis, as his emblem.

The first definite association of the fleur-de-lis with the heraldry of the French monarchy dates from the reign of the twelfth-century King Louis VII, hence the suggestion that the fleur-de-lis is a pun on the name Louis. It is also known that a fleur-de-lis formation was a Moslem motif and there is speculation that Louis VII was attracted to it while taking part in the Third Crusade. However, this may be coincidence, as such a formation is aesthetically obvious and might

easily be reached by different civilisations without outside influence. Furthermore the fleur-de-lis has a pre-heraldic history as a royal device in France, where it featured on crowns and sceptres. At the beginning of the eleventh century Robert II decorated the rim of his crown with fleurs-de-lis; and 200 years earlier a fleur-de-lis formed the finial of the Emperor Charlemagne's sceptre.

More intriguing are the attributed arms of King Pharamund – *Sable three frogs gold*. King Pharamund was reputedly the great-grandfather of King Clovis, and was said to have been descended from a river god. There is some indication that the Merovingian dynasty of France founded by Clovis paid special attention to the frog, either mystical or emblematic, and this may account for many ancient fairy stories where frogs turned

ABOVE: *White roses in the arms of Ludlow, confirmed at the Visitation of Shropshire, 1623.*

LEFT: *Fleurs-de-lis in the arms of Louis, Dauphin and later Louis XI of France. The dolphin in the arms and crest is a pun on his title of Dauphin; the Hyghalmen Roll, painted c.1450.*

RIGHT: *Three frogs in the attributed arms of King Pharamund, ancestor of the Merovingian kings of France.*

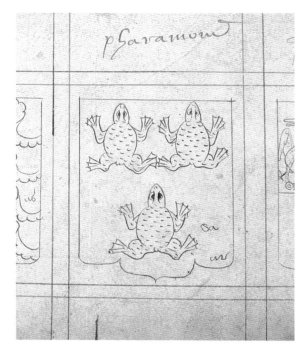

BELOW: *Christopher Barker, Garter King of Arms, granting armorial bearings to Thomas Bell in 1542. The decorative border includes the royal badges of Tudor rose and fleur-de-lis, together with native flowers and fruits.*

OPPOSITE PAGE, BELOW RIGHT: *Examples of flora and fauna, sometimes highly stylised, in the Fenwick Roll.*

water iris occupies the same habitat as the frog; and the one reflects the physical shape of the other. Whether this was recognised and the fleur-de-lis represents both the flower and a stylised frog, is a matter of speculation.

Before 1700, trees rarely appear in English heraldry. Of the 9000 shields in the sixteenth-century *Smith's Ordinary*, whole trees appear in only seven. Qualities of strength and endurance typified by the oak might, for example, have appealed, but clearly they did not. The tree was more often limited to a punning use until it obtained a new popularity in the eighteenth century, which was followed by a growing interest in flowers in the nineteenth. Heraldic use can therefore be seen as reflecting gardening tastes, from the period of Georgian landscape gardens to the herbaceous borders of the Victorians. Today, a wide range of flora is in use, particularly the non-European; the dogwood of North America, hibiscus, lotus and the Australian wattle and waratah flower are examples which are now well established in heraldry.

into princes and vice versa. This in turn may also have inspired the Flemings to call their French neighbours the nickname later revived by British sailors in the nineteenth century, translated as 'Froggy'. The golden

Nonetheless, if largely restricted to rose, fleur-de-lis and foils in pre-eighteenth-

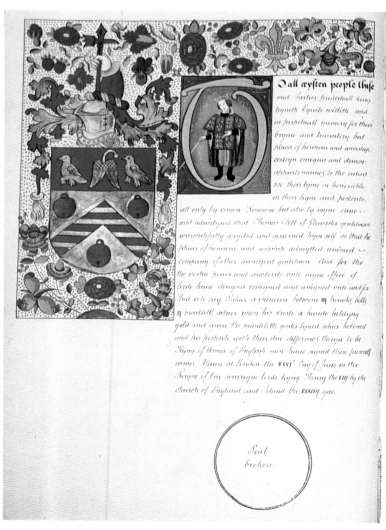

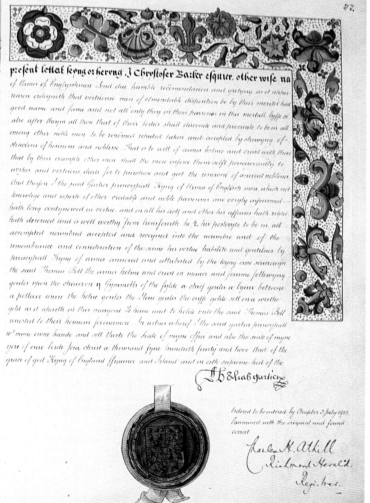

century shield and crest, the flower has featured on the periphery of heraldry as a decorative motif in the borders of Letters Patent issued by Kings of Arms when granting new armorial bearings. Floral borders to Letters Patent date back to the fifteenth century and feature the native flowers of the countryside, with campion, periwinkle, heartsease or wild pansy, honeysuckle, columbine and dog rose proving the most popular. Conspicuously absent are primrose, daffodil and cowslip. Heraldic principle precludes gold or yellow being used on silver or white, and vice versa, as they fail to stand out against each other and it seems to have extended to these non-heraldic borders. The columbine was one of the few native flowers to enter pre-eighteenth-century heraldry. Its use was limited to a handful of armorial bearings, including that granted in 1461 to the Company of Cooks. Its presence in this grant may result from a confusion with a type of ginger used for culinary purposes, known as 'colambyne' or 'columbyne', a native of Colombo. Alternatively, it may have been intended to act as a form of talisman or charm, the columbine

flower being held 'to be very medicinable for dissolving impostumations and swellings in the throat'. If this is so, then it represents a rare example of herbal law in heraldry, two sciences which otherwise remained far apart.

ABOVE: *Columbine in the arms of the Company of Cooks, originally granted in 1461, as entered at the Visitation of London, 1687.*

ABOVE: *Cloves, representing grocery, and badgers, notable for their good house-keeping, are combined in the armorial bearings of Tesco Stores (Holdings) Limited.*

RIGHT: *Australian fauna and flora exemplified in the unusual supporters – brush-tailed possums and eucalyptus trees – of the Zoological Board of Victoria, Australia. A helmeted honey eater features in the crest.*

colours of the Prince of Wales' Royal Canadian Regiment. Today it features in the Royal Arms of Canada, in the Canadian national flag, and is requested as a device by the majority of Canadians petitioning for a grant of new armorial bearings.

Fruit are largely confined to punning use, with a few exceptions. One such exception is the pomegranate, where its numerous seeds provide an allusion to the seeds of learning. Similarly, the hazelnut is the fruit of the hazel, the pre-Christian tree of wisdom; both of these are useful botanical charges for places of education and a welcome relief from the over-used open book and torch of youth.

With the exception of the Welsh leek, vegetables have been largely ignored by heraldry. Tudor livery reflected the leek's colours of green and white, and there is a contemporary reference to the thirteenth-century Welsh prince, Llewellyn the Great 'clad in robes of royalty, a robe of green and white silk'. In the fourteenth century, Edward, the Black Prince, ordered cloth of 'green and white' to make short, particoloured coats and hats for his Welsh troops, the first soldiers to appear on the continental battlefields in a national uniform. Although no medieval source described the leek as a Welsh emblem, its wearing was an established custom in Tudor times. Some complain about the twentieth-century intrusion of the more aesthetically pleasing daffodil as a national emblem, forgetting that the daffodil was known as St David's leek.

Zoology and botany are frequently combined, with an animal holding a flower or sprig in foot or mouth. However, a more imaginative combination dates from the thirteenth century: a lion or leopard's face *jessant de lys*. The traditional belief that it represents the English lion swallowing the French lily has been challenged, as the device first appears in the thirteenth century, when it was used by the Cantelupe family. The Latin word, *lupus*, suggests that the original animal was intended to be a wolf, thus providing a pun on the Cantelupe surname. However, this overlooks early blazon which refers to the lion or leopard as 'Lupard', which also provides a pun. The fleur-de-lis has been combined with the animal in twentieth-century heraldry by terminating the upper petals in animal heads in several recent grants. This combination of the two branches of natural history, zoology and botany, has considerable scope for future heraldic design.

Leaves attracted little interest in the Middle Ages but since 1700 their use in heraldry has been widespread. The maple leaf of Canada must rank as one of the more spectacular successes. The *Quebec Gazette* first refers to it as an emblem in 1805, and soon after it was incorporated as a device in the regimental

SEMPER · LIBERTAS

WE *Sir Anthony Richard Wagner, Knight Commander of the Royal Victorian Order, Garter Principal King of Arms, John Riddell Bromhead Walker, Esquire, Member of the Royal Victorian Order, upon whom has been conferred the decoration of the Military Cross, Clarenceux King of Arms, and Walter John*

7
ROYAL
HERALDRY

Henry Bedingfeld

The Royal Arms of England date back to about 1198. In that year, or perhaps a bit earlier, King Richard I Cœur de Lion had his second Great Seal made, showing three lions passant guardant in pale, and this device has been borne by English monarchs ever since. Before that date lions were certainly attributed to kings of England, but it is uncertain whether they were actually used in practice. Richard I's first Great Seal shows a lion rampant facing the sinister on the visible half of a curved shield; the invisible half is thought to have borne a similar lion facing the first. In these positions the lions are rearing up as though they are about to fight, the heraldic term for this being 'combatant'. The fact that King Richard did not continue with this design and changed it to the three lions makes it clear that heraldry was still in an experimental stage, and that designs were not strictly fixed.

We have seen that Geoffrey of Anjou bore six golden lions on a blue shield, but it is a curious fact that his father-in-law, Henry I of England, who apparently gave him the shield, did not, as far as we know, bear arms

himself, although descendants of his illegitimate sons, Robert, Earl of Gloucester and Reginald, Earl of Cornwall bore lions. Geoffrey of Anjou's son, Henry II, the first Plantagenet king, is not known to have borne arms either, but he has been attributed with two lions passant. Henry II's sons, on the other hand, did bear arms: John, during his father's lifetime, may have borne two lions passant guardant, Richard I's we have mentioned, and William de Longespée, an illegitimate son, bore the same arms as his grandfather Geoffrey of Anjou. After Henry II's death in 1189 his queen, Eleanor of Aquitaine, who died in 1204, had a seal cut the reverse of which shows a shield bearing the three lions.

Ingenious heralds of the later Middle Ages attributed fictitious armorial bearings to pre-armorial monarchs, from King Arthur onwards. Those assigned to Edward the Confessor, based on the design on the reverse of a penny coin minted in his reign, were later used with the Royal Arms by Richard II (1377-99) in a personal rather than a formal capacity, as he had a particular devotion to him. All the Norman kings of England were

BELOW: *Henry VIII, from the Westminster Tournament Roll, 1511.*

attributed a single Sagittary and sometimes three Sagittaries. Matthew Paris, in his thirteenth-century *Historia Anglorum*, attributed the three lions passant guardant to all the Norman kings, including King Stephen. All these attributions were retrospective; there is no evidence that they were ever used by the kings in their own days.

The Royal Arms of the three lions of England were used on their own until the fourteenth century. In 1337 Edward III claimed the throne of France, styled himself King of England and France, and quartered the French Royal Arms with those of England to emphasise the point. The ancient French arms were blue with gold fleurs-de-lis scattered throughout, and they were placed in the first and fourth quarters, the superior position, as the French monarchy was older than the English. In about 1400 Henry V of England reduced the number of fleurs-de-lis to three, to copy the practice adopted by Charles V of France in 1376. This new version of the quartered arms continued unchanged until Queen Mary married Philip II of Spain in 1554.

attributed two gold lions passant guardant on a red field. King Stephen, not a male-line descendant of the Norman royal house, was

LEFT: *Charles the Bold, Duke of Burgundy, who died in 1477.*

In about 1300 crests first made their appearance in England. It became the fashion to place a modelled object, frequently an animal or animal's head, on top and pointing in the same direction as the helmet. From the top of the helmet flowed a cape of material thought to protect the wearer from the heat of the sun or to deflect blows to the neck. The crest, with a wreath of twisted material, or a coronet, held the cape or mantling, as it became known, in position. The third Great Seal of Edward III shows for the first time a crest of a gold lion wearing an ancient crown standing upon a chapeau or cap of maintenance, an ancient cap of dignity made of red velvet and turned-up ermine. Henry VII continued to use this crest, but it was not until the reign of Henry VIII that an arched crown of crosses formy alternating with fleurs-de-lis became continuously used with the chapeau inside the crown. This is very much like the present royal crest, though there have been variations in the style of the crown in the intervening centuries.

Animal supporters, holding and guarding the shield, have been consistently used in the display of Royal Arms since the reign of Edward IV, but they have varied. Supporters have been attributed to earlier kings of England, from Edward III to Henry V, but their authority is considered doubtful. The antelope supporters attributed to Henry VI only appear on buildings completed after his death, for example the Eton Gateway and St George's Chapel, Windsor. However, an interesting discovery was made in 1895 when a copper jug was found in the palace of King Prempeh at Kurnasi in Ghana. It is now in the British Museum and clearly shows the Royal Arms of King Richard II with two lions reguardant as supporters. It has been dated to about 1390 from the couchant hart badge that appears on it, together with other royal badges. Further evidence, however, will be needed before it can be established that Richard II and other kings prior to Henry VI consistently displayed supporters.

The origin of supporters to shields is still unclear. It is probable that it was just a question of artistry; seal engravers, carvers and sculptors merely added beasts from favourite badges or the arms of associated families as a form of decoration. Early seals include animal decoration in the void between the shape of the shield and the circular rim. The custom of adding this extra decoration proved popular with the higher nobility. Increasing numbers of them adorned their arms in this fashion, and the king was no exception. Henry VI displayed two white antelopes, sometimes a lion and a panther, or antelope or heraldic tyger; Edward IV a black bull and white lion, a gold lion and a black bull, or a white lion and hart, or two white lions; and Richard III a white lion and a white boar, or two white boars.

When Henry Tudor came to the throne in 1485 as Henry VII, he chose as supporters two greyhounds, animals associated with the house of Lancaster from which he was descended. A few years later, a red dragon was substituted for one greyhound, presumably to emphasise his links with Wales. His son, Henry VIII, changed them to the more regal gold lion and red dragon. These were also used by his children, Edward VI and Queen Mary until her marriage to Philip II of Spain in 1554. Queen Mary's marital arms were supported by a black eagle (from the Hapsburg arms) and a gold lion.

Royal Arms are arms of sovereignty, and are borne in order to show the territorial possessions of the king or queen. The French quartering, however, represented a claim rather than actual possession. They are not

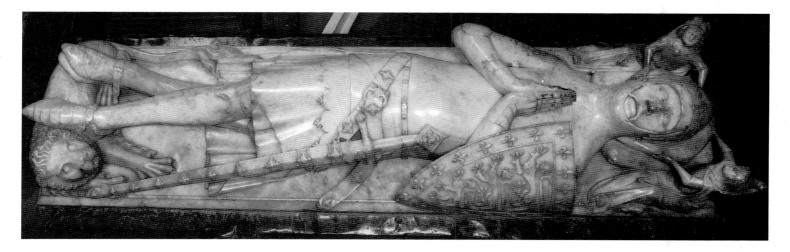

RIGHT: *The phoenix and falcon badges of Elizabeth I.*

FACING PAGE: *The arms of James I, with the crests of England, Scotland, France and Ireland.*

Queene Elizabeth *bare for her Badges the Phenyx Burnnge with this Motto* SEMPER EADEM *being a true type or figure of her Princely selfe which whilest she lived was the only Phenix living in the whole world.*

Her other Badge was a white Falcon Crowned houlding a Scepter and standing on a Stock or Roote of a Tree betwene 2 growing Branches of

BELOW: *Mary Queen of Scots married the Dauphin of France (later Francis II) in 1558.*

personal arms, which pass from father to son; upon a change of dynasty the new king gives up his personal arms to take on the symbols of his new sovereignty. This Henry Tudor, Earl of Richmond, did when he became king. Queen Mary Tudor, on the other hand, when she married King Philip II of Spain, bore the arms of her husband impaled with her own. This complicated piece of marshalling shows King Philip's sovereignty, through his wife, over England (and France) and Queen Mary's sovereignty, through her husband, over Castile, Leon, Aragon, Sicily, Granada, Austria, Burgundy (shown as ancient and modern), Brabant and with Flanders and Tyrol overall. Queen Mary was succeeded by her sister Elizabeth in 1558, who kept to the arms of France modern and England, but whose supporters became a royally-crowned gold lion and a red dragon; her adopted motto was *Semper Eadem* ('Always the Same'). When Elizabeth died in 1603 another dynastic change occurred when her Stuart cousin, James VI of Scotland, succeeded to the throne of England as James I. As King of England James bore in the first and fourth grand-quarters the arms of his predecessors, France modern and England; the Royal Arms of Scotland – *Or a lion rampant and a double tressure flory counter flory*

England

Scotland

France

Ireland

p. 105
v 168

RIGHT: *The Royal Arms of Great Britain and Hanover 1816-37, borne by George III, George IV and William IV.*

RIGHT: *The Royal Arms of Great Britain and Hanover 1816-37, borne by George III, George IV and William IV.*

FACING PAGE: *Attributed and actual Royal Arms from William the Conqueror until George III (1816).*

Gules in the second quarter, with Ireland in the third quarter – *Azure a harp stringed Argent*. The harp as a badge had previously been associated with Ireland when that lord-ship had been raised to a kingdom by Henry VIII, but when James I became king the harp was formally included as a part of the whole achievement to show King James' full sovereignty. James I retained the golden lion supporter of England and substituted his own unicorn supporter for Elizabeth's dragon. The unicorn first appears as a sup-porter to the arms of the kings of Scotland on the coinage of James III in the fifteenth century, but it is a single unicorn, sitting and holding the shield from behind; two unicorns on each side of the shield date from 1503, during the reign of James IV. Scottish sovereigns continued to use these supporters for the next century until James VI became King of England. The lion and unicorn are Queen Elizabeth II's supporters today, and they are blazoned, *a Lion guardant Or royally crowned proper and a Unicorn Argent armed tufted crined and unguled gorged with a coronet composed of crosses formy and fleurs-de-lis thereto a chain affixed and reflexed over the back all Or.*

The Royal Arms remained the same until 1688, although they were not used during the Commonwealth when Oliver Cromwell ruled England as Lord Protector and the royal family were in exile after the Civil War. The Stuart arms have survived in the arms of the descendants of Charles II's illegitimate sons. The Duke of Grafton bears them,

debruised by a baton sinister compony of six pieces Argent and Azure; the Duke of St Albans *debruised by a baton sinister Gules charged with three Roses Argent*; and the Duke of Richmond's arms have, instead of a baton sinister, *a bordure compony Argent and Gules charged with eight Roses of the second barbed and seeded proper.*

When Mary Stuart came to the throne in 1688, she reigned jointly with her husband William of Orange. The arms of William III and Mary II were the same as those of James I, with the addition of the arms of Nassau on a shield in the centre. This still exists today as the arms of the kingdom of the Netherlands and is blazoned, *Azure billety and a Lion rampant Or*. When Mary's sister, Anne, succeeded in 1702, she bore the Stuart Royal Arms (without the Nassau shield) until the Act of Union in 1707, which created the kingdom of Great Britain, necessitated another armorial change. The first quarter of the shield became England impaling (side by side with) Scotland, but the double tressure counter flory was dimidiated, that is, cut off, or omitted along the palar line; this coat was repeated in the fourth quarter. In the new scheme France was placed in the second quarter and Ireland remained in the third.

Anne was the last of the Stuart monarchs when she died in 1714, and was succeeded by George, the Elector of Hanover, Duke of Brunswick and Lüneburg and Arch Treasurer of the Holy Roman Empire, who became king as George I under the terms of the Act of Settlement of 1701. This again necessitated another change; the repeated fourth quarter in Queen Anne's arms were removed and replaced by the Hanoverian arms. The new quartering symbolised King George's German possessions: Brunswick (*Gules two Lions passant guardant in pale Or*), Lüneburg (*Or semy of hearts Gules and a Lion rampant Azure*), and Westphalia (*Gules a Horse courant Argent*) and, in the centre, the augmentation of the Arch Treasurer of the Holy Roman Empire (*an inescutcheon Gules charged with the golden crown of Charlemagne*). The latter augmentation was only borne by the king, not by other members of the royal family. (Curiously enough *The Times* still carries George I's arms on its masthead.)

Another change was necessary under the Act of Union with Ireland, and in 1801 the Royal Arms were rearranged. After nearly 500 years the opportunity was now taken to drop the French Royal Arms, and the quarterings now became (1) England (2) Scotland (3) Ireland and (4) England repeated; an

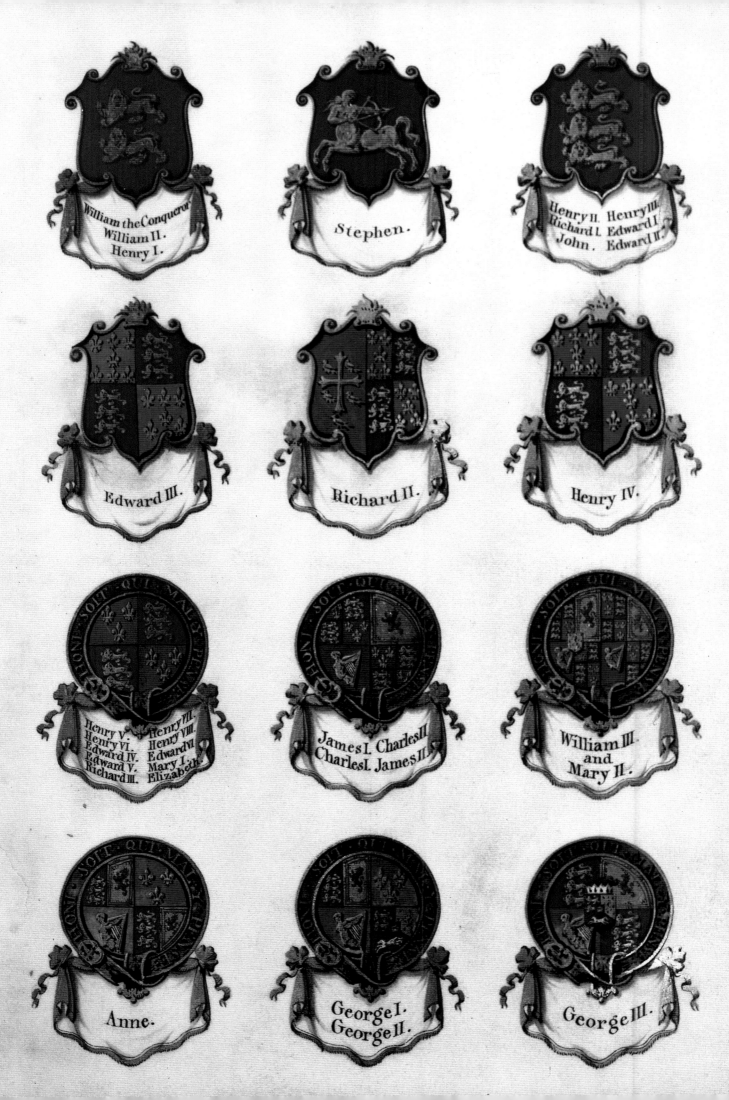

William the Conqueror. William II. Henry I.

Stephen.

Henry II. Henry III. Richard I. Edward I. John. Edward II.

Edward III.

Richard II.

Henry IV.

Henry V. Henry VII. Henry VI. Henry VIII. Edward IV. Edward VI. Edward V. Mary I. Richard III. Elizabeth.

James I. Charles II. Charles I. James II.

William III. and Mary II.

Anne.

George I. George II.

George III.

additional shield was placed in the centre with the arms of Brunswick, Lüneburg and Westphalia with the augmentation of the Arch Treasurer in the centre. As George III was also the Elector of Hanover, the central shield was surmounted by the Electoral bonnet. When, a few years later, Napoleon overthrew the Empire, and under the terms of the 1815 Congress of Vienna the Electorate became the kingdom of Hanover, a crown replaced the Electoral bonnet in 1816. The Hanoverian version of the Royal Arms exists today in the arms of the Earl of Munster, a descendant of an illegitimate son of William IV, though the crown has been removed and the whole is *debruised by a baton sinister Azure charged with three anchors Or*. The Royal Arms remained unaltered until William IV died and was succeeded by Queen Victoria in 1837. As Queen Victoria, as a woman, was prevented by Salic law from succeeding to the kingdom of Hanover, the Hanoverian shield and crown were removed from the Royal Arms. The resulting arms, quarterly England, Scotland, Ireland and England, have been borne

by Queen Victoria and every succeeding monarch until the present day.

In the chapter on the science of heraldry mention was made of cadency marks placed on shields to distinguish one son from another. Royal heraldry, however, has different rules and for many centuries the label of three points for sons of the monarch, each suitably differenced, has been employed. Originally, however, the Royal Arms were differenced with a bordure as well as the label. Of Edward III's sons Edward, Prince of Wales (the Black Prince) bore quarterly France ancient and England with a label of three points Argent; Lionel of Antwerp, Duke of Clarence (died 1386) bore the same shield with a label of three points Argent each point charged with a canton Gules; John of Gaunt, Duke of Lancaster (died 1399) bore France ancient and England with a label of three points Argent the points Ermine; Edmund of Langley, Duke of York (died 1402) bore a label of three points each charged with three torteaux (red roundels); and Thomas of Woodstock, Duke of Gloucester

BELOW: *English Royal Arms before 1400,* Flower's Ordinary*, 1520.*

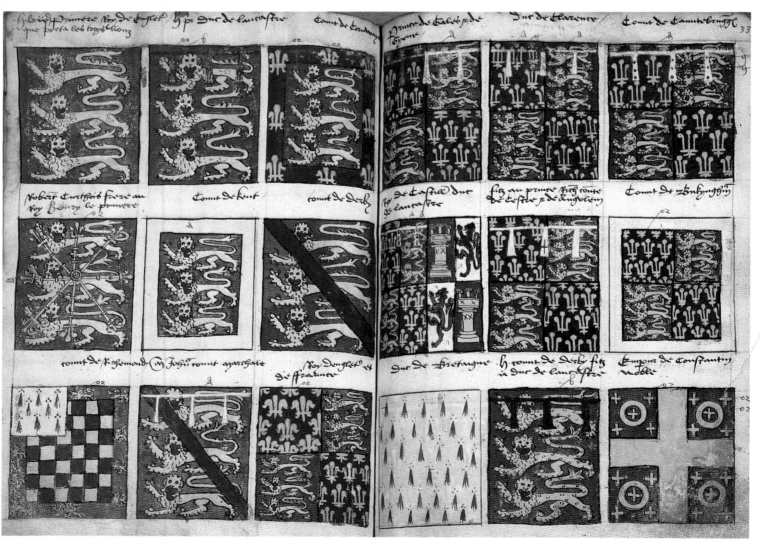

(murdered 1397) bore the Royal Arms with a bordure Argent.

John of Gaunt's illegitimate Beaufort children by Catherine Swynford, daughter of Sir Payn Roet, Guienne King of Arms, when later legitimated, bore the Royal Arms with a bordure compony Argent and Azure. The Somerset Dukes of Beaufort, illegitimately descended from the Beaufort Dukes of Somerset, bore the same arms, and the present duke continues to do so. Margaret Beaufort, daughter of John, Duke of Somerset and great-granddaughter of John of Gaunt, married Edmund Tudor, Earl of Richmond, and it is probable that this alliance induced Edmund Tudor to adopt the Royal Arms with a bordure Azure charged with alternating martlets and fleurs-de-lis Or. The son of this marriage was Henry Tudor, and the few drops of royal blood brought to him by his mother gave him his claim to the throne, which he successfully pursued in 1485.

The modern system of royal cadency relies entirely upon the label, children of a monarch having a label of three points, and grandchildren a label of five points, assigned only by Royal Warrant. King George V had four sons, and he issued a Royal Warrant in 1921 specifying the labels to be borne by them. His eldest son became Edward VIII (and upon his abdication in 1936 Duke of Windsor), his second son became George VI, his third son Henry became Duke of Gloucester and his fourth, George, Duke of Kent. The Duke of Gloucester was assigned a label of *three points Argent bearing a lion passant guardant Gules on the central point between a cross of St George on the outer points*; the Duke of Kent was assigned a white label of *three points each point charged with a blue anchor*. Their sons were later assigned white labels of five points; that of the present Duke of Gloucester bears *three St George's Crosses and two lions passant guardant Gules*, while that of the present Duke of Kent bears a label *charged alternately with three blue anchors and two St George's crosses*. The sons and daughters of the Dukes of Gloucester and Kent are not styled 'Royal Highness', and bear their fathers' arms. Queen Elizabeth, the Queen Mother bears the undifferenced Royal Arms impaling the arms of Bowes-Lyon, and the supporters are a *lion guardant Or imperially crowned proper* and a *lion per fess Or and Gules*. Her Majesty does not use a crest or motto.

King George VI ceased to be styled 'Emperor of India' upon India's independence in 1947, and when Elizabeth II suc-

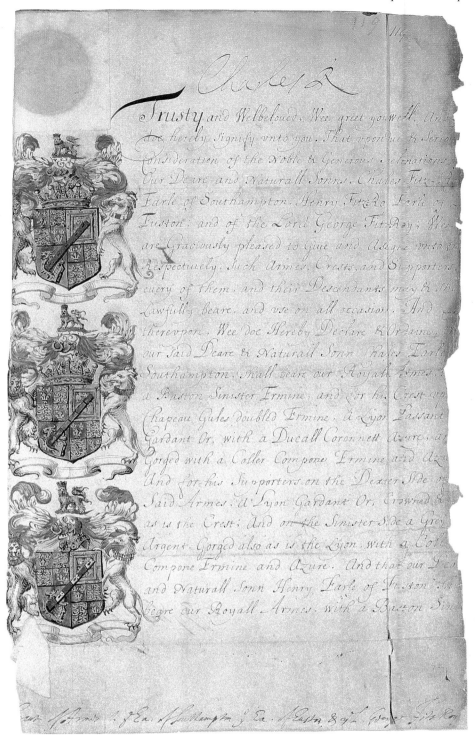

ceeded to the throne in 1952 the opportunity was taken to alter the heraldic royal crown. The imperial crown's high semi-circular arches were slightly depressed in the middle, reverting to the design used in the reign of Charles II.

The sovereign's arms are arms of sovereignty or dominion and cannot be quartered or impaled with those of his or her consort. The Duke of Edinburgh has borne since 1949: quarterly, (1) *Or semy of hearts Gules three lions passant in pale Azure crowned Gold* (the arms of Denmark); (2) *Azure, a cross Argent* (the arms of Greece); (3) *Argent two*

ABOVE: *The armorial bearings of the Earl of Southampton, the Earl of Euston, and of Lord George FitzRoy, natural sons of Charles II.*

123

pallets Sable (the family arms of Mountbatten); (4) *Argent on a rock in base proper a castle triple towered Sable masoned Argent each tower topped by a vane Gules* (Edinburgh). His crest is *Out* *of a ducal coronet Or a plume of five ostrich feathers alternately Sable and Argent*, and his supporters are *dexter the figure of Hercules proper* and *sinister a lion queue fourché ducally*

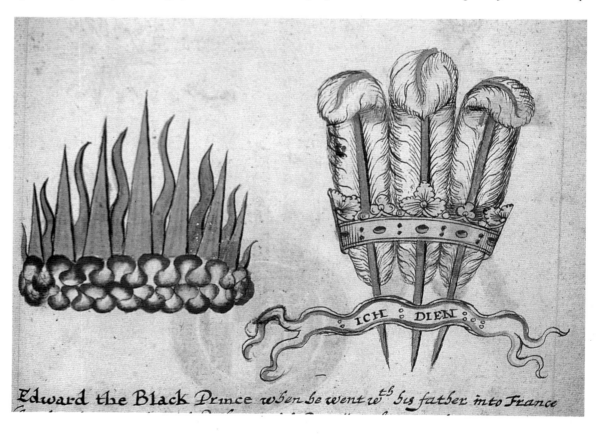

crowned Or gorged with a naval coronet Azure. His motto is: 'God is my help'.

The Prince of Wales bears the Royal Arms with a plain white label to indicate that he is the heir apparent to the throne, with an inescutcheon of the arms of the Principality of Wales ensigned (surmounted) by the heir apparent's coronet. His supporters are the same as the Queen's, but with a plain white label around the necks of the lion and unicorn and the lion wearing the prince's coronet. The crest shows a lion wearing the prince's coronet with a white label standing upon the coronet. In a full achievement of his arms, and below the shield, are the heir apparent's ostrich-feather badge, the arms of the Duchy of Cornwall and the badge of the red dragon of Wales. His motto is *Ich Dien* ('I serve').

The Queen's sister, Princess Margaret, Countess of Snowdon bears the Royal Arms on a lozenge differenced by a label of *three points Argent the centre point charged with a thistle slipped and leaved proper and each of the other points with a Tudor Rose.* Assigned by King George VI in 1944, the lozenge is ensigned by a princely coronet (with no crest) and the supporters are differenced as in the arms, the lion wearing a princely coronet rather than the royal crown.

The Duke of York and Prince Edward have been assigned labels of difference, respectively *a label of three points Argent the centre point charged with an anchor Azure, and a*

RIGHT: *The arms of the Black Prince at Canterbury Cathedral.*

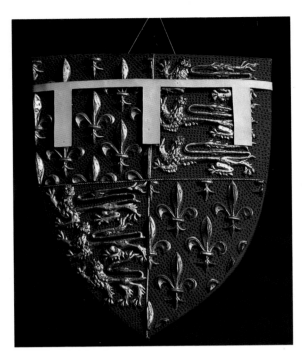

label of three points Argent the centre point charged with a rose Gules barbed proper thereon another rose Argent barbed and seeded proper. The Duke of York's daughters, like the sons of the Prince of Wales, have not yet been assigned arms. The Princess Royal bears arms on a lozenge with *a label of three points Argent the centre point charged with a heart Gules and each of the other points with St George's crosses.* The Princess Royal's children bear the arms of Phillips; they have no royal title and therefore follow the normal rules of heraldry rather than royal rules, although the shields are ensigned with a coronet the finials of which are composed of fleurs-de-lis and alternating strawberry leaves.

A display of the arms of male members of the royal family cannot show the arms of their spouses on the same shield as their own. Instead the spouse's arms are placed on a separate shield alongside, with the husband's supporters, helm, crest and motto. A wife may, however, impale her royal husband's arms with hers, as for example in the Princess of Wales' achievement. This shows the arms of the Prince of Wales on the dexter of the shield, impaling the arms of Spencer on the sinister, supported by the Princess' supporters, which are the Prince of Wales' lion supporter on the dexter, and on the sinister, a *Griffin Ermine winged Erminois beaked and legged Or gorged with a Prince's Coronet thereto a*

RIGHT: *The arms and badges of Richard II.*

Richard the Second when he intended his voyage into Ireland to subdue the rebelles were in...

chain reflexed behind the back and ending in a ring all of Gold (a derivation from one of her late father's supporters).

Royal badges have been used since the earliest stages of heraldry. They are always freestanding, in the sense that they are not dependent on shield or crest, and they are invariably simple devices. The earliest heraldic badge is the sprig of broom said to have been worn by Geoffrey of Anjou in his cap. The plant *planta genista* gave Geoffrey his nickname – Plantagenet – and was immortalised as the name of the dynasty which ruled England for over 300 years. The Plantagenet kings used this badge, sometimes combining it with personal devices. Henry II, for example, used the *planta genista*, a genet between two sprigs of broom and an escab-

BELOW: *King Edward IV, his Queen, Elizabeth Woodville, and the 'Princes in the Tower', c.1482, at Canterbury Cathedral.*

uncle; Edward I the *planta genista* and a gold rose; Edward III a sunburst issuing from a cloud and the base (or stock) of a tree showing roots (for Woodstock).

Ostrich-feather badges were very popular with Edward III and his descendants, and their origin is probably as a pun derived from his wife Philippa of Hainault whose father held the lordship of Ostrevans. Edward, the Prince of Wales (the Black Prince) bore as his shield for peace *Sable three ostrich feathers quilled and piercing scrolls Argent bearing the words* ICH DIEN; he used the Royal Arms on his war shield. Although he placed ostrich feathers on a shield, they were certainly regarded as badges; he described them in his will as 'nos bages des plumes d'ostruce'. (Incidentally, the myth that he captured the ostrich feathers from the blind King of Bohemia at the battle of Crécy has long been exploded.) His son, Richard II, used the feathers, as did John of Gaunt, Henry IV, Thomas, Duke of Gloucester, the Beauforts and other Plantagenets. Gradually they became, in Tudor times, the special badge of the heir apparent to the throne, whether or not he was created Prince of Wales. The

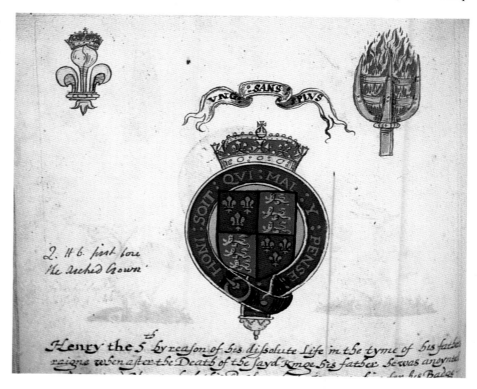

Prince of Wales bears this badge today as heir apparent, not as Prince of Wales.

The badges of the red rose of Lancaster and the white rose of York have come to symbol-

ABOVE: *Arms and badges of Henry V.*

FACING PAGE: *Badges of Henry VII.*

LEFT: *The armorial bearings of Henry VII.*

129

ise the fifteenth-century dispute for the throne between the rival branches of the Plantagenets, now known as the Wars of the Roses (a name coined by Sir Walter Scott). They originate in the gold rose borne by Edward I and in the red rose as differenced by his brother Edmund Crouchback, Earl of Lancaster. The Yorkists adopted the white rose as their symbol in their claim to the throne by virtue of their descent from Roger Mortimer, Earl of March, the senior descendant of Edward III. These badges still exist as royal badges; the red rose royally crowned is the badge of office of Lancaster Herald, while the white rose en soleil royally crowned is the badge of office of York Herald.

Richard III's badge was a white boar, the origin of which is obscure. It has been suggested that it was a pun on the Latin name for York, *Ebor*, but he never held the honour of York, nor was he the Duke of York. As Duke of Gloucester, however, he was governor of northern England during the reign of his brother, Edward IV (1461–83), and his seat of government was situated in Yorkshire, where he was very popular. It has also been

ABOVE: *The armorial bearings of Her Majesty Queen Elizabeth II, borne by each monarch since Queen Victoria.*

RIGHT: *The armorial bearings of Henry VIII.*

suggested that it is a pun on his royal title *Rex Anglie*, for *sanglier* is the French for boar, but he was known to have used a boar as a badge before he became king. In his play *Richard III*, William Shakespeare, the dramatist (and Tudor propagandist) used the pun, referring to Richard by his favourite device 'The wretched, bloody and usurping boar'.

It is said that during Richard's reign many inns displayed the white boar as a mark of allegiance to him, a common-enough practice at the time (and indeed now). After he was killed at the battle of Bosworth in 1485, the white boar inn signs were painted blue to mark a switched allegiance to the Earl of Oxford, whose badge it was, a commander in Henry VII's army at the battle.

Richard's opppressive reign prompted one Collingbourne of Wiltshire to produce a famous couplet:

The Cat, the Rat, and Lovel our Dog
Rule all England under a Hog.

The cat and rat referred to Richard's ministers, Sir William Catesby and Sir Richard Ratcliffe; Lord Lovel's badge was indeed a dog, and the hog referred, of course, to King Richard. The author of this rhyme paid for it with his life.

Mention must be made of the royal badges in use today. Her Majesty the Queen could,

LEFT: *The armorial bearings of the Duchy of Lancaster.*

of course, by right of inheritance, use any or all of the royal badges ever used by her predecessors. In fact, the badges in use today are limited to that of England, *the red and white*

LEFT: *The armorial bearings of Australia.*

A·MARI·VSQVE·AD·MARE

rose united, slipped and leaved proper ensigned with the Royal Crown; Scotland, *a thistle slipped and leaved proper ensigned with the Royal Crown*; Northern Ireland, *a shamrock leaf slipped vert ensigned with the Royal Crown*; and *a harp Or stringed Argent ensigned with the Royal Crown*; the United Kingdom, *the rose, thistle and shamrock engrafted on the same stem proper ensigned with the Royal Crown, and an escutcheon charged as the Union Flag ensigned with the Royal Crown*; Wales, *within a circular riband Argent fimbriated Or bearing the motto* Y DDRAIG GOCH DDYRY CYCHWYN ['The red dragon gives the lead'] *in letters Vert and ensigned with the Royal Crown an escutcheon per fess Argent and Vert and thereon a Dragon passant Gules.* The badge of the house of Windsor is: *On a mount Vert the Round Tower of Windsor Castle Argent masoned Sable flying thereon the Royal Banner the whole within two branches of Oak fructed and ensigned with a Royal Crown.*

The Prince of Wales' badge as heir apparent is *a plume of three ostrich feathers Argent enfiled by a coronet of crosses paty and fleurs-de-lis Or jewelled proper with the motto upon a scroll Azure fimbriated Or the words* ICH DIEN *in letters also Gold*, and his badge for Wales is *upon a mount Vert a Dragon passant wings elevated Gules gorged with a label of three points Argent.*

Her Majesty the Queen is styled in Great Britain as 'Elizabeth the Second by the Grace of God of the United Kingdom of Great Britain and Northern Ireland and of Her other Realms and Territories Queen Head of

Heraldry

RIGHT: Her Majesty The Queen's personal banner for use in New Zealand.

RIGHT: Her Majesty The Queen's personal banner for use in Canada.

134

the Commonwealth Defender of the Faith'. In her other realms the style varies, for Her Majesty is separately the Queen of Antigua and Barbuda, Australia, the Commonwealth of the Bahamas, Barbados, Belize, Canada, Grenada, Jamaica, New Zealand, Papua New Guinea, Saint Christopher and Nevis, Saint Lucia, Saint Vincent and the Grenadines, the Solomon Islands and Tuvalu. In Australia, for example, Her Majesty is styled as 'Elizabeth the Second by the Grace of God Queen of Australia and Her other Realms and Territories, Head of the Commonwealth'. In each of her independent realms, the Queen bears different armorial bearings to identify separate sovereignty and authority in each nation. In dependent territories of the United Kingdom which have armorial bearings, such as Hong Kong and the Falkland Islands, the arms are also borne by the Queen in right of these territories. Where a dependent territory has not had arms assigned to it, the Royal Arms of the United Kingdom are borne as arms of dominion and sovereignty. The Queen also flies a personal banner when in her realms other than the United Kingdom,

which shows her arms of that country surmounted by the initial letter E, ensigned by the royal crown upon a blue roundel surrounded with a chaplet of roses gold.

LEFT: *The arms of the Falkland Islands.*

135

Este es vn muy noble linage y procede de dos caualleros Andaluzes
el vno llamado Fernan Nuñez y el otro Aluar perez, destos salio
vn gran Capitan llamado Gonçalo Fernandez de Cordoua

8
INTERNATIONAL HERALDRY

Peter Gwynn-Jones

It was during the twelfth century that the nobility of Europe began to identify themselves by painting distinctive designs on their shields in bright contrasting colours. This marks the birth of heraldry. Common ground and personal contact were established between the knights of Europe through their affiliation to the Latin church and found a practical outlet in the Crusades.

In 1974 the author wrote an article entitled 'Heraldry and The Wider World' summarising the heraldic characteristics of different European countries, and it serves to quote from this article as follows. 'Much of the science and system of heraldry developed as part of a European rather than national culture. Nonetheless, there remained characteristics peculiar to different individual countries or groups of countries. The proliferation of crests found in Germany, Austria, and much of Switzerland contrasts with the British custom of a single crest and the absence of crests in France and the Iberian countries. In Eastern Europe, whole groups of families or territorial areas adopted the same armorial bearings, a form of clan affiliation unknown elsewhere. Similarly, the East favoured white charges set in a blue or red field, while the extreme West, that is, France and the British Isles, made extensive use of furs and favoured the powdering of their shields with small charges. Again, France and the British Isles were foremost in applying marks of difference to the shield to distinguish between several members or branches of the same family; further East this practice is usually absent.

Regional differences tended to become more emphasised as medieval civilisation gave way to the growth of nationalism and the evolution of strong centralised monarchies which took upon themselves the control of armorial bearings and appointed their own heraldic authorities. Special features of individual countries can now be more readily recognised.

BELOW: *German crests frequently reflect the charges used in the arms as can be seen in Povey's German Roll, painted in the early fifteenth century.*

each of its arms downwards in a concave curve is another ubiquitous characteristic of continental design. Hills and terraces emerging from the base may account for as many as one in 15 of all arms found on the European mainland; in the British Isles they are exceedingly rare. This difference is carried further, with other charges emerging from the sides or bases of shields. In the British heraldic world only the Ordinaries are treated in this way; other charges, whether floral, faunal or inanimate are left freestanding. The absence of any crests in the rendering of the arms of Notthaft, and the use of a coronet of the type borne by a French marquis, suggests that a strong French influence filtered into Bavaria, the homeland of this

LEFT: The arms of the Saxon family Hennenberg provide an obvious pun. The crest is typical of Teutonic heraldry, exaggerating and fancifying the human form, and is adorned with a panache of peacocks' feathers; painted in 1580.

BELOW: A Bavarian claret jug showing the armorial bearings of Notthaft of Podenstein. Hills or terraces and chevrons reaching the middle chief are typical features of continental European heraldry.

German or Teutonic heraldry extended its sphere of influence over Central Europe and spread northwards into Scandinavia. Its most striking characteristic lies in the design and treatment of crests. The majority of crests reflect the arms by repeating either the latter's charge or tinctures, or both, in a manner virtually unknown in the British Isles. There is also a predilection for wings and buffalo horns. The merging of crest and mantling in one flowing sweep is another readily recognisable and typical feature.

With the declining use of armorial bearings in a military context at the end of the Middle Ages, Teutonic Europe witnessed the marshalling of many arms on a single shield, each bearing its corresponding crest on a helmet. In the British Isles more than one crest is unusual, and in Latin Europe the use of crests has continuously declined or been abandoned altogether.' The armorial bearings of Notthaft of Podenstein 'exemplify features of design almost unknown in the heraldry of Britain and the latter's sphere of heraldic influence. Chevrons terminating at the top of the arms are a frequent form of continental treatment and contrast with the British custom of keeping the chevron apex in the centre; to embow a chevron and so sweep

RIGHT: *Dutch heraldry is characteristically simple, with single charges on the arms being frequent. From the* Edele Geslagten in de 7 Provintien, *painted 1738.*

140

family, and affected the way in which Bavarian nobility portrayed their arms.

Holland and Switzerland stand unrivalled in their widespread use of heraldry. Holland in particular is notable for the great esteem with which Dutch families regard their armorial bearings. Much of this was influenced by the Dutch republic of the sixteenth and seventeenth centuries. Many old medieval families, if not extinguished by the Wars of Independence, often fled to the Spanish Netherlands (modern Belgium), and their place was taken by republican traders and merchants who began an extensive adoption of arms. In comparison with other countries, Dutch heraldry is notable for its pleasant simplicity, many shields bearing only a single charge. In general one shield, one helmet and one crest are found; the practice of marshalling more than one shield in the form of quarterings is uncommon and the use of mottoes is rare.

Belgian shields can be recognised by the practice of suspending them by a strap from the helmet; and in the case of the Belgian nobility a gold medallion and collar is found about the helmet's neck.' Burgher arms which date from the late Middle Ages and the development of the Low Countries as Europe's commercial and industrial centre are characterised by the absence of helmets in Belgian burgher heraldry.

'In France the choice of charges and their arrangement bear close similarity to British heraldry. A major difference is the absence of crests. From the time of the Renaissance families tended to place only their coronets of rank upon their helmets; but by the eighteenth century the helmet had also been abandoned and coronets were placed directly above the shield.

The French revolution of 1789 saw the abolition of French heraldry which was replaced some 15 years later by a new Imperial heraldry.' As might be expected this was characterised by weapons and items of war reflecting the Napoleonic campaigns. Crests, helmets, supporters and mottoes were excluded, but a system of plumed caps to denote rank was introduced. Specific charges and arrangements of design were also laid down for the several grades of nobility and officials, and were even extended to civic heraldry. The plumed caps or toques were supplemented with Napoleonic precision by augmentations to the shield to denote rank. Civic heraldry was similarly graded, with towns being classified with their corresponding chief or canton charged with the symbols favoured by Napoleon, such as the initial N, the Imperial crown and bees.

'Spanish and Portuguese heraldry is characterised by the use of broad shields, often with borders. This practice dates back to earlier times when it was customary for a man to surround his arms with a border charged with single heraldic devices taken from the arms of his wife, or with her complete arms arranged as a series of small shields, usually numbering seven or eight.

Complicated schemes of quarterings have also evolved in Spain and Portugal, for it is

ABOVE: *French heraldry bears some similarity to that of the British Isles, but replaces crests with coronets of rank. From Hector le Breton, painted c.1600.*

141

held that a woman may transmit the arms of her family whether or not she is an heraldic heiress in the sense accepted in the heraldry of other countries. Crests are rarely found; but an adornment of ostrich feathers is frequently used instead. Other characteristics are the presence of mottoes on the shield itself and the occasional placing of gold on silver or vice versa in a manner quite contrary to heraldic principles elsewhere.

The heraldry of Italy reflects the troubled history of that country, which acted as a battlefield for successive German, French, Spanish and Austrian invaders. All these left

their mark. The rise of the northern city states and the general fragmentation of the country led to a certain duplication of armorial bearings, while the intense Italian cultural activity of the late Middle Ages and the Renaissance lessened the hold of medieval heraldry on the country; charges lack the stylisation found elsewhere and have obtained a more natural and classical form. The chief or top half of the shield often represents a political allegiance, the most frequent being charged with the fleur-de-lis of France and differenced by a label of Anjou, or the eagle of the Holy Roman Empire.

In spite of foreign intervention, Italian heraldry has developed certain characteristics distinctive to itself, in particular the use of almond-shaped or horsehead-shaped shields. The latter were possibly placed on the foreheads of horses at tournaments and resemble the head of a horse when viewed from the front. Crests are rare, but when found, they can obtain an extravagance as exemplified by the crests of Sforza and Dal Verme. Crest wreaths are noticeably thin and are often borne with coronets of rank, a combination rarely found elsewhere in Europe. The hillocks issuing from the base of the shield which are so characteristic of mainland European heraldry, have evolved into elongated pieces which are set one above the other to create a stylised formation found in many Italian arms.'

Central Italian heraldry has been much influenced by the Church. Many families deriving their titles from successive popes have alluded to this by incorporating papal insignia in their arms, notably the papal tiara and the crossed keys.

'Hungarian heraldry is closely akin to that of Austria and Germany, but differs in two particular respects. Firstly there is a marked preference for charges or devices associated with the Turkish wars, which were a perennial feature in Hungarian history from the fifteenth to the eighteenth centuries. More than 15 per cent of all Hungarian armorial bearings feature a gory decapitated Turk's head, usually well moustached and often turbanned. Sabres, swords and lances brandished by arms in armour, lions, gryphons or horsemen are all typical of the warlike quality of Magyar armory. The second characteristic is the occasional extravagance typified by the arms of Hajduboszormeny, charged with a firing gun beneath which are burning logs and above a friendly sun, the whole encircled by a green dragon bearing a patriarchal cross.

BELOW: *The arms of Pope Pius XII (left), Pope Paul VI (centre) and Pope John XXIII (right), showing characteristic Italian shield shapes and stylised hillocks or coupeaux.*

DAL VERME DI VERONA

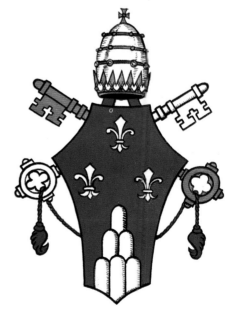

Designs such as these have a certain strangeness about them which seem to border on the eccentric to those accustomed to the more subdued taste found further west.

Poland separates itself from the rest of Europe by reason of the pre-heraldic runic signs which were later absorbed by heraldry and came to constitute its principal feature. These signs were in the form of straight lines or curves. While many remain strictly geometrical, others eventually evolved into a simple charge such as a cross, lance, horseshoe, or crescent. Many arms bearing these charges are not individual to one particular family, but pertain to a whole group of families; for example, nearly 600 families are known to bear a horseshoe enclosing a cross, a situation unlike anything found outside the sphere of Polish heraldic influence.

RIGHT: *The arms of Russian provinces, with Moscow in the centre, on the armorial achievement of Alexander II, Tsar of Russia; painted in 1857.*

144

Heraldry came late to Russia and was subsequently developed by external rather than internal forces. There was no medieval heraldry, and the simple divisions and charges characteristic of that period are absent. Charges such as animals have avoided stylisation and have retained a natural and arguably unheraldic form; sometimes this natural representation is extended to include a landscape environment. Most of these animals face to the sinister, the opposite direction to their counterparts in the heraldry of other countries. The earliest Russian heraldry is found in Lithuania, which was later to become part of Imperial Russia, and where the nobility began adopting armorial bearings of the Polish type in the fifteenth century. French and German influences date from the westernisation begun by Tsar Peter the Great at the end of the seventeenth century.' Peter established an heraldic authority with a Master of Heraldry in 1722, and 355 grants of armorial bearings were made during the eighteenth century.

Within the British Isles differences can also be discerned. In Scotland the granting of armorial bearings is vested by the Crown in Lord Lyon or Lyon King of Arms. The heraldry of Scotland has always been separate from that of England and has developed its

LEFT: *The horseshoe enclosing a cross formy is a combination characteristic of the armorial bearings of many Polish families. Here the Bath stall plate of Dr Conrad Swan, CVO, Garter Principal King of Arms.*

own characteristics. Mottoes, for example, are placed above the crest: in England they are placed beneath. The Scottish system of matriculation does not allow for the same

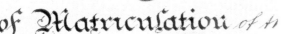

FAR LEFT AND LEFT: *George Coats and Andrew Coats, younger sons of Thomas Coats of Ferguslie and Maxwelton in the County of Renfrew, matriculated armorial bearings in Scotland in 1908 with suitably differenced bordures. In Scotland mottoes are placed above the crest.*

145

SEASA : PAIS

The lord Linyngstone:

RIGHT: *Scottish heraldry favours the use of wild men or savages as supporters. A demi savage wielding a club also features in the armorial bearings of successive Barons Livingstone; painted 1625.*

146

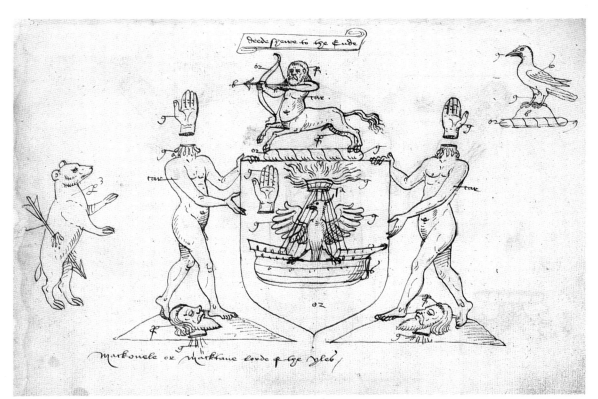

armorial bearings to pertain to all the male-line descendants of the grantee. Younger sons must matriculate and receive a suitably differenced grant of the armorial bearings; this frequently takes the form of a border. Scottish badges are confined to clan chiefs, whereas in England they have no such restriction and are permitted with any new grant of arms.

In Ireland the power to grant arms was once vested in successive Ulster Kings of Arms. On Irish independence this power was transferred to the new office of Chief Herald of Ireland; and the office of Ulster King of Arms was merged with that of Norroy King of Arms in England. Irish heraldry is similar to English medieval or late Tudor heraldry in its general simplicity. Ulster Kings of Arms were disposed to grant the arms of an English family to a person of the same surname in Ireland without proof of connection; and the arms were then often differenced with a trefoil slipped, representing the shamrock. Irish crests show a remarkable preference for the human arm, usually in armour, with the hand grasping a weapon. An analysis of *Kennedy's Book of Irish Arms* shows that approximately a quarter of Irish crests fall within this category.

Heraldry beyond Europe has been much influenced by the English. The cause is not solely past British expansion overseas; of greater significance is the retention of a heraldic authority under the Crown. Where-

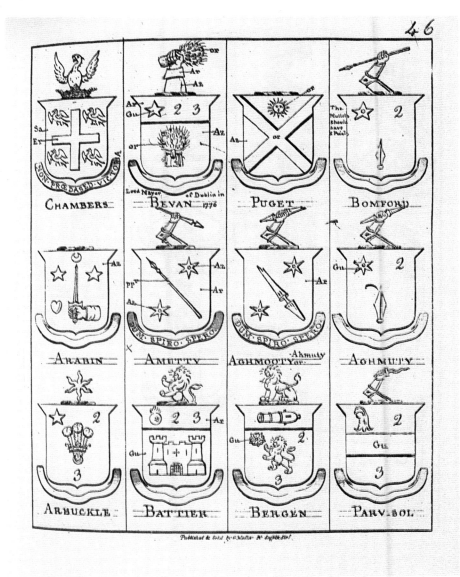

flecting that country's interest in heraldry, but is still subject to the jurisdiction of the English Kings of Arms.

Heraldry on the American continent arrived with the Spanish. Shortly after the first voyage of Christopher Columbus arms were established for the new continent and were borne on a banner at the marriage of Philip of Hapsburg to Joanna of Spain in 1496, alluding to the original name given to the territories on their discovery, 'The Kingdom of the Fifteen Islands'. Columbus described the vegetation of the West Indies as being green, red and brown, which was duly rendered in heraldic form. Thereafter central and South America retained the characteristics of Spanish and Portuguese heraldry, to which indigenous flora and fauna have been added, together with elements of the native Indian civilisations. After the independence movements of the nineteenth century, a number of charges suggestive of the new freedom were introduced, such as rising suns, caps of liberty and clasped hands of brotherhood.

English heraldry prevailed in North America, the first grant being in 1586 to the City and Corporation of Ralegh in Virginia;

ABOVE: *Armorial bearings granted to Tanganyika in 1962, placing the arms on an African shield.*

as such authorities have been generally swept away in continental Europe with the political upheavals of the last two centuries, the English Kings of Arms have continued to grant new armorial bearings to overseas subjects of the Crown. As members of the Royal Household, they are as much the heralds of Australia, for example, as of England. In this respect it is significant that the present Garter King of Arms is a Canadian citizen and holds a Canadian passport.

Living heraldry emanating from England in recent years has adapted to changing circumstances. Countries such as South Africa and Kenya have established their own heraldic authorities on becoming republics and have thus severed their connection with the Crown and the jurisdiction of the English Kings of Arms. In 1988 the Queen established a separate heraldic authority for Canada. The transfer of the right to grant armorial bearings to the Chief Herald of Canada allows for the continued granting of new armorial bearings to Canadian citizens and corporate bodies; and the close relationship between the English and Canadian granting authorities has ensured the smooth continuity of Canadian heraldry. New Zealand also has its own New Zealand Herald Extraordinary, re-

RIGHT: *The first instance of American heraldry: the 15 multi-coloured islands of the arms of the West Indies, borne at the marriage of Philip of Hapsburg to Joanna of Spain, 1496.*

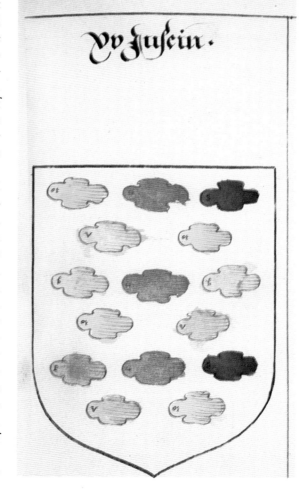

it related to the first English settlement on Roanoke Island, now sited in North Carolina. Although the original grant seemingly made by William Dethick, Garter King of Arms, has not survived, three drafts of the document exist at the College of Arms and include not only arms for the colony, but also for the governor, John White, and each of the 12 assistant governors. Thereafter heraldry was to remain largely dormant in North America, and it was not until 1694 that the first North American resident, Francis Nicholson, 'the Captain General and Governor in Chief of Their Majesties Province of Maryland One of the Chief Governors of a College or University now to be erected or founded in Virginia' received a grant of arms. Shortly afterwards, this university, the College of William and Mary, received its own grant.

In an attempt to further heraldry in America, Laurence Cromp, York Herald, was appointed Carolina Herald in 1705. This appointment is of academic interest only, as Cromp does not appear to have made any grants and provided no stimulus to American heraldry. Ten grants were made to colonists towards the end of the eighteenth century,

LEFT: *Armorial bearings of the College of Arms Foundation, with an 'American' coronet in the crest, featuring mullets (stars) and bars, devised in 1983.*

BELOW: *Indian supporters granted to Sir Jeffery Amherst, commander in chief of His Majesty's Forces in North America, 1761.*

RIGHT: *Armorial bearings of Newfoundland, granted 1638, with Indian supporters* apparaled according to their guise when they go to war.

but this increase in American activity was cut short by the Revolution. Although one or two grants had American connections during the nineteenth century, it was not until the present century that an agreement was reached whereby the English Kings of Arms could issue grants of honorary armorial bearings to American citizens who were able to establish male-line descent from a British subject. In consequence, heraldry in the United States has been revived and is on the increase. A further stimulus was given by an Earl Marshal's Warrant in 1960, which authorised the Kings of Arms to devise armorial bearings for American corporate bodies with the consent of the governor of the relevant state. These have included cities and counties, colleges, ecclesiastical bodies such as the Church of the Advent, Birmingham, Alabama and St Thomas' Church, New York, and leading commercial companies. Growth and interest in heraldry in the United States means that heralds are frequent visitors there; in addition, the College of Arms Foundation was established in the United States in 1983 to disseminate information about heraldry. The armorial bearings granted to the Foundation include a crest which incorporates a new style of American coronet composed of mullets and bars (stars and stripes).

Much American heraldry uses indigenous flora and fauna, but there are also allusions to American history, with figures such as eighteenth-century Virginian gentlemen and officers from the Civil War. The native American Indian and his artefacts are also popular, and featured in a grant to New-foundland as early as 1638. Sir John Borough, Garter King of Arms, granted supporters: *two Savages of the Clyme proper armed and appareled according to their guise when they go to war.* The continuous strife between European and Indian is manifest in the grant of supporters in 1761 to Sir Jeffery Amherst, the eighteenth-century commander in chief of the British Army in North America, and in the armorial bearings designed in 1764 for Joseph Hopkins of Maryland, commandant of the Queen's Regiment of American Rangers. The Amherst supporters are blazoned as, *On the Dexter side a Canadian Warr Indian of a Swarthy or bright Copper colour his exterior Arm embowed holding a Warr Axe proper Rings in his nose and Ears and Bracelets on his Arms and wrists Argent over his Shoulders two Buff Belts in Saltire one with his powder horn, the other his Scalping Knife before him a short Apron Azure tied around the Waist with a string Gules having also Blue Gaters seamed Or, the Legs fetterd and fastend by a Chain to the Bracelet on the exterior wrist. On the*

Sinister side a like Canadian holding in his exterior hand a Wand thereon a Scalp proper.

The grant to Joseph Hopkins is blazoned as *Sable on a chevron between two Pistols Or and a Silver Medal with a French King's Bust inscribed Louis XV a Laurel Chaplet in the Centre a Scalp and a Staff on the dexter and a Tomahawk on the sinister proper a chief embattled Argent; crest a rock over the top a Battery in perspective, thereon a French Flagg hoisted, an Officer of the Queen's* American Rangers climbing the said rock Sword in hand all proper. The recital states that 'the said Joseph Hopkins was the first Officer who landed at Louisburgh 8 June 1758 and killed and scalped the Chief of the St John's Indians and took from him an honorary medal given him by the French'. This grant was never entered in the official register at the College of Arms as it was 'never delivered nor entered, not having been paid for'.

BELOW: *Armorial bearings of Richs Incorporated of the City of Atlanta, an example of a devisal for an American commercial body, devised in 1966.*

A happier and less belligerent situation now prevails and is exemplified by the armorial bearings of the Mescalero Apache Tribe devised in 1986. This draws upon the precedent of placing arms on tribal shields established by grants of armorial bearings to several African countries. The shield contains tribal emblems and is ensigned with a Mescalero Apache mountain-spirit dancer's crown while mountain-spirit dancers feature in the supporters and badge.

American heraldry has thus survived the vicissitudes of past Anglo-American relations. Today it is contributing to the mainstream of new heraldic creation; it is to be hoped that this contribution will continue to increase and so enrich the culture and heritage of that country.

GLOSSARY

Achievement The complete armorial bearings displayed to show shield, helm, mantling, crest wreath or crest coronet, motto and, where applicable, supporters and compartment.

Addorsed Placed back-to-back. The wings of a bird when extended and almost touching each other behind the bird are termed addorsed. Also two animals back-to-back are so termed.

Adopted children May use their adoptive father's arms, but only by Royal Licence, with the difference of two interlaced links of chain.

Aesculapius, Rod of A snake entwining a rod. Frequently used as a charge by those in the medical profession. Sometimes called 'Aaron's Rod'.

Affronty An animal, monster or helm is so termed when facing the viewer.

Allerion An eagle displayed without legs or beak.

Annulet A ring.

Apaumy A hand or gauntlet is so termed when the palm is facing the viewer.

Arched (or enarched) An Ordinary that has been bent is arched or double-arched (or enarched).

Argent The heraldic metal shown as white or, rarely, silver.

Armed When an animal or bird's claws, talons, horns, beak or tusks are of a different colour to the rest of its body they are blazoned 'armed Gules/Argent' etc.

Armiger One who bears arms, abbreviated to arm. or armig.

Armorial bearings The same as an achievement.

Arms of office Arms borne by virtue of holding office. The Kings of Arms have such arms and can impale their personal arms during tenure of that office.

Astral crown A coronet composed of pairs of wings, each enclosing a mullet of six points and set upon a rim. Associated with the Royal Air Force.

At gaze A term used specifically for deer when standing and regarding the viewer.

Attired A term used to describe antlers of deer when of a different colour to the body.

Attributed arms Arms devised for persons who did not bear them, usually for those living in pre-heraldic times.

Augmentation A small device added to a shield, crest or supporters as a mark of honour, eg for victory in battle.

Azure The heraldic tincture blue.

Badge An heraldic device not associated with arms, crest or supporters, which an armiger may allow to be used by a stranger in blood, employee etc. Originally adopted in the Middle Ages for use by retainers, but since a revival in 1906 may now be granted by the Kings of Arms. An armiger may have more than one badge.

Banner A square or upright-oblong flag showing arms only. It is incorrect to place the whole achievement on a banner. *See also* standard.

Bar An Ordinary, the diminutive of a fess.

Bar gemel Twinned bars usually borne in pairs.

Barbed The sepals of the heraldic rose which appear between each of the five petals. Barbed proper means in their natural colours, ie green.

Barry An even number of bars on a shield. If more or less than six then the number must be specified, eg 'Barry of eight Argent and Azure'.

Barry bendy Divided barry and bendy.

Bar sinister A term used only by those ignorant of heraldry when trying to denote illegitimacy (*see* baton sinister).

Base An area at the bottom of the field.

Baton sinister A bendlet sinister couped or cut off at both ends running from sinister chief to the dexter base, used as a mark of bastardy, usually royal.

Bend An Ordinary, a diagonal strip running from dexter chief to sinister base. When charges are placed upon the shield in a diagonal position they are 'in bend', or 'in bend sinister'.

Bendlet A diminutive of the bend, ie narrower.

Bend sinister An Ordinary, a diagonal strip running from sinister chief to dexter base (*see also* bend).

Bendwise Charges lying in the direction of a bend without the bend being present.

Bendy Divided into an equal number of bends.

Bezant A gold roundel.

Bezanty When the field or charge is strewn with bezants it becomes bezanty.

Bicorporate When an animal or monster has one head attached to two bodies it is termed 'bicorporate'.

Billet An oblong rectangle, the same shape as a ticket (French = *billet*).

Billety Strewn with billets.

Blazon The technical language used to describe arms, crest, mantling, supporters and badge.

Blue Celeste A pale blue tincture, often associated with the Royal Air Force.

Bordure A border running round the edge of a shield which can be plain or charged with devices.

Brock A badger.

Caboshed An animal's head affronty chopped off at the top of the neck is termed caboshed.

Cadency, marks of A small device upon a shield and crest to denote different sons. There are nine such marks. They are also used to denote branches of families.

Caduceus A rod winged at the top and entwined with two snakes. Often confused with the Rod of Aesculapius.

Caltrap A device with three iron spikes so that when thrown onto the ground one spike is always uppermost. It was particularly effective against horses and was termed a 'cheval-trap'.

Canting arms Arms or crest providing a visual pun on the bearer's name (from the Latin *cantus*, song).

Canton A small square situated on the dexter chief corner; if in the sinister chief corner it becomes a canton sinister. Augmentations are often placed upon cantons.

Caparisoned A horse is thus described when fully furnished and decorated with bridle, saddle, armour etc.

Carnation A rare term, denoting a flesh-coloured tincture.

Cartouche The decoration sometimes found round the edge of shield or lozenge.

Celestial crown A crown with a rim, thereon sharp points each terminating with a mullet.

Chapeau A medieval hat of crimson velvet lined and turned-up ermine. It is the forerunner of the velvet cap inside the royal crown. Also called a cap of maintenance and cap of estate.

Chaplet A circular garland of leaves and four flowers, usually heraldic roses.

Charge A device or emblem placed on the shield or Ordinary.

Checky A chequerboard pattern of one tincture and one metal.

Chevron One of the Ordinaries, shaped like an inverted V or gable end of a house.

Chevronel The diminutive of the chevron.

Chevronny Divided into a multiple chevron pattern.

Chief An Ordinary, the top third of the shield. Charges placed in this position are said to be 'in chief'.

Chivalry, Court of The court of law where heraldic disputes can be settled. Presided over by the Earl Marshal of England.

Cinquefoil A stylised flower, having five petals or leaves.

Close A bird is described as close when its wings are folded.

Coat of arms This was originally the surcoat worn over armour depicting the arms of the wearer. Now it refers generally to the achievement or the shield of arms.

Collared Having a collar around the neck.

College of Arms This is the shorthand name of the Corporation of Kings Heralds and Pursuivants of Arms in ordinary to Her Majesty The Queen. It is also abbreviated to the Heralds College. The corporation was founded by King Richard III in 1484 and houses the offices of the officers of arms, together with their official records and collections. It is situated in Queen Victoria Street, London EC4V 4BT.

Combatant Two beasts or monsters facing one another in a rampant position are termed combatant.

Compartment Usually a grassy mound or solid base upon which the supporters stand so that they can perform their function of supporting the shield.

Compony A single row of rectangles tincture alternating with metal. A double row is termed 'countercompony'.

Conjoined The term used when charges touch one another or are joined together.

Corbie A raven, from the French *corbeau*.

Cornucopia The heraldic term for a horn of plenty.

Coronets (1) The crest coronet is not a coronet denoting rank, but forms part of the crest. This category includes the ducal coronet, the ancient coronet, the astral crown, the celestial crown, the mural crown etc, and others of recent invention such as a coronet the finials of which are alternating cinquefoils and crosses patonce.
(2) There are five coronets of rank, one for each of the five ranks of the higher nobility: Duke, Marquis, Earl, Viscount and Baron. These are placed immediately above the shield, below the helm and mantling. The royal crown, the Prince of Wales' coronet and the coronets of princes and princesses do, of course, denote rank but are not treated in the same way as those of nobility in heraldic display.

Cotises The bend, bend sinister,

fess, chevron, pale and cross when they have a pair of very thin 'bars' on each side are termed cotised. From the the French *côté*, side.

Couchant This describes a beast or monster lying down, but with its head up.

Counterchanged When a shield is divided by one of the lines of partition, the colours of the field and charges on one side are reversed on the other.

Couped When a beast or monster's head or limb is cut off cleanly with a straight line it is termed couped. This also applies to Ordinaries.

Courant Running at speed.

Coward A beast (or monster, rarely) with its tail between its back legs.

Crescent A new moon with horns uppermost. When the horns are pointing to the dexter, the term becomes 'increscent', when to the sinister, 'decrescent'. The cadency mark for a second son.

Crest An hereditary three-dimensional device situated on top of the helmet.

Crined When the hair of a beast or man is of a different colour to the body, it is termed 'crined', eg 'crined Or'.

Cross One of the Ordinaries. There are many different types of cross in heraldry.

Crusily When cross-crosslets are strewn (semy) over the field or charge, the term 'crusily' is sufficient.

Cubit arm An arm cut off below the elbow.

Dance This is a fess in the form of a wide zigzag pattern.

Dancetty A line of partition of a wide zigzag.

Debruised When a baton or baton sinister is laid over the shield it is termed as 'debruised by a baton'.

Dexter The right side of the shield as held by the bearer, but the left-hand side from the point of view of the spectator. Charges that are capable of facing one direction or another always face the dexter unless described otherwise.

Difference, marks of Synonymous with marks of cadency.

Dimidiation A form of marshalling long since abandoned. When two coats were impaled, the dexter half of the dexter coat was joined with the sinister half of the sinister coat. This could produce unfortunate results.

Displayed Birds, principally eagles, when shown with wings

spread open and wing tips uppermost are termed 'displayed'.

Dormant Asleep.

Double-queued A beast or monster having two tails.

Double tressure Twin thin lines following the edge of the shield. Principally known from the Royal Arms of Scotland, where the double tressure is flory counter flory, ie fleurs-de-lis alternatively, pointing outwards and inwards.

Doubled When mantling is blazoned, the lining is described as doubled of a metal.

Earl Marshal of England The great officer of state responsible for state ceremonial and the College of Arms. Also the judge of the Court of Chivalry. The title is hereditary with the dukedom of Norfolk.

Enfile To thread. A charge with a coronet around it is 'enfiling' the coronet, or the cornet is 'enfiled' by the charge. This term easily causes confusion.

Enhanced An Ordinary raised above its normal position.

Ensigned A shield or charge with a crown or coronet above it is termed as 'ensigned' by the crown or coronet.

Eradicated A tree pulled up to show its roots is termed eradicated.

Erased The head or limb of an animal or monster torn from its body and showing a jagged edge is termed erased.

Escarbuncle A charge comprising ornamental spokes emanating from a hub and usually terminating in a fleur-de-lis.

Escutcheon A small shield as a charge in arms, or an escutcheon of pretence if it is a form of marshalling whereby the marital coat is shown indicating that the wife is an heraldic heiress. Also termed inescutcheon.

Fess An Ordinary. A central horizontal strip about one-third of the height of the shield.

Fesswise Lying in the same direction as the fess

Field The background or surface of the shield.

Fimbriated An Ordinary or charge edged with a different colour.

Flaunches Enarched areas on both sides of the shield.

Fleam A stylised instrument for bloodletting.

Flory When the ends of charges terminate in a fleur-de-lis they are termed flory.

Forcene An adjective used to describe a horse rearing up but not rampant.

Fountain A roundel composed of six bars wavy Argent and Azure, to represent water.

Fourché A tail of an animal that is bifurcated.

Fret A mascle interlaced with a bendlet and a bendlet sinister.

Fretty Bendlets and bendlets sinister interlaced throughout the shield. This looks like netting.

Fructed A tree or plant bearing fruit, or bearing fruit of a different colour, is fructed of that colour.

Fusil A vertically-stretched lozenge.

Fusilly A vertically-stretched version of lozengy.

Gamb The lower part of a beast's leg.

Garb A wheatsheaf.

Garnished A term used for metallic charges, such as helmets, when edged with gold or silver.

Golpe A purple roundel.

Goutte A droplet representing liquid. The term 'goutty' shows droplets splashed upon the field, Ordinary or shield.

Grant of arms A legal document under the hands and seals of the Kings of Arms when exercising the Royal Prerogative, subject to the Earl Marshal's Warrant, granting an individual or corporation the use of armorial bearings or badge. Also called Letters Patent of Armorial Bearings.

Guardant A term used to describe animals and monsters as looking at the viewer.

Gules The heraldic tincture red.

Gyron Half a quarter of the shield, cut per fess and per bend.

Gyronny The shield divided quarterly and per saltire, the eight pieces in alternating tincture and metal.

Hatchment A funerary painting of the armorial achievement of a deceased person, painted on a square canvas (or wood) but turned 90° with points N, S, E, and W.

Haurient A term to describe a fish with head uppermost.

Heiress Or coheiress, a daughter or daughters without brothers (or without surviving brother *sans* issue) who can transmit arms to children as a quartering, providing the husband is armigerous.

Helmet The helmet is always shown in an achievement of arms as a reminder of the martial medieval origins of heraldry. The crest is fixed to the top of the helmet. It also denotes rank: a steel tilting helm denotes a gentleman or esquire (and is used in corporate heraldry), a steel helmet with visor raised denotes a knight or baronet, a silver helmet with gold bars as a visor denotes a peer, and entirely gold helmets are reserved for the sovereign and princes of the blood royal. The tilting helm faces the dexter unless an individual has two crests, when they can face each other; a knight's baronet's and peer's helm face affronty or to the dexter, and the royal helm is affronty only.

Honorary arms By an Earl Marshal's Warrant, the Kings of Arms are empowered to grant honorary arms to citizens of the United States of America if they can prove a descent in the male line from an ancestor who had been a subject of a British or English sovereign and who must first place such a descent on official record at the College of Arms. Grants of honorary arms may equally be made to foreign citizens already honoured by the Queen.

Hurt A blue roundel.

Impale A term used to describe a shield split vertically down the middle. A husband's arms placed on the dexter side, and a wife's arms placed on the sinister side of the same shield are impaled, showing a marital alliance. Likewise, the head of a corporation may do the same during his tenure of office only, showing the arms of the corporation on the dexter and his or her arms on the sinister, indicating a 'temporary marriage' to that office.

Issuant Issuing from, or coming out of. An animal, monster or other charge is termed as issuant when it arises or comes out of a crest coronet.

Jessed A falcon or hawk is termed 'jessed' if it has leather straps about its legs, and with bells attached it is 'belled and jessed'.

Label The cadency mark of the eldest son. Used in the past as an Ordinary or charge.

Langued Used as a description of the tongue of a beast when of a different colour to the body.

Lodged A deer when lying down is termed 'lodged'.

Lozenge A diamond-shaped charge (but see also fusil). Unmarried and divorced ladies depict their arms on a lozenge with or without a cartouche.

Lozengy A term used to describe a shield or charge as divided into a lozengy pattern, ie bendy and bendy sinister, with alternating tincture and metal.

Lymphad A term used to describe an ancient type of seagoing vessel with oars protruding, either in full sail or with sails furled.

Mantling A cape fixed to the top of the helmet, held in place by the wreath. Origins not definitely known. It is possible that it is a version of the Arab head-dress discovered by the crusaders and adopted by them. It is said that its purpose was to keep the sun off the neck, or to deaden blows aimed at the back of the neck. Maybe it was just decorative. It is now depicted in many artistic ways and adds great beauty to an achievement of arms. It is usually described as having a tincture on the outside, lined with a metal. An ermine lining is reserved for peers, and gold mantling-lined ermine is reserved for the sovereign and royal princes.

Marshalling This is the name given to the system whereby arms acquired by marital alliances may be added to the paternal coat by impalement or quartering. It also applies to arms of office impaled with personal arms.

Mascle A voided lozenge.

Masoned A term used to denote that the mortar in a brick or stone wall is of a different colour.

Maunch A stylised depiction of a lady's sleeve, cut off at the shoulder.

Memorial The term given to the petition made by one desiring a grant of arms, addressed to the Earl Marshal of England.

Metals The colours white (*Argent*) and gold (*Or*) are termed metals (see also tinctures).

Millrind The metal bracket used for holding a millstone in place.

Motto Usually expressing an uplifting sentiment which is adopted by a grantee, not granted to him. It can be in any language, but Latin, English or French are preferred. In an achievement it is placed upon a scroll below the shield.

Mullet A star of five points, unpierced. The cadency mark of the third son.

Murrey One of the stains, as opposed to the tinctures. A reddish-purple or mulberry colour.

Naiant Swimming; used to describe a fish swimming horizon-

tally (see also haurient and urinant).

Naval crown A coronet composed of billowing sails alternating with ships' hulls. Reserved in modern grants for senior naval officers.

Nimbus A halo.

Nowed Snakes and tails of animals when shown in the form of a knot are termed as 'nowed'. Also a type of cross with enlarged circular centre.

Octofoil The same as a cinquefoil, but with eight petals or leaves. The cadency mark of the ninth son.

Or The heraldic term for the metal gold.

Ordinaries a) The basic linear shapes upon a shield, ie the bend, bend sinister, chevron, chief, cross, fess, pale, pile and saltire.
b) An heraldic dictionary, arranged by the charges upon the shield, crest or badge, either in written form (blazon) or pictorial.

Orle Similar to a bordure, but set a little towards the centre of the shield.

Orle, in When charges are arranged around the edges of a shield, but not on a bordure they are termed 'in orle'.

Pairle When a shield is divided in the form of the letter 'Y', or inverted, it is termed 'tierced in pairle' or 'tierced in pairle reversed'.

Pale An Ordinary; it is a vertical band about one-third the width of the shield.

Palewise A charge lying in the direction of a pale.

Palisado crown A coronet in the form of a palisade.

Pall An Ordinary in the shape of the letter 'Y'. It is similar to the ecclesiastical vestment of the same name, or pallium.

Paly A shield divided into an equal number of vertical stripes is termed 'paly'.

Paly bendy A combination of paly and bendy.

Panache A fan of feathers, usually in the crest.

Parted Divided or 'party'.

Partition, lines of See illustration in the chapter on the science of heraldry.

Passant An animal or monster walking, with its dexter forepaw raised.

Paty A cross with the arms splayed towards the edge of the shield is termed 'paty' (or 'patee') or, in modern blazon, 'formy'.

Pean A black fur strewn with gold ermine spots.

Pellet A black roundel.

Pellety Semy of pellets.

Pendant A charge hanging from another is termed pendant.

Pennon A tapering lance-flag.

Pheon A broad arrowhead, the barbs engrailed on the inner edge, shown point downward unless described otherwise.

Pierced A charge pierced with a round central hole is so termed.

Pile An Ordinary, a triangular shape usually starting at the top of the shield with its point in base, but which can also be reversed or can come from either side of the shield.

Plate A white roundel.

Platy Semy of plates.

Potent An early term for a crutch. Ordinaries, particularly the cross, can have crutched ends.

Proper A charge depicted in its natural colours is so termed.

Purpure The heraldic term for the tincture purple.

Quadrate A cross with a square at its centre is termed a 'cross quadrate'.

Quarter A quarter of the shield, in dexter chief unless otherwise blazoned.

Quarterly A term used when describing a shield or charge divided into four quarters coloured with tinctures and metals.

Quatrefoil A four-leaved charge.

Queue fourchy A forked tail, as opposed to 'double-queued' which means two tails.

Quise, à la A bird's leg cut off at the thigh is so described.

Rampant An upright beast with its left hind leg downwards and its other legs splayed to the dexter.

Reflexed This term is usually applied to a chain or line where it is fixed to a collar around the neck of an animal, monster or human and is arranged or reflexed over the back of the creature.

Reguardant An animal looking backwards over his shoulder is reguardant.

Respectant Two animals facing one another. If rampant at the same time the term 'combatant' is used.

Reversed Turned upside-down from its normal position.

Rising A bird about to take off with wings stretched out is described as rising.

Roundel A disc with special names according to the colour – gold (*bezant*), white (*plate*), red (*torteau*), blue (*hurt*), green (*pomeis*), black (*pellet*), purple (*golpe*), barry wavy Argent and Azure (*fountain*).

Sable The heraldic tincture black.

Salient Animals leaping or springing are described as salient, except horses, which are forcene.

Saltire An Ordinary in the shape of an X.

Segreant Synonymous with rampant, but applied only to a gryphon when in this position.

Sejant Sitting down (not lying down).

Semy Charges evenly strewn over the shield or Ordinary are described as 'semy of . . .'

Sinister The left side of the shield when borne by the owner, the right side when viewed by the spectator.

Slipped Flowers, leaves, and small branches with stalks when pulled off the main stem, are so described.

Stains In addition to metals and tinctures, other colours are occasionally used: sanguine (a bloody colour), tenne (orange) and murrey (mulberry).

Standard This is a long tapering flag with a round end (split for knights, baronets and peers), showing the owner's arms at the hoist, and his badges or crest between his motto upon diagonal bands in the fly. This is not a banner.

Statant An animal standing with all four feet on the ground is so described.

Stock The stump of a tree.

Surcoat A long coat without sleeves, worn over armour, upon which was shown the wearer's arms, hence 'coat of arms'.

Tabard A short surcoat with broad sleeves. The royal tabard is now worn only by heralds on ceremonial duty.

Tierced A shield divided into three parts is so described, as in 'tierced in pairle'.

Tinctures The heraldic colours red (*Gules*), blue (*Azure*), black (*Sable*), green (*Vert*) and purple (*Purpure*) are described collectively as tinctures.

Trick When a pen-and-ink drawing of arms, crest, supporters or badge is shown with colours indicated by lettering, it is said to be 'tricked' or 'a trick'.

Trippant Deer when passant are described as trippant.

Tufted Beasts which have tufts of hair of a different colour are described as tufted of that colour.

Unguled When beasts have hooves of a different colour to their bodies, they are described as unguled of that colour.

Urchin The heraldic term for a hedgehog. It is also called a herisson.

Urinant A term used to describe a fish with its head downwards.

Vambraced A term used to describe a human arm when wearing armour.

Vert The heraldic tincture green.

Voided The heraldic term used to describe a charge which has had its centre cut out, to show only an outline with the background colour showing through, eg 'voided of the field'.

Volant A bird in the act of flying.

Vulned Wounded and showing droplets of blood.

Water bouget A stylised pair of leather bags, joined by a yoke, for carrying water.

Wodehouse A savage or wild man of the woods.

Wreath A circlet of twisted material, holding the mantling on top of the helmet, and disguising how the crest is fixed to the helmet. Conventionally it is depicted as having six twists alternating metal and tincture. When the blazon describes the wreath as 'of the colours', the first metal and first tincture described in the blazon are the colours to be used. A wreath can also be used as a charge, and an Ordinary may also be wreathed.

INDEX

Figures in *italics* refer to illustrations

achievement of arms 46
Adams, Robert, Governor of Coast of Malabar 69, 59
African countries heraldry 148, *148*, 153
Alliance and Leicester Building Society *101*
alphyn 89, *89*
America
 animals in design 102
 heraldry *111*, 148-53, *148-53*
 honorary grants to 73, 150
 Sir Isaac Heard's interest 39
 Washington family 10, 39, 56-7
American Indian
 Mescalero Apache tribe *151*, 153
 supporters 148, *149*, *150*, 151, *151*
Amhurst, Sir Jeffery *149*, 151-2
Andrew, Duke of York 125-6
animals
 crests 58-9, *59*, 64, 66, 69, *69*, *71*, *99*, *100*, *101*, *102*, 117
 postures 44
 shields 44, *44*, 56, 66, *66*, 75, 99-100
 supporters 101-2, *101*, 117
 see also lion
Anjou
 account of Geoffrey Plantagenet's ceremony of knighthood in 14
 origins of heraldry 10
Anne, Queen 120
Anne, Princess Royal *125*, 126
Anstis, John, Garter King of Arms 38, 68
antelope 83-4, *84*, 117
application procedures for the granting of arms 76
Argent (white tincture) 42, 56
Ashmole, Elias, Windsor Herald 39
Australia 135, 148
 animals in design 102, *110*
 armorial bearings *131*
 birds 75
 grantees 73, *110*
 Queen's personal banner for use in *133*
Austrian heraldry 138, 143
Azure (blue tincture) 42, 52, 56

badges *26*, 28, 42, 63, *72*, 73-4, *87*, 120
 royal *55*, *59*, *117*, *118*, *124*, 127, *127*, *128*, 129, *129*, 130-1, 133

bagwyn 63, 67, 69
banners *15*, 18
 Queen's *133*, 34, 135
battle of Agincourt 28, 34
battlefields, twelfth century use of heraldry on 10, 11, 18
Bayeux Tapestry 52, 54
Beaufort, John, Duke of Somerset and Earl of Kendal 83, *83*, 106
Bedingfeld, Henry, Rouge Croix Pursuivant *27*, *39*

Belgian heraldry 141
Benolt, Thomas, Clarenceux King of Arms 35, 64, 66, 100
bestiaries, medieval 80, 82, 83, 84, 85, 86, 87, 89, 92, 95, 98, 99, 100
Bigot Roll 16
birds *44*, *55*, 56, 57, *57*, 62, 64, *64*, 74, 75, 87-8, *89*, 94, *95*, 99, 100, *100*, *101*, 102-3, *103*, *118*
blazon of shield 16, 18
 Royal Arms 42
 steps in 42-6
bonacon 85-6
Bowyers Company *12*
Broderers Company *108*
Bruce, Robert 58, *59*
Bruges, William 28, 34
Burke, Henry Farnham, Rouge Croix Pursuivant 73

cadency, marks of 46, *46*
 Royal 122-3
caladrius 94-5, *95*
Camden, William, Clarenceux King of Arms 38
Canada 71, 135, 148
 armorial bearings of *132*
 grantees 73
 maple leaf 110
 Queen's personal banner for use in *134*
cases before the Court of Chivalry Scrope v Grosvenor (1385-90) 32
catoblepas 94, 95
charge on shield 43-4, *44*, 55-6, 57, 60, 66, 138, 139, 141
 legends relating to charges appearing in medieval armorials 56, 57-9
Charles II 38, 120, 123
Charles, Prince of Wales 125, 126, 133
Charny, Geoffrey de
 treatises on chivalry 20-1
checky arms *15*
 Waleran seal and shield 12
 Warenne banners and shields 12, *15*
chevrons 12, 14, 43, *43*, 44, 48, 60, 64, 66, *71*, 72, 139
Chinese phoenix 90, *91*, 92-3, 95, *95*
chivalric ideal 10, 20, 21
 thirteenth and fourteenth century treatises on 20-1
Cinque Ports arms 48
cinquefoil *55*, 57, 106, 108
City of London 32, 81, 90
Clare family shields 12, 14, *16*
Clarenceux King of Arms 11, 28, 35, 37-8, *40*, *50*, 56, 64-6, *67*, 68, 100, *101*, *108*
Clothworkers Company 60, *60*, 62
Clovis, King of the Franks 107
cockatrice 80, 81-2, *82*, 83
cognate heraldry 55, 56, 57, 60, 63, 64, 75
College of Arms 32, 35, *36*, 63, 65, 67, 73
 application for arms to, present-day method 76
arms, description of 44

Monograph of the London Survey Committee, 1963 27
 residences *29*, 32
 series of grant volumes 37
College of Ophthalmologists *93*
Comnena, Princess Anna 52, 54
Cooke, Robert, Clarenceux King of Arms *40*, 65-6, 67, *67*, 68, 100
Cooks Company 109, *109*
Cordoba, Gonzalo Fernandez *137*
corporate heraldry 34, *38*, *39*, 48, 60, *60*, 62, 67-8, *67*, 71, 73, 74, 75, 76, *88*, *91*, *101*, 103, *103*, *104*, *108*, 109, *109*, *110*, 150, *152*
Corporation of Clergymen's Sons 67-8, *67*
county visitations by heralds 28, 35, 38, 66, 67
 1530 Commission controversy 35, 37
Court of Chivalry 32, 35
crescent 55, *55*
crests *6*, *11*, 42, 46, *63*, 64, *65*, 66-7, 69, 83, 93, 99, 109, 138, *138*, 139, *139*, 141, 142, 145, 147
 animals on 63, 67, 69, *69*, *71*, *96*, *99*, 100, *100*, *101*, *102*, 117
 birds on 62, *64*, 67, *100*, *101*
 monsters on *59*, 67, *81*, *82*, *85*, 87, *88*, *89*, *91*, *92*, 94, *95*
cross 43, *43*, 44, *44*, *53*, 54-5, *54*, 64, 66, 72
Crusades 52, 107, 138

de Bado Aureo, John 52
deflecting devices 55-6
design of arms for grantee, present practice 76
Dethick, William, Garter King of Arms *25*, 149
dexter 42
Diana, Princess of Wales 126-7
dimidiation 48
dragon 78, 81, *81*, 83, 117, 118, 120
Drapers Company 34, 60
Duchy of Cornwall *124*, 125
Duchy of Lancaster *131*
Dugdale, John, Windsor Herald 68
Dugdale, Sir William, Garter King of Arms *28*, 38
Dutch heraldry *140*, 141

Earl Marshal 32, 35, 76, 150
Edward the Confessor 114
Edward I 48, 106, 129, 130
Edward III *25*, 34, 48, *59*, 107, 115, 117, 122, 129, 130
Edward IV *6*, 117, *127*, 130
Edward VIII, Duke of Windsor 123
Edward, Prince, son of Elizabeth II 125-6
Edward the Black Prince 58, 110, 122, *124*, *126*, 129
Eleanor of Aquitaine 114
Eleanor of Castile 48, *112*, *125*
Elizabeth I 118, *118*, 120
Elizabeth II *36*, 120, 123, *130*, 131, 133, *133*, *134*, 135

Elizabeth, Queen Mother 123
enfield 63, 67, 89
ermine 12, 42, 75, 105
escarbuncle 54
events in grantee's life used for determining arms 69-71

Falkland Islands 135, *135*
Fenwick Roll *61*
fess 14, 43, *43*, 60, 63, 64, 66, 72
field 42-3, 44, 45
fish 98, 99, 103, *107*
FitzGerald monkey legend 58-9, *59*
fleur-de-lis 45, 48, 74, 106-7, *107*, 108, *108*, *111*, 115, 117, 126, 142
flora *38*, *55*, 57, 75, 106-7, *106*, 108-9, *108*, *109*, 110, *111*, 139, 151, *see also* fleur-de-lis, rose
France
 blazon 42
 corporate status acquired by royal heralds 28
 crests, absence of 138, 141, *141*
 medieval times, origins of heraldry in 10, 12, 14, 26
 Royal Arms 46, 48, 107, 115, 120
frog 104, 107-8, *108*
fur 42, 105, 138, *see also* ermine, vair

Garter ceremonies, Windsor *29*, *30-1*, 34, 37
Garter King of Arms *25*, 28, 34, 35, 38, 39, 62, 63-4, *63*, 65, 66, 68, 73, 86, 96, 100, 148, 149
George I 38, 120
George III 122
George V 123
George VI 123, 125
George, Duke of Kent 123
German heraldry *11*, 12, 26, 138, *138*, 139, *139*, 143
glossary 154-7
Glover's Roll 16, 42
granting of arms 34, 35
 present-day procedure 76
greyhound 64, 72, 117
gryphon *44*, 71, 72, 80-1, *80*, 83, 95, 143
Gules (red tincture) 42, 56
Gwynn-Jones, Peter, Lancaster Herald *27*

Hanoverian arms 120, 122
Hartwell, William 103, *104*
Hawley, Thomas, Clarenceux King of Arms 64-5, *66*, 100, *101*
Heard, Sir Isaac, Garter King of Arms 39
heathcock 87-8, *89*
helmet 46, 99, 117, 139, 141
Henry I 14, 98, 114
Henry II 14, 114, 127
Henry III 16, 46, 57
Henry IV *127*, 129
Henry V 28, 34, *55*, 115, 117, *129*
Henry VI 117
Henry VII 32, 35, 45, 64, 83, 117, 118, 123, *129*, 131
Henry VIII 35, 100, *114*, 117, 120, *130*

Henry, Duke of Gloucester 123
heralds, medieval times 11, 21, *24*
    compiling of rolls 16, 18, 32
    first mention in literature 24
    grades 26-8
    minstrels, relationship between
        24-6
    tournaments, functions at 11, 24,
        25-6, *25*, 32
Heralds' Roll 98-9, *98*
Heralds' Visitations *28*, 35, 38, 66, 67
    1530 Visitation Commission
        controversy 35, 37
Hervey, William, Clarenceux King of
    Arms *50*, 65, 66, *108*
Holborn Law Tutors 76, 77
Holles Ordinary *16*, *105*
Holwell, John Zephaniah, Governor
    of Bengal *68*, 69
Hong Kong
    armorial bearings 135, *135*
    University of 73, *95*
human arm 66, 72, 93
Hungarian heraldry 143-4

Il faut Faire Pursuivant 28
impalement 48
inanimate charges 44, 57, *58*, 60, *60*,
    63, 74, 75, *75*, 139
Indian, Native American
    Mescalero Apache tribe *151*, 153
    supporters *149*, *150*, 151, *151*
inheritance of arms 32
    heredity devices 10, 11
insects 103, *104*
Ireland 120
    heraldry *25*, 147, *147*
    Royal Arms 120, 122
Italian heraldry 142-3, *142*

James I 118, *119*, 120
Japan Tobacco (UK) Limited *88*
Jean, Marmoutier monk 14
jousting *20*, 24, *25*
Keen, Maurice 18, 20, 21
King, Gregory, Lancaster Herald 38-9
Kings of Arms see Clarenceux, Garter,
    March, Norroy King of Arms
knights 10, 11, 14, 16, *19*, 20, *20*, *21*,
    24, 26, 56, 80, 138
    chivalric ideal 10, 20, 21
Knights of the Garter
    arms *30-1*, *33*, 46
    ceremonies *29*, *34*, 37

Lancaster Herald *27*, 28, 38, 130
Lancelot du Lac, Sir 24
legends relating to charges appearing
    on medieval armorial
    achievements 56, 57-9
Legh, Roger 28, 35
leisure pursuits representation 75-6,
    76
Letters Patent 34, 35, *35*, 38, 63, 69,
    71, 109
Lillywhites Limited *38*
lion *44*, 46, 47, 48, 56, 57, *61*, 66, 71,
    72, 98, *98*, 99, 110, 114, 118, 143
    in Royal Arms 42, 114-5, 117, 120,
    125
local authorities *35*, 44-5, 48, 73, 76,
    92, *95*, 104, *105*
Louis VII, King of France 107
Louis XI, King of France 28, *107*
lozenge *18*, 46, *61*, 75, 125, 126
Lull, Ramon
    treatise on chivalry 20, 21
lynx *93*, 94

magnates in twelfth century 10-11, 12,
    25, 26
male gryphon 84, *84*, 86, *86*
mantling 46, 139

maple leaf 75, 110
March King of Arms 35
Margaret, Princess, Countess of
    Snowdon 125
marshalling of arms 46-9, *62*, 118,
    139, 141
martlet 57, *57*, 74, 99
Mary I 32, 115, 117, 118
metals 42, 44, 46, 56
minstrels, relationship to heralds 24-6
mollusc 105
monkey charge of FitzGerald family
    58-9, *59*
monsters 44, 63, 80-90, 92-5
    on crests 67, *81*, *82*, *85*, *87*, *88*, *89*,
        91, *92*, *94*, *95*
    postures 44
    supporters 63, *78*, *80*, *83*, *84*, *86*,
        87, *90*, *92*, *93*, *95*, 120
Montfort, Simon de, Earl of Leicester
    57, 107
moorcock 87-8, *89*
mottoes *28*, 46, *59*, 118, 125, 141, 142,
    145
Mowbray's Roll *53*
mullet 55-6, 66, 74, *149*
mythical beasts *see* monsters

Nelson, Viscount and Viscountess *45*
New Zealand 135, 148
    armorial bearings of *133*
    birds in design 102
    grantees 72, 73, *73*
    Queen's personal banner for use in
        134
Norfolk, Duke of 7
Norroy King of Arms *25*, 35, 38, 67,
    147

occupational heraldry *39*, 60, 62, *63*,
    64, 65, 72, 75, 76, 77, *93*, *103*
Or (gold tincture) 42, 52, 56, 142
Order of the Bath 20, 38
Ordinaries 16, 18, 43, *43*, 55, *55*, 56,
    58, *61*, 64, 66, 68, 72, 75, *105*,
    108, 139
    diminutives of 43-4
origins of heraldry 10-12, 14-6, 18,
    20-1, 138
overseas grantees 72, 73, *95*, 148, 150

Painter Stainers Company *91*
pantheon 63, 67, 89, *90*
panther 86-7, *87*, *88*
papillonny 75-6, 77
Paris, Matthew, Benedictine monk of
    St Albans
    histories 14-6, *17*, 115
partition lines 43, *43*, *45*
Pharamund, King 107, *108*
Philip, Duke of Edinburgh 123-5
Plantagenet, Geoffrey, Count of
    Anjou and Maine 14, *14*, 98, 114,
    127
Plantagenet, Richard, Duke of York
    106
poems
    evidence of early heraldry in 12, 18,
        25
    first mention of herald in 24
Polish heraldry 144, *145*
pomegranate *44*, *108*, 110
popes, arms of 143, *143*
Portuguese heraldry 141
punning heraldry   57, 58, *58*, 60, 62,
    63, *63*, 64, *64*, 65, 75, 83, 101,
    103, 105, 106, 108, 110
Purpure (purple tincture) 42
pursuivants *24*, 26, *26*, 27, 28

quartering *18*, *47*, 48-9, 115, 117, 141

Radclyffe, William, Rouge Croix 37

regulation of the use of arms 32
Richard I 114
Richard II 32, 34, 114, *116*, 117, *126*,
    129
Richard III 28, 62, 117, 130-1
rolls of arms *9*, 11, 14-6, *17*, 18, 35,
    42, *53*, *61*, 98-9, *98*
romances 10, 18
    evidence of early heraldry in 10, 12,
        18, 25
rose 106, *107*, 108, *108*, 129, 130
Rouge Croix Pursuivant *27*, 28, *35*,
    37, *39*, 73
roundels 45, 48, 54, 64, *100*
Royal Arms *1*, *2*, *6*, 98, *111*, 114, 120,
    120, *121*, *122*
    blazon 42
Royal Philharmonic Orchestra 75
Russian heraldry *144*, 145

Sable (black tincture) 42, 56
salamander *59*, 86, *87*
Salters Company *60*
saltire 43, *43*, 44, *61*, 66
Sclater 75, 103, *104*
Scotland
    heraldry 145, *145*, *146*, 147, *147*
    Royal Arms of 118, 120
Scott-Gatty, Alfred, Rouge Dragon
    Pursuivant *72*, 73
sea monsters 90, *90*
seals 10-11, 12, *12*, *13*, 14, *21*, 48, 80,
    114
Secret or Segret Pursuivant 28
Segar, William, Garter King of Arms
    65, 86
Seymour, Jane 86, *87*
shield
    Bayeux Tapestry 52, *52*, 54
    blazon of 16, 18, 42-6
    charge on 43-4, *44*, 55-6, 57, 60,
        66, 138, 139, 141
    medieval battle and tournament
        shields 10, 11, 14, *15*, 18, 52, 54
sinister 42
Smith's Ordinary 55, 56, *58*, 108
snake *59*, 81, *100*, 103-4
Spanish heraldry *137*, 141, *142*
Stephen, King 115
supporters 28, 42, 46, 63, 64, 83, 93,
    103, *110*, 141, *151*
    American Indian *149*, *150*, 151, *151*
    animals *59*, 64, 99, *101*, *110*, 117,
        118, 120
    monsters 63, *78*, *80*, *83*, *84*, *86*, *87*,
        90, *92*, *93*, *95*, 120
swan in cognate heraldry 56
Swiss heraldry 138, 141

Tennyson, Lord Alfred 71
Tesco Stores (Holdings) Limited 75,
    110
Textile Institute 102, *103*
tincture 42, 44, 46, 52, 54, 56, 139
toad 104, *105*
tournaments, use of heraldry at 10, 11,
    20, 24, 25-6, *25*, 32, 34
trees 106, 108, *110*
Troyes, Chrétien de
    writings of 24
tyger 84, *85*, 89
Tyger Pursuivant 28, 32

unicorn 80, 82-3, *83*, *95*, 120
University of Cambridge 44

vair 42, *42*, 105, *105*
Vanbrugh, Sir John, Clarenceux King
    of Arms 37-8
Victoria, Queen 122
visitations to counties by heralds *28*,
    35, 38, 66, 67
    1530 Commission controversy 35,

Wagner, Sir Anthony, Clarenceux
    King of Arms 11, 16, 24, 56
Waleran, Count of Meulan and Earl
    of Worcester 12
Walford's Roll 16, 18
Warenne Earls of Surrey 12, *13*, *15*
Warren, Ralph, Lord Mayor of
    London *63*, 64
Washington family 56-7, *56*
werewolf 92
William III and Mary II 120
Wimbledon, All England Lawn
    Tennis and Croquet Club 74
Wolsey, Cardinal Thomas *80*
women, rules for 46
Wriothesley, Thomas, Garter King of
    Arms *62*, 63-4, *63*, 65, 66, *96*,
    100
Writhe, John, Garter King of Arms
    35, *62*, 63, *63*, 64

yale 83, *83*

ACKNOWLEDGMENTS

The publisher would like to thank Martin Bristow for designing this book, Judith Millidge and Clare Haworth-Maden for editing it, Stephen Small for the picture research, Pat Coward for compiling the index, and Godfrey New Photographic for many of the photographs reproduced here.

The authors would like to thank the following for their assistance in the preparation of this book: the Chapter of the College of Arms for permission to reproduce illustrations from the College Records and Collections; the Duke of Norfolk, Earl Marshal; Robert Yorke, Archivist at the College of Arms; Jane Nickels, Assistant Librarian at the College of Arms; Robert Parsons, Linda West and Gillian Barlow, for providing artwork; Herr Heinz Waldner; Dr Elizabeth Hallam; Lady Garrod; Mary-Rose Rogers; Beryl Pendley, Clerk of the Ordinaries at the College of Arms, for her general assistance and acting as referee between the authors.

The following individuals and agencies provided the illustrations:

Gillian Barlow: p.76 top four, 93T (based on College of Arms Carta Marina), 100 top left and top right (based on College of Arms MSS Vincent 187/258 and H13/81), 111 bottom three, 130B, 143 bottom three. **Henry Bedingfeld:** p.11B, 27B, 35, 39T, 48T. **Bibliothèque Nationale, Paris:** p.11T. **Graham Bingham:** p.1, 2 all three, 6 both, 7, 120, 130B. **British Library:** p.12BR, 17, 19, 20, 21T, 25T, 42, 115T. **Canterbury Cathedral:** p.126T, 127B. **College of Arms:** p.8 (Heralds' Roll), 15 (Flower's Ordinary 2G9/105 & 6), 16B (Holles Ordinary), 18 top and bottom (Holles Ordinary), 24 (Westminster Tournament Roll), 25B (Old Grants 2/90), 26, 27 top left and top right, 28 (C36/58), 29T, 37, 38 (Lillywhites Ltd), 39B (Pickering Kenyon), 40, 45B, 46B (M7/62), 48B, 49, 50 (L10/28), 53 (2 L12/7b), 54 (E16/34), 55 top (Jenyn's Ordinary/24b) and bottom (M10/129), 56 (C14/44), 58 top (Smith's Ordinary/34b) and bottom (2G11/1b), 59 top left (Vincent 152/50b) top right (Stall Plates of the Knights of the Garter, St John Hope, 1901, No. LXXII) and bottom (Vincent 152/57), 60 top right and top left (L6/17) and bottom (I 2/62), 61 (Fenwick Roll, Rows 118-121), 62 top (Vincent 153/10b) and bottom (Vincent 153/23), 63 top (Misc. Grants 7/401) and bottom (L10/99), 64 (L10/59), 65 top (Vincent 168/206 & 21) and bottom (L10/58b), 66 (Grants II/449), 67 top (Hare's Ordinary/109b) and bottom (Grants III/250), 68 top (Grants XV/293) and bottom (Grants X/455), 69 top (SML 33/193) and bottom (Grants VIII/148), 70 (Grants XI/21), 71 top (Grants XXXVII/65) and bottom (Grants LXII/292), 72 top (Grants LXII/228) and bottom (Standards I/20), 73 (Culham), 74 (All England Lawn Tennis and Croquet Club), 75 (Royal Philharmonic Orchestra), 76 bottom (Grants CXXXVII/306), 77 (Grants CXLVII/322), 78 (Vincent 152/95), 80 (Vincent 152/92b), 81 (Stall Plates of the Knights of the Garter, St John Hope, 1901, No. VII), 82 (Old Grants 2/79), 83 top (Order of the Bath Vol. 3/104) and bottom (Stall Plates of the Knights of the Garter, St John Hope, 1901, No. LXVIII), 84 top (B 19/25) and bottom (G 2/46), 85 (D 15/2), 86 (Grants LXII/174), 87 top (Grants CXXXIX/51) and bottom (M7/17), 88 (Japan Tobacco (UK) Ltd), 89B (Roberts), 90 top (Grants III/119b) and bottom (L 10/106), 91 (1H 7/59b), 92 top (Grants CXLII/196) and bottom (Vincent 182/111), 93B (CLIII/181), 94 (Grants CLIX/15), 95 top (CXLVIII/62) and bottom (Grants CXXX/136), 96 (L 10/108), 98 top (Heralds' Roll/23) and bottom (2G9/38), 99 (Vincent 152/80), 100B (L10/105b), 101 top (Grants II/453), bottom left (BEDN/48b) and far left (Grants CLI/195), 103 (Grants CXIV/21), 104 top left (153/42), top right (M9/42) and bottom (Grants CLIII/36), 105 top (Grants CXLIII/37) and bottom (EDN 31/351 & 2), 106 (L 10/110), 107 top (C 20/326) and bottom (IM 5/126), 108 top (L 8/1) and bottom (Old Grants 2/77), 109 top (K 9/442) and bottom (Arundel 3/96), 110 top (CXL 11/211) and bottom (CXLVI/102), 111T (Foreign Arms 2/117), 114/115B (Westminster Tournament Roll), 118 top and bottom, 119, 121 (Bath Book/11), 122, 123, (R23/119), 124 top and bottom, 125B, 126B, 127T, 128, 129 top and bottom, 130T, 131 top and bottom, 132, 133 top and bottom, 134 top and bottom, 135 top and bottom, 136 (Hector le Breton/10), 138 (B23/58b & 59), 139T (Vincent 171/27), 140 (Edele Geslagten in de 7 Proviinten/96), 141 (Hector le Breton/15), 142 top (Famiglie Celebri Italiane, Pompeo Litta Vols. 2 & 5) and bottom (Spanish Certificates of Arms), 143T (Famiglie Celebri Italiane, Pompeo Litta Vols. 2 & 5), 144 (Young Collection Vol. 922), 145 bottom left and right (Scotland III/28 & 34), 146 (EDN Scotland's Nobility/51), 147 top (Vincent 172/162b) and bottom (Kennedy's Book of Irish Arms/45), 148 top (I 82/257) and bottom (Arms of Foreign States/21), 149 top (Foreign Arms 2/172) and bottom (Grants X/324), 150 (Misc. Grants 4/7), 151 top left (SML 34/15), top right (Foreign Arms 2/176), bottom (Foreign Arms 2/69), 152 (Foreign Arms 2/63), 153 (Foreign Arms 2/113). **Keith Ellis Collection:** p.34. **Peter Gwynn-Jones:** p.89T, 102, 139B. **Michael Holford:** p.52. **Hulton-Deutsch Collection Ltd:** p.29B. **Lichfield Studios:** p.36. **Lichfield Studios/ Museum of London:** p.125T. **Magdalen College, Oxford University:** p.21B. **Musée de Tessé, Le Mans:** p.14. **Robert Parsons:** p.12T, 44B all 11. **Courtesy of the Public Record Office:** p.12BL, 13. **Royal Collection, Reproduced by Gracious Permission of Her Majesty the Queen:** p.30/31. **Salisbury Cathedral:** p.16T. **Nigel Shuttleworth:** p.10. **Dr Conrad Swan, CVO:** p.145T. **Linda West:** p.43 all 17, 44 top 10, 45T, 46 top three, 47 all three. **By courtesy of the Dean and Chapter of Westminster:** p.57, 112, 116, 117. **Reproduced by permission of the Dean and Canons of Windsor:** p.22, 33.

FOR FURTHER READING

Heralds and Heraldry in the Middle Ages, A R Wagner, Oxford University Press, 1956.

Historic Heraldry of Britain, A R Wagner, Oxford University Press, 1939.

A Catalogue of English Medieval Rolls of Arms (Aspilog a I), A R Wagner, Society of Antiquaries, 1950.

Rolls of Arms, Henry III (Aspilogia II), T D Tremlett, H S London and A R Wagner, Society of Antiquaries, 1967.

Chivalry, Maurice Keen, Yale University Press, 1984.

Lines of Succession, Jiri Louda and Michael Maclagan, Orbis Publishing Ltd, London, 1981.

Die ältesten Wappenbilder, Heinz Waldner, Herold, Berlin, 1992.

The Plantagenet Chronicles, Dr Elizabeth Hallam (ed), Weidenfeld & Nicholson, 1986.

The Complete Peerage, GEC, St Catharine's Press, 1910-40.

Eight Rolls of Arms, Gerard J Brault, Pennsylvania State University Press, 1973.

The College of Arms Monograph, Walter H Godfrey CBE, FSA, FRIBA, assisted by Sir Anthony Wagner, KCVO, DLitt, FSA, Garter King of Arms, with a complete list of the Officers of Arms, prepared by the late H Stanford London FSA, Norfolk Herald Extraordinary, 1963.

Paston Letters and Papers of the Fifteenth Century, Norman Davis (ed), Oxford University Press, 1971 and 1976.

Heralds of England, Sir Anthony Wagner, KCVO, DLitt, Garter King of Arms, HMSO, 1967.

The Records and Collections of the College of Arms, A R Wagner, Burkes Peerage, 1952.

Boutell's Heraldry, revised by J P Brooke-Little, CVO, Norroy and Ulster King of Arms, Frederick Warne & Co Ltd, 1983.

An Heraldic Alphabet, J P Brooke-Little, CVO, Norroy & Ulster King of Arms, Macdonald & Co, 1973 and 1975.

Canada: Symbols of Sovereignty, Conrad Swan, York Herald of Arms, University of Toronto Press, 1977.

The Romance of Heraldry, by Wilfrid Scott-Giles, Fitzalan Pursuivant Extraordinary, J M Dent & Sons Ltd, London, 1967.

Animals and Maps, Wilma George, Secker and Warburg, 1969.

The Magic Zoo, Peter Costello, Sphere Books, 1979.

The Naming of the Beasts, Wilma George and Brunsdon Yapp, Duckworth, 1991.

Medieval Beasts, Ann Payne, The British Library, 1990.

The Heraldic Imagination, Rodney Dennys, Clarkson N Potter Inc, New York, 1975.